TO LIVE IN THE NEW WORLD

TO LIVE IN THE NEW WORLD

*A. J. Downing and American
Landscape Gardening*

Judith K. Major

THE MIT PRESS
CAMBRIDGE, MASSACHUSETTS
LONDON, ENGLAND

©1997 Massachusetts Institute of Technology

All rights reserved. No part of this book may be reproduced in any form by any electronic or mechanical means (including photocopying, recording, or information storage and retrieval) without permission in writing from the publisher.

This book was set in Bembo by Graphic Composition, Inc., and was printed and bound in the United States of America.

Library of Congress Cataloging-in-Publication Data

Major, Judith K.
   To live in the New World : A. J. Downing and American landscape gardening / Judith K. Major.
     p. cm.
   Includes bibliographical references and index.
   ISBN 978-0-262-13331-9 (hc.: alk. paper)
978-0-262-63360-4 (pb.)
   1. Downing, A. J. (Andrew Jackson), 1815–1852. 2. Landscape architects—United States—Biography. 3. Landscape architecture—United States—History—19th century. 4. Landscape gardening—United States—History—19th century. 5. Downing, A. J. (Andrew Jackson), 1815–1852. Treatise on the theory and practice of landscape gardening. I. Title.
SB470.D68M36   1997
712′.092—dc20   96-36407
                                        CIP

The MIT Press is pleased to keep this title available in print by manufacturing single copies, on demand, via digital printing technology.

TO MY HUSBAND JIM

*this time, for giving me
strength and courage*

viii Acknowledgments

2 Introduction

PART I

7 LANDSCAPE GARDENING AS A FINE ART
The Treatise *of 1841, 1844, and 1849*

1

10 THE TREATISE: *Aspirations and Audience*

11 *To Garden Finely*
17 *The Love of Home*
21 *Who Does Not Love the Country?*
26 *Country Gentlemen and Large Landed Estates*
30 *Amateurs and Professionals*
33 *A Studied and Polished Mode*

2

36 ALMOST EVERYTHING IS YET BEFORE US: *The 1841 Edition*

38 *The More Exquisite Beauty of Natural Forms*
43 *Here, Where Nature Has Done So Much*
46 *General Beauty and Picturesque Beauty*
53 *Imitation in the Fine Arts and the Beau Ideal*
61 *The Superior Beauty of Expresssion*

3

66 ON HIS NATIVE HEATHER: *The 1844 Edition*

70 *The Reading of the Past*
73 *Comparatively Little Having Yet Been Done*
78 *Expression: The Master Key*
80 *The Graceful and the Picturesque*

4

86 LET THE PRINCIPLES BE PRESERVED: *The 1849 Edition*

87 *American Rural Gems*
91 *The Beautiful and the Picturesque*
95 *The Finest Form of a Fine Type*

PART II
99 LANDSCAPE GARDENING AS A HARMONY
BETWEEN THE REAL AND THE IDEAL
The 1846–52 Horticulturist *Editorials*

5
106 THE HORTICULTURIST: *Aspirations and Audience*

106 *Moderate Establishments*
109 *Republican Simplicity*
113 *The Moral Effects of the Fine Arts*
119 *The Spirit of Emulation*
124 *Citizens Turning Country-Folk*
126 *Novices, Amateurs, and Professionals*
129 *Wisdom Conveyed in Pleasant and Familiar Words*

6
136 A THEORY AND PRACTICE ADAPTED

137 *A National Taste in Gardening*
141 *Economy in Gardening*
148 *The Neglected American Plants*
154 *The Type of All True Art in Landscape Gardening*

7
158 AFTER TWENTY YEARS TRIAL

167 Appendix: *Horticulturist* Editorials
185 Notes
217 Bibliography
233 Index

ACKNOWLEDGMENTS

My interest in A. J. Downing began in 1983 at the University of Pennsylvania, and I remain greatly indebted to several professors on that faculty. David Leatherbarrow encouraged me to study the connection between eighteenth- and nineteenth-century architectural theory and Downing's ideas on landscape gardening; David Brownlee, a meticulous editor who taught me discipline in writing, and Christa Wilmanns-Wells, the first at Penn to listen and to understand, continue to give unstintingly of their advice, encouragement, and friendship.

While following the trail of a footnote during my first semester, I discovered the treasures of the Library Company of Philadelphia and its neighbor the Historical Society of Pennsylvania. A 1987 Summer Research Fellowship in American History and Culture allowed me the luxury of a thorough study of their Downing letters and collections of nineteenth-century American books, diaries, and periodicals. I am especially obliged to Jim Green, assistant librarian, and Ken Finkel, then curator of prints. A 1989 Dumbarton Oaks Summer Fellowship in Landscape Architecture provided a blissful summer in the Garden Library immersed in the old-world texts that

Acknowledgments

inspired Downing. I thank Linda Lott and Annie Thacher for their help. In 1993 I was awarded the Samuel H. Kress Publication Fellowship administered by the Architectural History Foundation to fund the preparation of this book.

I am grateful to the staff at the Library Company of Philadelphia, where Phil Lapsansky helped with the complications of gathering illustrations; the Historical Society of Pennsylvania; the Library of the Pennsylvania Horticultural Society; the Manuscript Collection, Houghton Library, Harvard University; the Weigel Library, Kansas State University; the Spencer Research Library, where Anthony Jacobs was of great help, and the Kansas Collection, University of Kansas Libraries; Stacey L. Sherman and Valerie Zell at the Nelson-Atkins Museum of Art, Kansas City, Missouri; Richard H. Smith at the National Archives and Records Administration, College Park, Maryland; Sylvia Fitzgerald, Chief Librarian and Archivist, and Cheryl Piggott, Archivist, Royal Botanic Gardens, Kew, England; the Lindley Library at the Royal Horticultural Society, London, England; the Central Library, City of Liverpool, England; and Margaret M. Sherry, Reference Librarian/Archivist in the Rare Books and Special Collections, Princeton University Libraries.

During my twelve Downing years, I have benefited from the teaching, assistance, or moral support of many people, including Dean Emeritus G. Holmes Perkins, Julia Moore Converse, Peter McCleary, Marco Frascari, Joseph Rykwert, Anne Whiston Spirn, Mark Laird, Georges Teyssot, Joanna Lombard, Saralyn Reece Hardy, Kent Spreckelmeyer, Leland E. Warren, Joseph Disponzio, Pat Tiller, and Matthew Abbate and Jim McWethy at the MIT Press. Richard Longstreth, Marlene Heck, and Joy Stocke read various parts of the manuscript, and their suggestions were of great value. Donald Worster led the Hall Center for the Humanities 1993 Faculty Seminar in which seven of my colleagues at the University of Kansas participated, and all offered thoughtful comments on the *Horticulturist* portion of the manuscript. I reserve a special appreciation for John Dixon Hunt—the scholarly rigor of his work remains the measure for my own, and his keen and generous counsel has helped to bring this book to light.

Finally, thanks to my friends who were a lifeline during the hot summer months of 1995, to my brother, mother, and father—and especially to Jim, Corbin, Sarah, Adam, and McGee.

TO LIVE IN THE NEW WORLD

INTRODUCTION

In 1852 Andrew Jackson Downing, the country's premier author and practitioner in landscape gardening and editor of the monthly *Horticulturist and Journal of Rural Art and Rural Taste,* was reflecting upon the difference between American and British gardening. On his travels throughout the eastern seaboard states, Downing met with constant reminders of the obstacles to American progress in horticulture, and he abhorred the fact that the country's gardening was almost entirely in the hands of foreign-born practitioners. "When a man goes into a country without understanding its language," Downing mused, "he is likely to comprehend little of the real character of that country." Remaining ignorant of the language, manners, and customs, a person would never be more than an "alien in a strange land." One could not stubbornly adhere to old-world prejudices and customs and hope "to live in the new world" as a contented and successful citizen. Since the 1841 publication of his *Treatise on the Theory and Practice of Landscape Gardening,* Downing's conviction had been growing steadily that the art of landscape gardening required similar adaptations to the language, manners, and customs of Americans and to the character of the country's indigenous landscape.[1]

Ironically, what most branded Downing as an American-born author was hidden from the reading public, for he signed his correspondence and published works simply "A. J. Downing" (fig. 0.1). Born October 31, 1815, ten months after General Andrew Jackson's celebrated victory over British troops at the Battle of New Orleans, Downing avoided an embarrassing connection to the former hero. His wife Caroline (née DeWint) was the grandniece of John Quincy Adams, who was ousted from office by Jackson in the vicious 1828 presidential campaign and who remained his sworn political foe. Downing's in-laws were decidedly Whig—a party supported by wealthy northern businessmen and, by the early 1840s, by upwardly mobile farmers and merchants, all of whom were Downing's likely readers and clients. A. J. further distanced himself from his namesake by "respectfully and affectionately" dedicating his 1841 *Treatise* to "the distinguished patriot, statesman, and sage" John Quincy Adams. He perhaps alluded to the burden of being allied in name only with the mudslinging politician and military man when he inserted this gentle reminder into his opening *Horticulturist* editorial: "Angry volumes of politics have we written none; but peaceful books, humbly aiming to weave something more into the fair garland of the beautiful, and useful, that encircles this excellent old Earth."[2]

Such a body of work was the natural outcome for an author who described himself as "a man born on the banks of one of the noblest and most fruitful rivers in America . . . whose best days have been spent in gardens and orchards." Downing's father Samuel had made a living as a wheelwright, but at the time of his youngest son's birth he owned an established nursery business in Newburgh, New York, a village on the west bank of the Hudson River. Downing was remembered as uncommonly bright for his years; showing an interest in botany, mineralogy, and insects at the age of fifteen, he left school a year later and pursued studies on his own. In this regard, he was fortunate in the area's great botanical variety; more native species of trees could be found in the Hudson Valley than in the British Isles. Proximity to the city of New York and the ease of transportation encouraged an increasing number of elegant summer residences and family seats along this majestic

0.1

Portrait of A. J. Downing. Frontispiece in *Horticulturist* (November 1852). Author's collection.

stretch of the Hudson River. According to his wife Caroline, whose own family's Cedar Grove was directly across the river from Newburgh, Downing's acquaintance with several cultivated and distinguished neighbors during his youth "had no doubt much influence in strengthening his naturally refined taste & generous nature." The English architect Calvert Vaux related the circumstances in which his partner became skilled in his future profession: "His taste early induced him to turn his attention to the improvement of grounds and gardens [and] for several years he seemed to retire as it were within himself and during that time he must have been a very close student." Downing remained in Newburgh, at first to run the family nursery, then to build a home and conduct horticultural experiments within his four and a half acres, and finally to devote himself to writing and his landscape gardening and architectural practice (fig. 0.2). Thus, the spectacular natural setting of New York's Hudson Highlands, where dramatic ramparts lined both banks for a distance of fifteen miles, was a significant factor in the life of the landscape gardener who promoted an American version of the British picturesque style. Downing lived and worked in the midst of the type of landscape that he recommended to his readers—where nature assisted in the creation of beautiful homes and gardens (figure 0.3).[3]

While this is not a biography of Downing, the people, events, and experiences that gradually shaped his thinking on landscape gardening are central to the story. One of those persons, the prolific Scottish author and landscape gardener John Claudius Loudon, lived with the same intensity during his sixty years as Downing did in his thirty-seven. "In this progressive age," Loudon admonished, "a man who has the means of existence to procure by his labour or his talent ought to be learning every day of his life. If he stands still for a moment, the world will march on without him." Downing, like his mentor Loudon, was learning each day of his life—from books and periodicals, travel, colleagues and friends, his nursery business and landscape gardening practice, and his own writings and editorship of the *Horticulturist*. As a friend remarked after Downing's death, "his taste and his common sense . . . were well balanced, and they kept pace and enlarged and brightened, to his dying day." A critical inquiry into Downing's ideas must take this intellectual growth into account.[4]

0.2

Residence of the Author, Newburgh, N.Y. In *Treatise* (1841). Author's collection.

Downing developed his theory and practice of landscape gardening in three editions of the *Treatise* and in a series of monthly editorials for the *Horticulturist*, which he edited from July 1846 until his death on July 28, 1852. His other works, including *Cottage Residences* (1842), *The Fruits and Fruit-Trees of America* (1845), and *The Architecture of Country Houses* (1850), are considered only in relation to these two publications, which when examined chronologically reveal Downing's increasing awareness that, however much the new nation could benefit from European precedent in the fine art of landscape gardening, he had to move beyond a respectful adherence to certain traditional principles. He made successive changes to the *Treatise* to add material of a more national interest, and he modified its theoretical framework to take advantage of the expressive potential in the country's indigenous landscape. Nevertheless, this work remained true to Downing's highest aspirations: to guide country gentlemen—with enough money, time, and taste—in the creation of ideal homes and pleasure grounds. Downing claimed that the *Treatise* was adapted to North America;

Introduction

however, the "new starting ground" announced in the second edition was less fertile for American landscape gardening than the *Horticulturist* proved to be. In the *Horticulturist* Downing "spoke American" and offered men and women a message of moderation and simplicity, encouraging them to practice economy, to use America's rich natural resources wisely yet artfully—to be content with a little cottage and a few fine native trees. Downing ultimately accommodated a republican as opposed to an aristocratic rural art.

There are significant differences among the 1841, 1844, and 1849 editions of the *Treatise,* and Downing's views on landscape gardening can be only partially and imperfectly known without a thorough analysis of the *Horticulturist*. The editorial of January 1849 (the date of the introduction to the *Treatise*'s last edition) and those that followed monthly until his death almost three and a half years later are particularly important. They present Downing's most mature treatment of the subject and span a third of his career as America's most renowned horticulturist and landscape gardener. The changes in the 1844 and 1849 editions of the *Treatise,* when studied in conjunction with the *Horticulturist* editorials, show that Downing moved

0.3

View from Ruggle's House, Newburgh. (Hudson River.) In N. P. Willis, *American Scenery,* vol. 1 (1840). The Library Company of Philadelphia.

toward a more realistic assessment of American capabilities and resources and adjusted his theory and practice accordingly.

Downing has been securely established as the popularizer of an American landscape gardening. Luther Tucker, proprietor of the *Horticulturist*, needed no stronger term than "American" to praise his former editor a month after his death: "Mr. Downing was an American, and all his thinking and acting tended toward the welfare and elevation of his country." However, this appellation has never been sufficiently explained. His genius partly lay in a talent for invoking the proper sentiments, as did other mid-nineteenth-century inspirational writers, teachers, ministers, and politicians. When Downing reviewed the work of a contemporary, he was impressed if he detected an American voice and found an honest clarity in the writing; his comments often seemed to highlight his own rare abilities. For example, he praised the clergyman Henry Ward Beecher as "*a man of his time*—who utters the thoughts, and interprets the language, of the great struggling heart of the nineteenth century." In a glowing review of a manual by Asa Gray, a prominent botanist and Harvard professor of natural history, Downing used the opportunity to mock pedantry—that fondness for displaying one's knowledge by introducing hard technical names on every possible occasion. He believed that a person's specialized knowledge would be sought when needed and was, in fact, better appreciated and understood "from its not being intruded at inappropriate seasons." His humorous example was typical of what his readers had come to expect: "Only a very young botanist, therefore, will cry out *Hypericum perforatum*, whenever he passes through a field filled with Johnswort!" In the *Treatise* and the *Horticulturist*, Downing's theory and practice of landscape gardening were placed under the light of ideas and values that Americans understood and embraced. Thus did that art of civility and elegance begin to live contentedly and successfully in the New World.[5]

PART I

LANDSCAPE GARDENING
AS A FINE ART

The Treatise *of 1841, 1844, and 1849*

A. J. Downing's *Treatise on the Theory and Practice of Landscape Gardening, Adapted to North America* was recognized immediately as "the first work of the kind, of any considerable pretensions, [to] come from the American press." As one reviewer remarked, Downing had "neither companion nor rival," for none of his countrymen had written a book devoted entirely to this subject. Two earlier publications contained only brief sections on landscape gardening: *American Gardener's Calendar* (1806), by Bernard M'Mahon of Philadelphia, devoted a chapter to "The Pleasure, or Flower-Garden"; and Thomas G. Fessenden's *New American Gardener* (1828) included the Brooklyn nurseryman and practitioner André Parmentier's "Landscapes and Picturesque Gardens" between descriptions of the "Jerusalem Artichoke" and "Lavender." Although Downing referred to Parmentier's work as a "short treatise," the three-page essay merely touched upon "how ridiculous it was . . . to apply the rules of architecture to the embellishment of gardens."[1]

Downing was only twenty-five when the *Treatise* appeared in the spring of 1841, but in the preceding ten years he had gained extensive professional experience as a horticulturist, in partnership with his brother Charles until 1837 and then as sole proprietor of his Newburgh, New York, Botanic Garden and Nursery, and he quickly assumed a position of leadership in American horticultural societies. Downing had also been publishing articles since the early 1830s in American, French, and English periodicals on an impressive variety of topics including ornamental trees and shrubs, new methods of heating by hot water, the cultivation of hedges, protection against hail storms, and the progress of American horticulture and gardening. In July 1841 the critic for the *North American Re-*

view correctly surmised that Downing possessed "much more than the mere requisites for making a book about gardening." Praising the author of the *Treatise* as "an enthusiast, as well as a practical artist," Charles Francis Adams reported: "He speaks of effects to be produced from given causes, not from what he may have read of them in books, or seen in pictures and highly-colored engravings, but from personal observation and experiment."[2]

As early as 1836, Downing described his "first conception" of the *Treatise* in a letter to C. M. Hovey and P. B. Hovey, Jr., editors of the *American Gardener's Magazine:* "a book to be entitled 'Arboriculture, or the Culture and Management of Forest, Ornamental and Fruit Trees, with their adaptation to Landscape Gardening, the Orchard, the Arts, &c." Soon after, Downing remarked to readers of what had become C. M. Hovey's *Magazine of Horticulture* that landscape gardening was the least understood branch of horticulture in the United States:

In truth, we have but barely made a commencement . . . and as the examples already existing on this side of the Atlantic are but rare, and this branch of the art chiefly in the hands of the proprietors themselves, we shall probably have to witness a great variety of attempts, which will not always be followed by the most successful results as to effect: but the public feeling is alive to improvement on this subject, and we hope much from the general good taste of the proprietors who usually make themselves acquainted with the best European authors on the subject.[3]

By October 1838, as Downing told the Hoveys, he had nearly completed the book now tentatively titled "The Improvement of Country Residences, &c.":

About half the work will be occupied with a description of all the finest hardy ornamental and forest trees of both hemispheres, with remarks on their effect in landscape gardening, both singly and in composition, (groups, &c.) The remainder may be called a short treatise on modern Landscape Gardening—the arrangement of plantations—disposition of grounds—architectural decorations, buildings, &c. . . . I conceive that, with the increasing spirit of improvement in the country growing up among us, it will not be found ill-timed.

When Downing wrote to New York architect Alexander J. Davis two months later, he was still "busily engaged in preparing a work for the press"—which he now described in substance as "Landscape Gardening and Rural Residences." The shift in the book's core subject can be reasonably explained by Downing's acquisition of J. C. Loudon's *Suburban Gardener* (1838) during the fall of that year, for it was in this work that Loudon elaborated on the gardenesque, the theory of imitation, the recognition of art, and landscape gardening as a fine art. The profound influence of the *Suburban Gardener* was evident in Downing's first edition of the *Treatise*.[4]

However, an additional two years would pass before the *Treatise* appeared; a contemporary remembered the discouraging circumstances under which Downing pursued publication, suggesting that the art of landscape gardening was so unappreciated in America that the manuscript remained for some time without a publisher. More likely, and as Downing himself pointed out, easy access to the best English works precluded the necessity of books on the same subjects in the United States. This was the general state of affairs in the 1830s. The French observer Alexis de Tocqueville remarked that England supplied American readers with most of the books they required, and Harriet Martineau, an Englishwoman who also visited the United States during this time, blamed the depression in American literature on the lack of international copyright laws. She acer-

The Treatise of 1841, 1844, and 1849

bically reported that booksellers would not remunerate native authors when they could "purloin the works of British writers." Another factor, according to Martineau, was the American public's "strong disposition to listen to the utterance of the English in preference to the prophets of their own country." The enthusiastic reception of Downing's *Treatise* was evidence that Americans were ready to listen to one of their own.[5]

The *Treatise* should be recognized as part of the response to intensifying demands for a national American literature. Authors and critics alike challenged those who suggested that foreign books could meet all of the country's wants. In an oration delivered in the summer of 1837, Ralph Waldo Emerson assured the young scholars in his audience: "Our day of dependence, our long apprenticeship to the learning of other lands, draws to a close." Two years later, the nationalistic *Democratic Review* called the propensity to imitate foreign nations "absurd and injurious" and asked, "Oh, when will [our literature] breathe the spirit of our republican institutions?" Writers who contributed to this magazine argued that their literature ought to be strongly American, fitted to "the New Man in the New Age." This same magazine celebrated Downing's *Treatise*, declaring that its publication could be regarded "as constituting an era in the literature of this country."[6]

Notices of America's tardy initiation into the civility of fine gardening were numerous. J. C. Loudon was quick to label the *Treatise* "a masterly work of its kind, more especially considering that it was produced in America." Others recognized Downing as a new-world master spirit who combined the proper birthright with the best of classical tradition and modern European gardening. Reviews noted with conspicuous pride that a native author had produced a fine art treatise, but the *North American Review* also offered more pragmatic reasons for the book's success:

> The English works, which are to be found in great variety, and some of them very splendid, are worse than useless in many respects upon this side of the Atlantic; for they are predicated upon a state of society and manners, a climate, an extent of private fortunes, and a scale of prices of labor and materials, so wholly different from what is known here, that any luckless wight who ever commenced operations upon the faith of what he read in them, must have had occasion before he ended, to repent in more ways than one of his misplaced confidence.[7]

Downing admitted in the book's preface that he often heard such complaints; consequently, the *Treatise* was written for America and "the peculiar wants of its inhabitants." One critic recognized this particular contribution, commenting that Downing had done for America what Sir Uvedale Price, Thomas Whately, and J. C. Loudon could not do. Despite America's veneration of Price's *Essay on the Picturesque* (1794), Whately's *Observations on Modern Gardening* (1770), and Loudon's numerous volumes including *An Encyclopedia of Gardening* (1822), none of these British works satisfied the charge that the new nation's rural arts "must grow directly out of the wants and the position of the people; not of some other people, but of this people."[8]

1

THE *TREATISE*

Aspirations and Audience

The *Treatise* responded directly to the charge that foreign books were not adequate guides for the nation's landscape design. Downing invoked popular cultural issues that Americans of the 1840s could embrace; as did other writers interested in the art of persuasion, he used emotional manipulation to appeal to the heart as well as the head. For example, the *Treatise*'s pretensions backed national pride in American progress. Downing purported that the Atlantic seaboard states possessed "all the luxuries and refinements that belong[ed] to an old and long cultivated country," and reviewers concurred with his appraisal of the rapidly improving conditions. They hailed the publication as evidence of "a growing disposition to elegance" and as an indication that an American class now existed that could devote time and energy to "the more liberal and elevated arts." Downing told landowners with this newly acquired leisure that the art of landscape gardening responded to their desire to render their own property attractive, made domestic life more delightful, and increased local attachments. Thus, the *Treatise* embraced the freehold concept and ideals of domesticity and stability. With a bond forged between these sentiments and landscape gardening, the improvement of house and garden was turned into a patriotic act. Finally, the American love of rural life was satisfied in the practice of rural embellishment; no greater pleasure, Downing promised, could be derived by the person who "plucks life's roses in his quiet fields."[1]

The presumed proprietor of these quiet fields was the country gentleman of leisure. An estate of fifty to five hundred acres would suffice for what Downing deemed landscape gardening in its proper sense. Men capable of carrying out exemplary improvements were rare, however; wealthy Americans apparently had more money than taste, practical experience, or knowledge of correct principles. The 1841 preface carried a rebuke to those who fancied themselves amateur landscape gardeners; rather than employ professional talent, they planned and arranged their own residences, often with poor results and a great waste of time and money. The *Treatise* therefore had a dual, seemingly self-contradictory intention: it acted as a do-it-yourself guide for amateurs but was also concerned with establishing a respect for professional landscape gardeners and a market for their services.[2]

Whatever its purpose, the *Treatise* had to exhibit a high style of writing to take its place among comparable European works, and Downing's countrymen were not disappointed. Americans were more ready for the refinements of civilization than foreign observers credited; one reader commented, "How opportunely, then, has Mr. Downing come forward with his instructive and delightful volume." This elegant book proudly refuted what the sculptor Horatio Greenough saw as the old-world inclination to concentrate unfairly on America's "anti-poetical tendency." In an essay titled "Remarks on American Art" (1843), Greenough complained, "Seeing us intently occupied during several generations in felling forests, in building towns, and constructing roads, she thence formed a theory that we are good for nothing except these pioneering efforts."[3]

Downing's perception was similar, for he dryly remarked to a friend in 1842: "The Landscape Gardening treatise . . . seems to have startled the Europeans, who can hardly believe that we have any thing but log houses." Political image makers in Washington were partially to blame for this misconception. Although in truth a large proportion of the population still lived in log cabins, these crude dwellings had not been looked upon as a symbol of republican simplicity and of America's humble beginnings until the 1840 "Log Cabin and Hard Cider" presidential campaign of William Henry Harrison and John Tyler (fig. 1.1). If one also finds in Downing's comment an allusion to the often quoted observation by Francis Bacon—"When ages grow to civility and elegancy, men come to build stately, sooner than to garden finely; as if gardening were the greater perfection"—then Downing's charge as apostle of refinement in landscape gardening is clear. Downing had not only to struggle against the Old World's imperfect knowledge of America's accomplishments but to counteract Americans' own tendency to extoll the common and uncultured aspects of their character.[4]

To Garden Finely

As a refined taste in architecture and landscape gardening traditionally indicated a civilized and elegant society, the *Treatise*'s preface opened with an assertion of America's rapid strides in both of these arts: "The evidences of the growing wealth and prosperity of our citizens have become apparent in the great increase of elegant cottage and villa residences on the banks of our noble rivers, [and] throughout our rich valleys" (fig. 1.2). Downing was not solely boasting about the buildings, for he stressed that architectural beauty must be considered jointly with the beauty of the landscape and that residential structures, in particular, were meant to be component parts of the general scene.[5]

Six years earlier, the *New-York Mirror* had reported

THE *TREATISE*: Aspirations and Audience

1.1

This Log Cabin. Political cartoon (1840). The Library Company of Philadelphia.

on the economic changes reflected in its readers' domestic arrangements. The weekly stated that increased commerce in the city so enhanced property values that housing costs had grown intolerable. High rents and the new ease of rail transportation to and from the city in turn enhanced the lure of the country's pure air and water, "not to mention the numberless enjoyments . . . such as gardens, fruit-trees, lovely walks, and rides." Life's necessities were being succeeded by its delights and refinements as civilization progressed—at least along the Atlantic seaboard.[6]

Downing agreed with contemporaries such as Susan Fenimore Cooper, author of *Rural Hours* (1851), that the "first rude stage of progress" had passed. With their primary wants such as food and shelter satisfied, people were beginning to think about the conveniences and pleasures of permanent homes. In reviewing Downing's work, Parke Godwin remarked the end of "a period of doubt, of struggle, of incessant bodily exertion." The *Trea-*

12

To Garden Finely

tise honored the country's self-conscious pride in its achievements and established a strong connection between the rural arts and American progress.[7]

While Downing boasted that easterners were starting to concern themselves with urban amenities and tasteful country houses, he admitted that another part of the population had more basic cares: "In the far west the pioneer constructs his rude hut of logs for a dwelling, and sweeps away with his axe the lofty forest trees that encumber the ground" (fig. 1.3). In 1841, forty-eight wagons reached Sacramento—the first large group to emigrate to California; one year later, a major party headed for the Oregon territory from Independence, Missouri. A pioneer woman named Johnaphene Faulkner recorded that for many of these westward-moving people any shelter at all was welcome. A settlement old enough to boast a log cabin, she remembered, was an improvement on a tent, which in turn was an improvement on the camp of boughs and poles erected on a site the first day. The pioneer and agriculturist Solon Robinson gave advice to these western emigrants grounded in his firsthand knowledge of conditions during the first years in a new habitation. He enumerated the "fixins" of a house composed of rough logs and cautioned readers of the *Cultivator*

1.2

Belmont and Waterworks, Mount Pleasant, Fairmount Park, Philadelphia. In A. Kollner, *Bits of Nature and Some Art Products in Fairmount Park at Philadelphia, Pennsylvania* (1878). The Library Company of Philadelphia. Belmont was built c. 1755 on the Schuylkill River.

THE *TREATISE*: *Aspirations and Audience*

to dispose of all articles of luxury and to invest the proceeds in improved farming implements and valuable stock and seeds. Downing knew that these homesteaders, who faced life in shacks with dirt floors and canvas ceilings, in dark dugouts, or in dirty brown soddies, did not have the time or energy "to cultivate a taste for Rural Embellishment," but his acknowledgment of these enterprising spirits in the West was another boost to the national ego, and provided a measure of just how far civilization had advanced in the older parts of the United States (fig. 1.4).[8]

Downing's countrymen were declaring that the time had come for "prosecuting the nobler pursuits." Horatio Greenough regretted that Europeans did not understand what the United States had accomplished in its struggles with the hard-

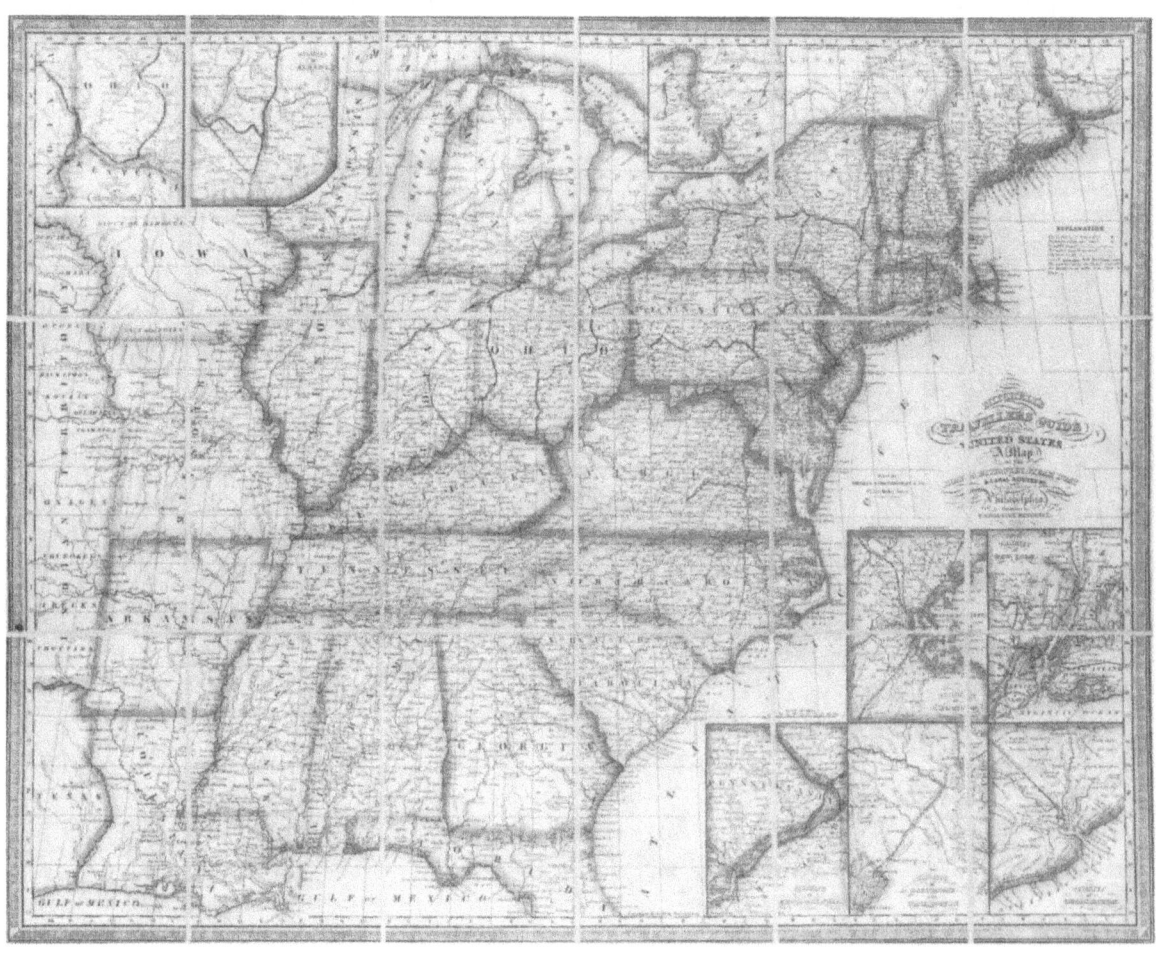

1.3

U.S. map. *Mitchell's Traveller's Guide* (1843). The Library Company of Philadelphia. The state of Missouri, on the border of Indian Territory, was the "far west" of the United States.

To Garden Finely

1.4

Homestead with sod buildings (n.d.). Kansas Collection, University of Kansas Libraries.

ships of an untamed continent and with the disadvantages of colonial relations. He complained that America was taunted because "there were no statues or frescoes in our log-cabins" and was pronounced unmusical because men "did not sit down in the swamp with an Indian on one side, and a rattlesnake on the other, to play the violin." Greenough could not foresee that America would be occupied with only the basic necessities its whole life just because the infant nation had been absorbed with feeding itself.[9]

Foreign travelers throughout the 1830s consistently remarked on the "thousand special causes" that fixed the American mind upon purely practical objects and not upon polite literature and the fine arts: "Behold how [the American] makes his way over the rocks and precipices; see how he struggles in close fight with the rivers, with the swamps, with the primeval forests." The *Democratic Review* offered a response: who had heard of a nation in the first half-century of its existence, engaged in a struggle for its liberties, that devoted much time to laying out flower gardens or transplanting shrubbery? The American fathers first did battle for freedom, justice, equality, and right and could not busy themselves with founding schools in the fine arts or adorning Bunker Hill with parterres of roses.[10]

THE *TREATISE*: *Aspirations and Audience*

Some observers suggested that the popular reception of Downing's book was gratifying evidence that American indifference to taste was coming to an end. Other indications of this progress in landscape gardening are found in the letters of the author Washington Irving, as he kept a friend informed of changes in the countryside near his Hudson River cottage. In the summer of 1847 he wrote: "This neighborhood is daily growing more and more beautiful, from the improved taste in building, in decorating grounds, in setting out trees &c." In diary notations during the 1840s, Philadelphians Joseph Sill and Sidney George Fisher wrote of the progress in building observed on their travels. Geneva, New York, was a pretty town, according to Sill, with beautiful sites for private villas. He also recorded a day trip just outside Philadelphia, where he noticed many recently erected, handsome villas (fig. 1.5). Fisher considered the country residences in the neighborhood

1.5

Sweet Briar Mansion, in 1843. Fairmount Park, Philadelphia. In A. Kollner, *Bits of Nature and Some Art Products in Fairmount Park at Philadelphia, Pennsylvania* (1878). The Library Company of Philadelphia. Sweetbriar was built in 1797 on the Schuylkill River.

of Albany, New York, and along the Hudson River far superior to any near Philadelphia. On a drive of eight miles on both sides of the Hudson in the fall of 1847, he passed many tasteful villas and cottages, all of them with handsome grounds planted with trees. He recognized the influence of Downing's books in these improvements. From the South, the Swedish author Fredrika Bremer reported in 1850: "Here, where [Ralph] Waldo Emerson's name is unknown . . . I hear Mr. Downing's name coupled with objects of beauty, and hear the same words in South Carolina that I heard under the snowy roofs of Concord in New England: 'Mr. Downing has done much good to this country!' "[11]

The good that Downing accomplished was twofold. For a young country anxious to justify itself, he provided a treatise on the civilizing art of landscape gardening—proof that Americans were ready to enter and enjoy a civilized society. Second, while acknowledging recent advances, he linked future national progress to a deeper and more active interest in the rural arts, thereby encouraging an American aesthetic culture in home embellishment.

The Love of Home

Patriotism is inseparably connected with "the love of home" in the *Treatise*. Downing declared his belief in the power of the individually owned home to contribute to familial security and contentment and to strengthen the nation at large by increasing attachments to native soil. Seeking to promote the freehold concept, Downing stipulated that the adornment of one's own property would afford more permanent satisfaction than any other employment or recreation: "To have a 'local habitation,'—a permanent dwelling, that we can give the impress of our own mind, and identify with our own existence,—appears to be the ardent wish, sooner or later felt, of every man." He expressed the lure of the individual home with a biblical phrase: "To sit under our own vine and fig tree, with no one to make us afraid." This obsession struck visitors to the United States, among them Harriet Martineau, who noted that the possession of land was the aim of all action and the cure for all social evils: "If a man is disappointed in politics or love, he goes and buys land. If he disgraces himself, he betakes himself to a lot in the west. . . . If a citizen's neighbours rise above him in the towns, he betakes himself where he can be monarch of all he surveys. An artisan works, that he may die on land of his own."[12]

Downing boasted in the *Treatise* that the United States had a larger class of intelligent and well-educated independent landholders than did any other country, compensating for the lack of landscape gardens as splendid as those in Britain. Writing from England in 1850, Downing reminded Americans that their ability to buy land placed them in an enviable position. He related a conversation with an old woman who had sons in the New World; she emphasized that they had *bought land* and were doing famously. Downing added: "For a working man to own land, in a country like [England], where the farmers are almost all only tenants of the few great proprietors, is to their minds something like holding a fee simple to part of paradise."[13]

The value of home was proclaimed both privately and publicly, in Edenic sentiments. The Philadelphia merchant Joseph Sill recorded in his diary: "I consider that a Home to a man is every thing." Late in life, Caroline Downing's great-uncle John

THE *TREATISE*: *Aspirations and Audience*

Quincy Adams wrote regretfully that the concept of "sweet home" was unintelligible to some and blamed the ease and speed of modern travel. Adams reflected on the multiple associations of the English word *home*—for him, it consisted of elements that formed "the choicest and purest enjoyments of human life." A writer for *Graham's Magazine* shared Adams's sensibilities: "'Home, sweet home!' How many holy and beautiful memories are crowded into those three little words. How does the absent one, when weary with the cold world's strife, return, like the dove of the deluge, to that bright spot amid the troubled waters of life." The *Treatise*'s frontispiece portrayed this ideal image: Blithewood was the Hudson River residence of Robert Donaldson, his wife, child, and dog (fig. 1.6).[14]

Some viewed a quiet home as the antidote to the restless, feverish activity that pervaded the country. The author James K. Paulding urged his countrymen to seek "in the quiet shades of life that gentle existence of mingled labor, amusement and contemplation which, when accompanied by a taste for rural pleasures and occupations affords as fair a chance for a happy, useful and contented life." An admirer of the *Treatise* agreed with Downing that the multiplying bonds that joined citizens with the soil would support civil institutions. Contrasting the man with a few roods of soil (approxi-

1.6

View in the Grounds at Blithewood, Dutchess Co., N.Y. Frontispiece in *Treatise* (1841). Author's collection.

mately one-half acre) to the migrating boarder in the fifth story of a city hotel, the *Democratic Review* asked if it were not inevitable that the man who viewed his relations to the government from a fixed locality would feel a closer tie to his native land. Moreover, crime statistics purportedly showed that a vast proportion of offenses were committed by persons who did not own land. Also appearing in this magazine were poems that addressed the power of home to soothe the weary and to still the American wanderlust. A few lines from Mrs. St. Leon Loud suffice: "From a far green valley ye come! ye come! / Speak to the wanderer, voices of home!"[15]

These arguments were meant to counteract the general "restlessness"—a term consistently linked to the population of the United States. In 1852 the clergyman and philosopher Henry P. Tappan admitted: "We are a restless people from the very conditions of our country. We seek for change and dare fortune." Disturbed by his countrymen's impermanence and lack of home feeling, Tappan criticized their tendency to build homes with the idea of future speculation instead of seeking wealth as a means of creating a home to find repose. A recent immigrant agreed that Americans distinguished themselves by their restlessness; although this drive had opened a successful career to thousands of men possessed of nothing but energy, it had also extinguished for many the calm enjoyment of what they did have. Lydia Sigourney, an editor for *Godey's Magazine,* labeled it "the restlessness and din of the rail-road principle."[16]

The American fever to be continuously "going ahead" and the fixation on what in 1845 would be termed "manifest destiny," disturbed Downing (fig. 1.7). He was certain that this "restless spirit of emigration" was damaging to his country's social and domestic happiness. In the 1841 preface to the *Treatise,* Downing offered a quotation from an author whom he identified only as "the most philosophical writer who has yet discussed our institutions." Although he did not mention Alexis de Tocqueville by name, Americans most likely recognized the author of *Democracy in America* as the source of these sentiments: "In the midst of the continual movement which agitates a democratic community, the tie which unites one generation to another is relaxed or broken; every man readily loses the trace of the ideas of his forefathers, or takes no care about them."[17]

It was proverbial among visiting foreigners as well as native-born commentators that Americans were "the most changing people in the world." Former British naval officer Captain Marryat expressed it thus: "All is transition, the waves follow one another to the far west." Another British traveler,

1.7

A War President. Political cartoon (1848). The Library Company of Philadelphia. The term *manifest destiny* (see soldier's sword) appeared in print for the first time in 1845 in reference to the annexation of Texas. General Zachary Taylor, a hero of the Mexican War, was elected president in 1848.

THE *TREATISE*: *Aspirations and Audience*

Charles Augustus Murray, became convinced that restlessness was a national feature: "A New Englander or Virginian, though proud and vain of his state, will move off to Missouri or Illinois, and leave the home of his childhood without any . . . symptom of regret." Americans viewed this idiosyncrasy both positively and negatively. When Henry Meigs and Lewis F. Allen addressed audiences on the subject of agriculture, the former proclaimed "an indisputable commission to subdue and to till [our own immense continent]" while the latter feared that the constant search for "a fresh spot in a strange and newer land" would be carried out at the sacrifice of stability. Not surprisingly, Downing pondered an unfortunate horticultural result of his countrymen's restlessness: the American brand of impatience, which made a few years of waiting seem endless, explained why hundreds of country places were bare: it required "an age" for forest trees to mature.[18]

In the summer of 1847, Downing wrote again of the country's "spirit of unrest." Concurring with Tocqueville and others, he recognized this as a national trait. The grand and exciting aspect of this spirit had settled the states with unparalleled rapid-

1.8

The Place We Hear About. Political cartoon (1849). The Library Company of Philadelphia. The country's "spirit of unrest" was exacerbated by the discovery of gold in California in 1848.

ity, but Downing also saw a disagreeable effect. Restlessness deprived his countrymen of the dignity of repose and made their lives socially and physically uncertain—like a tree that has been transplanted from place to place and shifted to a different soil every season (fig. 1.8). Downing quoted Tocqueville:

At first sight, there is something surprising in this strange unrest of so many happy men, restless in the midst of abundance.... In the United States a man builds a house to spend his latter years in, and sells it before the roof is on; he brings a field into tillage, and leaves other men to gather the crops; he embraces a profession, and gives it up; he settles in a place, which he soon after leaves, in order to carry his changeable longings elsewhere.[19]

Nathaniel Parker Willis, editor of the weekly *Home Journal,* which addressed "the circle around the family table," noted the lamentable readiness with which housekeepers sold out and the rareness of old homesteads. He suggested that his "plastic and rapidly maturing country would be bettered by a more careful culture of home associations" and urged poets and preachers to join in popularizing this culture. Willis's friend Downing was doing his best to promote domesticity. He offered guidance to those Americans who valued their houses and gardens, and he counted on these rural Edens to fix habits and elevate character. With a comfortable and elegant habitation, a country gentleman would find domestic life delightful and be charmed into remaining in one spot. His own enjoyment heightened and his patriotism strengthened, he would become a better citizen, and the nation would prosper. How could Americans resist this call?[20]

Who Does Not Love the Country?

As Downing well understood, the benefits of rural retirement amid the beauties of nature had attained the level of moral truth in America: "As a people descended from the English stock, we inherit much of the ardent love of rural life and its pursuits." He stated that out of this love, which to some degree naturally existed in the minds of all men, had grown the practice of landscape gardening. Downing reiterated untiringly in the *Horticulturist* that a desire for rural pleasures was the predominant passion of more thoughtful and educated Americans, referring to the rural homes of prominent men such as Henry Clay and Daniel Webster to illustrate his point that "with us, country life is a leading object of nearly all men's desires."[21]

It would be easier to ask "Who does not love the country?" as did *Godey's Magazine* than to document the numerous American poems, essays, diaries, and letters that evoked a passion for rural life during the mid-nineteenth century. "Rural" was called "the purest adjective, in its associations, in the language" (fig. 1.9). In American genre painting as well, rural life and agrarian society provided the most potent and persistent theme at this time. The ideal of a rural retreat modeled on those in classical Roman writings was no mere literary or artistic concept but influenced the fathers of the republic. Horace's Sabine Farm with its little house and fields, garden and vineyard, and flocks and herds on a hospitable site materialized in the country homes of American gentlemen.[22]

Washington Irving's Sunnyside was a recognized retreat cited by Downing and others. "There is scarcely a building or place more replete with interest in America," the *Treatise* proclaimed; "[it is]

THE *TREATISE*: Aspirations and Audience

1.9

Rural Life. In *Graham's American Monthly* (November 1847). The Library Company of Philadelphia.

one of the most secluded and delightful nooks on the banks of the Hudson" (fig. 1.10). A reference to Sunnyside even found its way into lines of humorous verse printed in *Godey's* during the dog days of summer:

The town looks like an ogre,
   The country like a bride;
Wealth hies to Saratoga,
   And Worth to Sunny-Side.

Irving's personal correspondence indicated that he preferred this "little nookery" to the royal salons of Europe; he returned with obvious eagerness in 1846 after a four-year absence as United States minister to Spain. Quickly slipping back into a quiet life, he contentedly counseled a friend who talked of setting up a residence in the country: "Cultivate rural habits and tastes and occupations.... A rural retreat when it is a man's own, and of his formation produces a new set of pleasures and interests."[23]

Hardly an enthusiast of rural life failed to invoke the English poet William Cowper's line from *The Task* (1785): "God made the country, and man made the town." Although the line became "as familiar as household words," neither Downing nor scores of other writers hesitated to quote it again and again because it "expressed so pithily what all observers and lovers of nature have felt." In Cowper's poem, health and virtue abound in the fields and groves, not threatened as they are in the town. A writer for the *New-York Mirror* found this "moral analysis" to be correct: "The perspective of the career of rational and graceful pleasure must be bounded by the scenery of rural-life."[24]

This deliberate and often exaggerated comparison between country and city life in America became commonplace. In truth, there were pitifully few green resorts in New York City; exceptions included the twenty-one-acre Battery and the meager open space in front of City Hall (fig. 1.11). Similarly, the nation's second- and third-largest cities, Philadelphia and Boston, had made little

1.10

Residence of Washington Irving, Esq. In *Treatise* (1841). Author's collection.

1.11

The Park and City Hall, New York. In N. P. Willis, *American Scenery,* vol. 1 (1840). The Library Company of Philadelphia.

provision for public recreation and health. Their close, crowded streets swarmed with people, and the shouts of newsboys and peddlars competed with the noisy clutter of omnibuses, carts, and wagons with iron wheels rolling over granite pavement. Understandably, a sense of contracted space was central to representations of the city. For a poet in *Godey's,* "city life" meant being "cooped up forever amid piles of brick," and New York was "most compactly / Of brick and mortar made." In *Nature* (1836) Ralph Waldo Emerson pictured the tradesman and the attorney emerging from "the din and craft of the street," their bodies and minds "cramped by noxious work or company." Emerson considered nature medicinal and believed that as soon as these men saw the sky and the woods, they would find themselves: "The health of the eye seems to demand a horizon. We are never tired, so long as we can see far enough."[25]

However, a certain ambivalence emerged in the attitude toward city life. Delights available in a civilized urban area were missed in the country in spite of a love of retirement. A writer for the *New-York Mirror* recognized that depending upon individual tastes and habits, both the country and the city had advantages: "Some love the noise and

THE *TREATISE*: Aspirations and Audience

bustle of the city, and have a decided aversion to everything green. . . . [Some] would repudiate the garden of Eden for the dear, shady side of Broadway: the wilderness of brick and stone has more charm for these than the richest forest scenery, and Wall-street is preferable to West Point." Downing reluctantly recognized that it was "needful in civilized life for men to live in cities," but his strong prejudice for country life was apparent to his readers. All sensible men, he told them, gladly escape from the city because "in the United States, nature, and domestic life, are better than society, and the manners of towns." The enjoyment drawn from rural pleasures was supposedly free of "the loss of moral rectitude." When Downing added parenthetically "(unlike many other amusements)," it was clear that he was referring to immoral *urban* amusements. A Mississippi correspondent wrote in support of Downing's position, saying that a man's birthplace had an important bearing on conduct and usefulness. Country-born-and-bred men would always speak of their homes with much fondness and refer to beautiful landscapes, playgrounds, and even the "moss-covered bucket" with great love (fig. 1.12).[26]

An ever-changing diversity of people began to live in cities during this time, and some reformers saw this heterogeneity as a threat to their political vision of an educated society of yeoman farmers who embodied the public virtues. For others, urbanization and industrialization were the root of all evil; the new forms of urban life were signs of the erosion of thrift, piety, prudence, and self-reliance. Tocqueville, visiting America in 1831, was disturbed by the size and nature of the population in Philadelphia and New York. In Tocqueville's eyes, the urban "rabble" was "even more formidable than the populace of European towns" and threatened the republic's security (fig. 1.13).[27]

A variety of material portrayed the extravagance and dissipation of young men who left good rural situations to pursue ruinous courses in the cities. Downing recommended one such book to his readers: In *European Agriculture* (1847), Henry Colman warned of the urban evils of avarice, ambition, and "a feverish thirst for notoriety and excitement," which he vividly contrasted to the rewards of agriculture. The *Democratic Review* applauded Downing's writings for articulating the pleasures to be gained from horticultural pursuits and a country life—as opposed to urban pursuits

1.12

The Old Oaken Bucket. In *Boston Miscellany of Literature & Fashion* (January–July 1842). The Library Company of Philadelphia.

and town life: "All classes find a new joy in turning their backs on cities . . . [and] the conventionalities and outside vanities that glitter and mislead and bewilder there. . . . [Nature] would turn off their eyes from sunsets of machinery, lamp-light and screens." These observations could have accompanied the urban scenes entitled *Corner Loungers* and *The Card Players* illustrated in an earlier issue of this magazine (figs. 1.14, 1.15). Numerous essays and stories repeated this theme: "Town and Country Contrasted," published in *Godey's,* left no doubt as to the author's preference for rural life: "There crime stalk[s] not . . . there the giddy crowd draws not into its vortex of dissipation and riot the unthinking and inexperienced youth." In a fictional account of a young man's downfall published in the *Columbian Magazine,* Mrs. C. H. Butler compared Paris to Erebus—a place of darkness in the underworld on the way to Hades.[28]

The cultivator of the soil was purported to be "much more liable to be right and pure in thought and action than the dweller in the city." The influence of agriculture and horticulture was much the same because "a sanative virtue" was thought to arise out of the soil—out of nature. Lovers of nature, it readily followed, were the strongest lovers of virtue. An open sky, a waterfall,

1.13

The Times. Political cartoon (1837). The Library Company of Philadelphia.

25

THE *TREATISE*: Aspirations and Audience

clouds, flowers, and fields (textbooks in the hand of the Great Teacher) encouraged all that was best in people and quickened their moral sensibilities. The "Book of Nature" was comparable to the fine arts as a tutor in taste; the frontispiece for Warren Burton's *District School as It Was* (1852) illustrated the difference between "man's mean school-house of timber and masonry" and the "school-room of creation" (fig. 1.16). The author Catharine Maria Sedgwick regretted that some had not been awakened to these insights and suggested: "Those who love and understand this word, written in trees and running brooks, should condescend to be its teachers to the young and unobservant." Perhaps it was to her friend Downing that Sedgwick directed this request in 1848, for he had a reputation for "kindling up an admiration for sylvan scenes and natural beauties."[29]

Country Gentlemen and Large Landed Estates

In the *Treatise,* Downing sought "by rendering familiar . . . most of the beautiful sylvan materials of the art, and by describing their peculiar effects in Landscape Gardening, to encourage a taste among general readers." However, an extensive rural property of fifty to five hundred acres was required to realize the full capabilities of the art, and a landholder needed funds and time to embellish it properly. Therefore, the main audience was logically "the country gentleman of leisure"—whom Downing believed would find "rational pleasure" in landscape gardening. The *Democratic Review* boasted that "men of leisure, opulence and education" were multiplying in the United States, and a serious inquiry was needed as to how they could devote their resources for the common benefit.

1.14

Corner Loungers. In *Democratic Review* (August 1843). The Library Company of Philadelphia.

1.15

The Card Players. In *Democratic Review* (November 1843). The Library Company of Philadelphia.

Downing set himself the task of convincing these gentlemen that the best way to spend their accumulated wealth was in building and gardening.[30]

With such a narrow segment of the American population as the audience and with such lofty aspirations for the extent of land ownership, why did the *Cultivator* proclaim that the *Treatise* must be heartily welcomed by "every friend of rural improvement"? A partial answer can be found in this comment from the *Democratic Review*:

> Notwithstanding [Downing's] endeavors to the contrary, we suspect most of his plans are on a scale implying expenditures beyond a safe economy for any but a limited class. . . . Not that he should abate one jot from the high standard of a pure taste; not that he should concede anything to false principles in the art. . . . Real artists must guide and sway, or there will be no lofty attainments. . . . Great models must rise to plead silently with their subduing eloquence.

Without lofty aspirations such as Downing's, there could be no lofty attainments. The *Treatise* taught the principles of landscape gardening as a fine art, and if the ultimate expression as manifested in the large estate was unattainable by most Americans, Downing assured them that this art, unlike others, was not exclusionary. A collection of pictures, for example, was shut up in a private gallery, but a collection of sylvan and floral treasures surrounding the country residence of the man of taste was "confined by no barriers narrower than the blue heaven above and around them." These groves and gardens would provide eloquent models for emulation; the taste and treasures would "creep beyond the nominal boundaries of the estate, and reappear in the pot of flowers in the window . . . of the humblest cottage by the way side."[31]

Downing reformulated his conviction for the *Horticulturist* audience: "To place before men reason-

1.16

Frontispiece in Warren Burton, *The District School As It Was* (1852). The Library Company of Philadelphia.

able objects of ambition, and to dignify and exalt their aims, cannot but be laudable in the sight of all." As an example of how people of fortune and refinement could diffuse taste and elegance to the lower classes, Downing liked to show visitors a beautiful little house and garden in his neighborhood that was owned by a common working man (fig. 1.17). Washington Irving told a similar story. In England, he observed the manner in which the influence of taste could flow down from "high sources" and pervade "the lowest levels of the public mind," because the laborer looked to the residences of people of fortune and refinement for guidance in embellishing his thatched cottage.[32]

Downing took for granted that a "first-class" existed in America. The country as a whole by no means accepted the egalitarian overtones of the Jeffersonian ideal of simple agrarian communities—a hierarchy of classes and a status system both had the weight of centuries behind them. According to Downing, refinement—not money—begat status. An editorial written in 1851 offers the clearest statement of his ideas on social class. He recognized the higher social and artistic elements lying dormant within every man: "Every laborer is a possible gentleman, not by the possession of money or fine clothes—but through the refining influence of intellectual and moral culture." Refined taste entitled a person to enter the ranks of the first class. In Downing's eyes, true progress for America lay in advances in education and culture—"common enjoyment for all classes, in the higher realms of art, letters, science, social recreations and enjoyments." Downing was assuming, of course, that everyone wanted access to these higher realms. In placing before country gentlemen the principles of landscape gardening by way of the *Treatise* and by encouraging them to set an example with their improvements, Downing believed that he would reach the owner of even the smallest cottage. He was able to accomplish this in at least one instance. When a young couple named Sarah and J. I. Taylor moved to Princeton, Illinois, in 1852 and decided to build a home, they modeled Greenwood Cottage after one shown in Downing's *Country Houses* and followed the precepts of the *Treatise* in the surrounding three-and-a-half-acre landscape. When Sarah Taylor described her house and garden in a 1905 newspaper article, she included a lengthy quotation concerning "the love of home" from the 1841 preface and declared herself and her husband to be "disciples of A. J. Downing."[33]

The faith that advancement was always possible in the New World offers another clue to the book's popularity; its readers included those who *aspired* to be country gentlemen of leisure and believed that such an attainment was achievable. Supposedly, Americans possessed an equality of condition as a result of unparalleled equality of opportunity. This egalitarian thesis held that few men in the United States were either very poor or very rich, and those who were rich were typically self-made,

1.17

A Workingman's Cottage, of Humble Means. Frontispiece in *Horticulturist* (September 1846). Author's collection.

born to humble families. Also, because work was exalted over status, class barriers were loose and insignificant. Captain Marryat told of a boy who held a traveler's horse and later became president of the United States—Martin Van Buren, in office from 1837 to 1841. Michael Chevalier perceived the message of American society to the poor man as: "Work . . . work, and at eighteen years of age, although a mere workman, you shall get more than a captain in Europe. You shall live in plenty . . . and be well-lodged." While one scholar has shown this characterization of America to have been mythical—there *were* extremes of wealth and poverty and little vertical mobility—Downing professed to believe in society's fundamental egalitarianism. Trusting that in America integrity and hard work would be rewarded, Downing assured his readers that a fine house and grounds need not foster "the pride of the few, and the envy and the discontent of the many." In some countries, wealth was limited to only a small minority, but because American laborers were much better paid than their counterparts in England, he maintained that the industrious man could rise to an independent position and be a landowner. In reference to these ambitious but still struggling proprietors, the *Treatise* recognized that there were many who had "neither room, time, nor income, to attempt the improvement of their grounds fully." Downing hoped, however, that no one would think his acreage too small "to feel willing to add something to the general amount of beauty in the country." In making readers aware of the principles and capabilities of the art, Downing sought to inspire even those with limited means to infuse tasteful design into their work.[34]

As the name implied, however, the *Treatise* addressed landscape gardening as a fine art, and Downing carefully differentiated landscape gardening from gardening in its common sense. He did not deny the value of an orchard to gratify the palate or a flower garden the eye and nose, but the landscape garden appealed to "that sense of the Beautiful and the Perfect." For this art to appear to advantage it required an extended surface; its lines had to lose themselves indefinitely and unite agreeably and gradually with those of the surrounding country. Thus, only large estates could rank high in landscape gardening. Downing conceded, however, that most of the art's beauty and all of its charm could be enjoyed in ten or twenty acres—if they were fortunately situated and well treated. America was lucky in this regard: the villa residences along the country's stunning rivers and lakes could be successful with only a few acres of tasteful foreground because they could appropriate the adjacent landscape.[35]

Downing's *Cottage Residences* (1842) specifically addressed Americans with only small parcels of ground; Design One was placed within a quarter-acre site. But a quotation by the German poet and dramatist Johann Wolfgang von Goethe that Downing selected for the book's preface showed his unwavering determination to instill all persons with a love of beautiful forms and a desire to assemble this beauty around their daily lives: "Men are so inclined to content themselves with what is commonest, so easily do the spirit and the sense grow dead to the impression of the Beautiful and the Perfect, that every person should strive to nourish in his mind the faculty of feeling these things, by everything in his power, for no man can bear to be wholly deprived of such enjoyment; it is only because they are not used to taste of what is excellent."[36]

THE *TREATISE*: Aspirations and Audience

The American examples of fine gardening that Downing described in the *Treatise*'s "Historical Notices" were primarily large estates in New York State, including the one thousand-acre Geneseo (the Wadsworth family seat on the Genesee River) and the one thousand two hundred-acre Kenwood (the residence of Joel Rathbone south of Albany)—landscapes appealing to the sense of the Beautiful and the Perfect. However, suburban cottages in the environs of Boston were recommended as exemplars for a class of residence that Downing predicted would become more numerous than any other in the country. Although these cottage grounds could have only "almost every kind of beauty and enjoyment," Downing granted that the owner of a few acres who personally directed the curve of every walk, selected and planted every shrub and tree, and watched their progress would receive a more intense degree of pleasure than one who only supervised a vast estate.[37]

Downing did not want to discourage those who owned merely one acre or less; if they would embellish in accordance with "propriety" and not aim at overly ambitious and costly improvements, they could delight their neighbors with "the good taste evinced in the tasteful simplicity of the whole arrangement." For Downing, propriety was equally applicable to landscape and architecture. *The Architecture of Country Houses* (1850) proposed that an entirely satisfactory house in the country was one in which there were not only pretty forms and details but meaning in its beauty in relation to a person's position, character, and daily life. On this subject of propriety or decorum, Downing was adhering to centuries-old architectural theory. To some Americans his opinions seemed antidemocratic; but traditional wisdom was the same from the ancient Roman architect Vitruvius to Downing's contemporary Prince Pückler Muskau, who wrote: "The ponderous castle . . . does not suit the merchant; but is in accordance with the aristocracy." For republican America, Downing advised that a house should be built and the grounds laid out according to the wealth of the proprietor and in reference to his business. The *Treatise* cautioned that even those with extensive property should be concerned with decorum and simplicity: "If the proprietors of our country villas, in their improvements, are more likely to run into any one error than another, we fear it will be that of too great a desire for display—too many vases, temples, and seats,—and too little purity and simplicity of general effect."[38]

It was crucial that this class—country gentlemen with large estates—set an example worthy of emulation because Downing believed that in America taste was contagious. Once appreciated and established in one part of the country, taste would be quickly disseminated. Although he had witnessed "an abundance of specimens of bad taste [and] a sufficient number of efforts to improve without any real taste whatever," Downing was optimistic; he suggested that these cases simply indicated that the amateurs of the art were still more numerous than its professors. The *Treatise* was offered to those individuals "at a loss how to proceed."[39]

Amateurs and Professionals

It took a poet, or at least someone with imagination, taste, and good sense, to be a skillful professional, according to Nathaniel Parker Willis, who wrote about his own amateur experiments in landscape gardening at Idlewild, his Hudson River estate (figs. 1.18, 1.19). In *Out-Doors at Idlewild* (1855) he analyzed the kind of talent needed to

Amateurs and Professionals

1.18
Title page for N. P. Willis, *Out-Doors at Idlewild* (1855). The Library Company of Philadelphia.

1.19
Frontispiece in N. P. Willis, *Out-Doors at Idlewild* (1855). The Library Company of Philadelphia.

look at fields and woods and tell what could be made out of them. To lay out paths, clump woods, plant avenues, and lay brooks among foliage and greensward took experience looking "at Nature wild in contrast with Nature improved." Willis recalled that Downing had been such a genius.[40]

But even Willis, a great admirer of Downing, did not consider it necessary to engage Downing's professional services, although he admitted that "few

books can be more expensively misapplied, than the treatises on landscape-gardening." Downing's *Treatise* bemoaned this general inclination: "Professional talent is seldom employed, in Architecture or Landscape Gardening, but almost every man fancies himself an amateur, and endeavours to plan and arrange his own residence. . . . it is not surprising that we witness much incongruity and great waste of time and money." The inexperienced, Downing warned, would be liable to fall into the error of a want of breadth and extent: "Their designs, like the sketches of a novice in drawing, are cramped and meagre." The *North American Review* similarly remarked that comparatively few had the means to employ a professional to lay out their grounds, and the do-it-your-selfers would begin with a favorite plan as coarse and rude as their first attempts in landscape painting would be, simply through ignorance of artistic principles. The magazine suggested the *Treatise* for guidance.[41]

To gain legitimacy for the nascent profession, Downing strove in the *Treatise* to invest landscape gardening with the status of landscape painting— one of the sister fine arts. It is important to understand that he made a living from design commissions and publications. Like his mentor, the Scottish landscape gardener J. C. Loudon, Downing had a great respect for the designation "fine art." Both wanted to associate it with their profession, for the term was synonymous with "elegant art, art of imagination, art of taste." As works of art, their landscape gardens would be acknowledged as creations of artists and would more likely procure further commissions. Downing may have mystified this art in the *Treatise* to induce aspiring amateurs to seek professional advice. For example, his readers learned that a familiarity with the grand principles of landscape gardening was of prime importance in successful practice: "To attempt a great work in any art, without knowing either the capacities of that art, or the great schools or modes by which it has previously been characterized, is but to be groping about in a dim twilight without the power of knowing, even should we be successful in our efforts, the real excellence of our production, or of judging of its merit comparatively, as a work of taste and imagination."[42]

Under discussion here, of course, was that elusive standard of "taste," a frequent topic of inquiry in eighteenth- and nineteenth-century European treatises. Edmund Burke, for example, had prefaced his *Philosophical Inquiry into the Origin of Our Ideas of the Sublime and Beautiful* (1757) with a discourse on taste, defining it as "that faculty or those faculties of the mind which are affected with, or which form a judgment of, the works of the imagination and the elegant arts." Essentially, it was refined judgment. According to Burke, taste was improved exactly as a person improved his judgment, by extending his knowledge, by steady attention, and by frequent exercise. Downing offered the meaning of "correct taste" as the combination of sensibility to the beautiful and good judgment that allowed a person to compare rapidly, discriminate, and give due rank to each object among many beautiful ones.[43]

The *Treatise* convinced a number of its readers that their own tastes were not sufficiently refined. Downing's practice prospered after its appearance, and in November 1841 he wrote to John Jay Smith, a librarian and amateur horticulturist in Philadelphia with whom he carried on a correspondence until his death: "I have been employed to a very considerable extent this season in giving designs for laying out grounds . . . and Landscape Gardening bids fair to become a profession in this country." The following year he was kept away from home on constant business trips and could boast, again to Smith: "My art is flourishing." He had commissions to design the asylum grounds at Utica, New York, and private places in four states: Boston, Massachusetts; Albany, Long Island, and Staten Island, New York; New Haven, Connecticut; and two unspecified locations in New Jersey.[44]

A Studied and Polished Mode

By 1849 Downing was America's preeminent practitioner, but comments in the diary of the Philadelphia gentleman Sidney George Fisher reveal the latter's prejudice against landscape gardening as a "profession" rather than a tasteful leisure occupation for gentlemen amateurs. Fisher met Downing at a party and recorded his disappointment: "Like his books better than himself. He is a Yankee not thoroughbred. Landscape gardening with him is a profession & not a liberal taste, and he talks with a professional air. I dislike 'bread-studies' & artizanship, & the smell of the shop destroys my pleasure in any subject however interesting in itself." Perhaps the complaint revealed more about the state of Fisher's own finances, for he also wrote disparagingly of the twenty-dollar per diem that Downing received for advising on the siting of his brother Charles Henry Fisher's house in Philadelphia. Charles Henry was a millionaire and could well afford Downing's fee; Brookwood was built in 1851 at a cost of approximately $50,000. Sidney George Fisher had to be content spending $3.50 for the *Treatise* and planning his own improvements. Others were not so judgmental, however, and had the money to seek out Downing's professional advice. In 1850 he was asked to design the buildings and carry out the landscape improvements at Matthew Vassar's Springside in Poughkeepsie, New York, and won the prestigious commission to design the public grounds in Washington, D.C.[45]

It was clear to Downing, however, that the majority of landowning Americans wanted to carry out their own improvements because—like his friend Willis at Idlewild—they found great satisfaction in the challenge or because they could not afford to do otherwise. Whatever the reason, amateur landscape gardeners previously had to look to European books for guidance; as of 1841, they had access to Downing's *Treatise,* which placed before them directions and guiding principles to assist in laying out their grounds.

A Studied and Polished Mode

To impress upon his countrymen as well as old-world critics the worth of this native-bred *Treatise,* Downing crowned his appeal "with the wreaths of an elegant and graceful style," liberally sprinkling the text with lines of poetry (mostly British; William Cullen Bryant was the lone American voice) and foreign phrases (mostly French). American reviewers were particularly proud of this evidence of the precociousness of their "infant nation." One labeled Downing "this Sir Joshua Reynolds of our rural decorations," pairing his writings with the acclaimed *Discourses on Art* delivered late in the eighteenth century to the Royal Academy. Downing's own desire for credibility can be gleaned from this comment: "From considering us as a mere liberated colony, a fourth rate nation, mostly living in log houses, and semi-civilized in customs, a few years have obliged Europeans to observe that there is a moral, intelligent and physical weight in America." Even the *Democratic Review,* that bastion of support for an American national literature, singled out the *Treatise*'s two sections on deciduous and evergreen ornamental trees, declaring: "The interspersed classical and poetical references, make the chapters devoted to [trees] among the most delightful."[46]

This "studied and polished mode of expression," so satisfying to most of Downing's audience, drew criticism from an agricultural publication (fig. 1.20). In an otherwise complimentary review of the second edition, the *Cultivator,* a monthly from

THE *TREATISE: Aspirations and Audience*

1.20

Masthead for the *Cultivator,* a monthly agricultural journal published in Albany, New York. The Library Company of Philadelphia.

Downing's home state of New York, suggested that "a more terse and vigorous style" would improve the work: "To readers like us, educated between the plow-handles, it would be pleasant to have the various extracts in French, Spanish, Latin and Italian, rendered into English, the only language which, having once learned, we have not become somewhat rusty in." If the reviewer had been more observant, he would have noticed that one change had already occurred: "the wildest *paysage*" of the first edition was rendered into English for the second, becoming "the wildest landscape."

This one translation is a mystery, for the high tone and cultured language of the *Treatise* remained through its two revisions. As an American critic remarked: "The effect of reading such graceful and interesting essays is often to create a taste of the kind where none had previously existed." This was precisely the effect desired as Downing struggled to raise his countrymen's ideas on the fine art of landscape gardening "above the level of their own accustomed vision."[47]

2

ALMOST EVERYTHING IS YET BEFORE US

The 1841 Edition

Bold type announced on the title page of Downing's 1841 *Treatise on the Theory and Practice of Landscape Gardening* that the work was "Adapted to North America," and the preface repeated the claim that the suggestions for embellishing the nation's rural residences were adjusted "especially to this country and to the peculiar wants of its inhabitants." With great finesse Downing demonstrated his understanding of the particular conditions and issues facing his American audience. However, the accolades greeting this indigenous treatise belied the fact that the landscape gardening theory and practice, as presented in this first edition, relied on ideas borrowed—and barely adapted—from the Old World.[1]

The *Treatise* was positioned between the American cultural camps of tradition and invention; at the time, a deference to customary European ways and the desire for a distinctive American identity battled it out. This debate had been critical since the American Revolution, when a whole way of life was altered and a new axis for politics and culture established; Europeans and Americans alike repeatedly asked how much was to be retained or modified, how much invented. The dangerous point at which admiration turned into submission was hard to fix, and in 1847 a contributor to *Literary World* attempted to distinguish between craven theft and "honorable allegiance": "Imitation is natural, or rather, we should say, was formerly pardonable, from our social and political condition. . . . Hence the frequent charge of Plagiarism, upon which, as between authors of original merit, little account is always to be placed—for what may appear to be a theft to minds of coarse perceptions, might, perhaps, be held by the great originals as simply a proof of honorable allegiance to themselves."²

Downing's work was a product of these tricky circumstances. Although one historian has accused him of being "a shameless plagiarist of English landscape and gardening literature," this is a harsh judgment against an author who admitted an honorable allegiance to his sources. Downing could not attempt a book such as the *Treatise* without an obeisance to the Old World, particularly to the mother country, whose taste in rural embellishment many felt to be unrivaled. "I have availed myself of the works of European authors," he admitted, "especially those of Britain, where Landscape Gardening was first raised to the rank of a fine art."³

The contents indeed conformed to the traditional European treatises on the subject. A section called "Historical Sketches" opened the work with a statement explaining "the object of landscape gardening," followed by a description of the ancient and modern styles, a brief account of the origins of the modern natural style, a list of recommended European landscape poets and writers, and examples of the art abroad and in North America. Section 2, "Beauties of Landscape Gardening," laid down the nature and principles of landscape gardening as an imitative art. Next, in order, were "Wood and Plantations" and a chapter each on deciduous and evergreen ornamental trees, vines and climbing plants, the treatment of ground and walks, water, rural architecture, and embellishments. An appendix contained instructions for transplanting trees and a lengthy essay on a moderately sized suburban residence near London, originally published in *Gardener's Magazine*.⁴

The modifications that Downing made to the book's first two sections are the most important in understanding his attempt to reconcile his theory and practice of landscape gardening with American conditions. The 1841 "Historical Sketches" revealed a young author with an exaggerated sense that tasteful gardening rested solely on the "modern" eighteenth-century developments in English gardening known by the terms "natural" or "irregular." The history of gardening summarized in this edition concentrated on those who had overthrown the opposing style, variously called "ancient," "formal," or "geometric." The list of exemplary British estates and authors devoted to landscape improvement contained no surprises; and with the infant nation so short on history and Downing himself such an inexperienced traveler, American examples were few.⁵

In the preface Downing acknowledged his obligations and gave thanks to his "valued correspondent, J. C. Loudon . . . the most distinguished gardening author of the age." His debt to this Scotsman was great, and nowhere was it more evident than in the section titled "Beauties of Landscape Gardening." However, Downing also was responding to other crosscurrents in aesthetics of different origins and opposite tendencies, and his first attempt to define the art for his American readers was a tentative mixture of terms and definitions from the late-eighteenth-century picturesque controversy, Loudon's theory of imitation in landscape gardening (which combined classical idealist aesthetics, French and British academic doctrine, and his own "gardenesque"), and the Scottish philosopher Archibald Alison's concept of expression. Downing's text evinces a dichotomy between a logical system that valued reason and sought an ideal beauty in nature and a philosophy that looked to the imagination to discover the individual spirit and expression of natural objects. The basic way in which the 1841 *Treatise* failed to adapt itself to America was a result of Downing's accommodation of Loudon's fundamental principle of landscape gardening—namely, "the recognition of art." This led Downing to favor foreign plants over his own country's loveliest indigenous flowers, shrubs, and trees in order that the designed landscape would be recognized as a work of art.[6]

The More Exquisite Beauty of Natural Forms

Downing paid homage on page one to the European gardening literature that substantiated his own preference for the eighteenth-century English modern/natural/irregular style as opposed to the ancient/formal/geometric style. Lines from Jacques Delille's 1782 poem *Les Jardins* provided an epigraph, and the opening words were from the British author Barbara Hofland's *White-Knights*

2.1

View of White Knights from the Woods. In Mrs. Hofland, *A Descriptive Account of the Mansion and Gardens of White-Knights* (1819). The Library Company of Philadelphia.

The More Exquisite Beauty of Natural Forms

(1819): "'Our first, most endearing, and most sacred associations,' says the amiable Mrs. Hofland, 'are connected with gardens; our most simple and most refined perceptions of beauty are combined with them'" (fig. 2.1). Delille's poem, for the linguistically educated Americans who could read French, compared the two modes of gardening: one geometric and imposing an order upon nature; the other respectful of nature. The first was a proud despot who imposed rules on trees and water; the second treated with indulgence nature's charming caprices, noble negligence, and irregular step. For those more visually inclined, the vignette decorating the first letter of the *Treatise* illustrated the two scenes (fig. 2.2). On the left, a straight road led through parallel rows of trees, offering a vista of a classically styled residence; on the right, the approach wound gracefully through a variety of plantations toward a villa with a picturesque outline.[7]

Delille, a Frenchman who preferred the art of William Kent to that of André Le Nôtre, was bound to be admired by the British and subsequently by Downing. Delille's *Les Jardins* criticized the extravagant and autocratic Louis XIV's Versailles, and although Downing cited this garden as the finest example of the geometric style and praised Le Nôtre as a distinguished artist, he too was disdainful of Versailles's kind of beauty, remarking: "Almost any one may succeed in laying out and planting a garden in right lines and may give it an air of stateliness and grandeur, by costly decorations." While everyone could appreciate the cost and labor incurred in such a garden, Downing suggested that only those with a cultivated and refined mind could "realize and enjoy the more exquisite beauty of natural forms."[8]

Downing reiterated his opinion on the geometric style in other sections, dismissing it in even stronger words: "The results evince a fertility of invention and odd conceits, rather than the exercise of the faculty of taste, or imagination." Geometric layouts were attained "in a merely mechanical manner," he declared, "with but little study or theory upon the subject." Unlike his American predecessor Bernard M'Mahon, Downing made no mention of the rules of perspective or the optical theories involved. Barbara Hofland, whose words provided Downing's opening paean to the garden, was also a passionate admirer of natural landscape gardening and was equally willing to consign "to oblivion the yew-clipped hedges, trim borders, and various puerile absurdities" of former days (fig. 2.3). When Downing did make concessions to the geometric style—praising "lengthy and majestic avenues . . . forming long shadowy aisles" or the formal and curiously knotted gardens for their pleasing associations with William Shakespeare and Edmund Spenser—he managed to belittle it at the same time by pairing the mode with the word *quaint*.[9]

2.2

The vignette decorating the first letter O of the *Treatise* (1841), illustrating the formal and natural styles of gardening. Author's collection.

39

ALMOST EVERYTHING IS YET BEFORE US: *The 1841 Edition*

2.3

View of White Knights from the New Gardens. In Mrs. Hofland, *A Descriptive Account of the Mansion and Gardens of White-Knights* (1819). The Library Company of Philadelphia.

Downing's stance on the natural versus geometric style did not adhere to Loudon's, although their views often coincided. Throughout his writings, Loudon expressed respect for the older mode of gardening; he considered it equal to the modern fashion and just as natural and tasteful. For public squares or small gardens bordered by straight lines, Loudon advised that the geometric style was unquestionably the best and condemned the prejudices of so-called authorities who were captivated by the novelty of the irregular style and could do no justice to any other. "We should suppose," he also speculated, "that, where there is so much natural woody scenery, it would be desirable frequently to introduce the geometric style as forming the greatest contrast to it." Downing, though surrounded by wooded scenery, noted that this was only true "as regards the mass of uncultivated minds."[10]

Downing could appeal to the authority of over 125 years of European literature for his pointed attacks on geometric gardening. Reviewing the history of gardening in his opening section, Downing especially honored Joseph Addison and Alexander Pope for "substituting in the minds of the British public a taste for the natural style." Addison, whose essays on the "Pleasures of the Imagination" appeared in the *Spectator* in 1712, has been credited with initiating and directing eighteenth-century aesthetic speculation concerning the response of the mind to works of nature and art. Downing, however, seemed less interested in the complexities of the analysis that ran through ten numbers of the *Spectator* than in Addison's tribute in one issue to "the rough careless Strokes of Nature" as opposed to "the nice Touches and Embellishments of Art." Downing simply noted that Addison effectively showed the "superiority of the beauty of natural expression." The less well-read in his audience could not judge how effectively, for Downing failed to quote Addison's comments about plantations "laid out by the Rule and Line": "Our Trees rise in Cones, Globes, and Pyramids. We see the Marks of the Scissars upon every Plant and Bush. . . . I would rather look upon a Tree in all its Luxuriancy and Diffusion of Boughs and Branches, than when it is thus cut and trimmed into a Mathematical Figure." Downing freely appropriated from this passage when he described the modern class of landscape artist: "Laying down the shears of the old gardeners, he feels that there is a grace and beauty in [the tree's] free and unshorn luxuriance, infinitely above that of the tree, clipped according to the rules of a formal art."[11]

Downing also praised Alexander Pope's *Guardian* essay of 1713, stating that Pope had pointed out "in a masterly manner . . . the absurdities of the ancient style." Pope's barbs in this particular essay were directed at "monstrous attempts" at verdant sculpture that turned trees into awkward topiary figures of men and animals. When Downing argued for the superiority of plantations in the natural mode, he alluded to this work: "In these [formal] gardens, nature was tamed and subdued, or as some critics will have it, tortured, into every shape which the ingenuity of the gardener could suggest . . . verdant statues, pyramids, crowing cocks, and rampant lions." In the 1731 "Epistle to Lord Burlington," Pope elaborated on his vision of the landscape designer who consulted "the Genius of the Place in all," and Downing quoted a couplet from this poem to illustrate how only an unenlightened taste would prefer a geometric arrangement of trees to more pleasing intricacies:

Grove nods at grove, each Alley has a brother,
And half the platform just reflects the other.[12]

Reciting the litany of important gardening figures, Downing praised other participants in this "natural" revolution, including Francis Bacon ("Of Gardens," 1625); John Milton (*Paradise Lost,* 1667); and William Kent. In this, he followed the lead of Loudon in the *Encyclopedia of Gardening* (who quoted William Mason). Downing also relied on Loudon when he brushed aside assertions by "continental authors" that the English had borrowed their ideas of the natural style from the Chinese. Referring to the gardens illustrated in William Temple's *Upon the Gardens of Epicurus* (1692) and William Chambers's *Designs of Chinese Buildings* (1757), Downing conceded that Chinese gardens were characterized by great irregularity, but he found them, as did Loudon, "full of littlenesses and puerile conceits, far below the standard of natural beauty aimed at by the English." Given Downing's disturbing asides in the *Horticulturist* concerning "the fair outside and the treacherous heart of the Asiatics" (rather typical of the time's racial and ethnic stereotyping), it is not surprising that he resented any reference to an Anglo-Chinese fashion.[13]

For those who wished to pursue the subject further, Downing recommended a selection of authors "whose works were devoted to the improvement of Landscape Gardening in the modern or natural style"; the list included George Mason's *Design in Gardening* (1768); Thomas Whately's *Observations on Modern Gardening* (1770); William Mason's *The English Garden* (1772–81; Downing gave the date of publication as 1782); Uvedale Price's *An Essay on the Picturesque* (1794); Horace Walpole's *On Modern Gardening* (1780; listed as 1782); Humphry Repton's *Observations on the Theory and Practice of Landscape Gardening* (1803; listed as 1795, the year of his *Sketches and Hints*); R. L. Girardin's *De la Composition des Paysages* (1777; listed as 1783, the date of the English translation by Daniel Malthus); and Jacques Delille's *Les Jardins* (1782; listed as 1820).[14]

Downing quoted Thomas Whately and Jacques Delille throughout the *Treatise* on subjects ranging from plantations to the treatment of ground and water. In *Observations on Modern Gardening,* Whately counseled readers that "the whole range of nature" was open to them; it was their business "to collect into one place, the delights which are generally dispersed through different species of country." He maintained that nature was perfected by a design technique employing selection and arrangement; the gardener applied his art to the control of natural forces as powerful as the sun. "Every degree of light and shade, from a glare to obscurity" was manageable partly through the number and partly through the texture of the chosen trees. Although rocks were too vast and stubborn to submit to control, according to Whately, the gardener could add or remove certain parts, and by improving the soil between the rocks, vegetation could relieve the dreariness of the scene. A cavity in the rocks, if made easily accessible, could suggest ideas of "protection from the bitterest inclemencies of the sky, and even of occasional refreshment and repose." Despite his emphasis on control, Whately believed that art was carried to excess in the classical French interpretation of improving nature. When ground, wood, and water were reduced to mathematical figures, art became "principal" as opposed to "accessory," thereby excluding nature. He condemned this practice as a mischief brought about "not by the use but the perversion of art." Although Whately conceded that architecture required symmetry, this attribute could not be transferred to the garden because the objects of nature required variety and freedom. The task of the landscape gardener was interpreted by Delille, Downing's favorite French poet, to be in line with Whately's improver. Speaking with Nature's voice, Delille urged Genius to listen: "My uncompleted works beg for your skill." Improving the countryside over which he flew, Genius reunited, divided, lightened, softened, or revealed the beauties that lay sleeping in the varied scenes. Delille's artist only corrected and refined the features sketched by Nature.[15]

The modern style, as described by these authors, was carried to its greatest perfection in England, and Downing referred his readers to several of the country's noble residences: Blenheim, Warwick Castle, Woburn Abbey, Ashridge (mistakenly called "Ashbridge"), and Chatsworth were selected from many splendid examples. Downing perhaps followed Whately's lead in choosing Blenheim and Woburn Abbey. He would not have personal knowledge of any of the estates until the summer of 1850, when he visited Warwick Castle, Woburn Abbey, and Chatsworth during a trip to England. Downing deemed no continental European gardens worthy of mention in the *Treatise* because the geometric style still prevailed there.[16]

Here, Where Nature Has Done So Much

Despite his own lack of travel experience, Downing lectured that nothing was more instructive than a personal inspection of tastefully embellished country seats: "In examining such, the mind is at a single view more fully impressed with the beauties of the art and its capabilities, than by ten times the amount of time spent in investigating the theory without any such practical illustrations." He cautioned, however, that it was highly improbable that the United States would ever have such magnificent landscape gardens as those abroad because there was no class of men whose wealth was hereditary. Downing was referring to his country's inheritance laws and their effect upon American estates. At the time of the American Revolution, English laws concerning primogeniture were abolished in almost all states, and an exclusive right of inheritance no longer belonged to the eldest son. First prescribed in the state of New York in 1786, the rule stipulated that the property of a man dying intestate passed to his heirs in direct line. If he had only one heir, he or she alone received the entire succession; if there were several heirs, they shared the succession equally among themselves, with no distinction of sex.[17]

Foreign visitors and Americans alike noted the influence of these changes upon the social conditions of the republic. Alexis de Tocqueville observed that the equal division of a father's property among all his children had two effects: it brought about a revolution of property because possessions were parceled into smaller and smaller shares; and, indirect consequences tended to destroy large fortunes and domains: "When the idea of family becomes vague, indeterminate, and uncertain, a man thinks of his present convenience, he provides for the establishment of his next succeeding generation and no more." Harriet Martineau saw the situation in a more positive light, observing a national bias against large estates that favored one child in the inheritance. She found it "an admitted truth . . . that enormous private wealth is inconsistent with the spirit of republicanism." Wealth was power, and large amounts of power were not supposed to rest in the hands of individuals.[18]

According to contemporary reports, large estates rarely remained undivided beyond the second generation. In an account sent to Loudon's *Gardener's Magazine* in 1832, the foreman at Bartram's Botanic Gardens, Philadelphia, noted the effects on American horticulture:

The law of primogeniture is (with all its monstrosities) the best friend of gardening. No such law exists in this country . . . and I know of nothing that feels the loss of this so much as horticulture. There is more than one instance, in the vicinity of Philadelphia, of fine houses and gardens going to wreck, from the individual of the family to whom they were left not being able to support the expense.[19]

Downing tried to console his readers for the lack of enormous estates, claiming that America had "a larger class of independent landholders . . . than any other country in the civilized world." Yet his list of American showplaces was lamentably short, and he regretted that "in so far as regards the literature and practice of Landscape Gardening as an art, in North America, almost every thing is yet before us." In the *Treatise*'s "Historical Sketches," Downing recommended only thirteen American country residences with reputations for elegance (perhaps a nod to the original thirteen colonies); all were located in Atlantic seaboard states—and he had yet to visit most of them. Five of the seats had been previously cited in Loudon's *Encyclopedia of Gardening* (1835); although Loudon mentioned several in the deep South, Downing ventured only as far as Philadelphia. Mount Vernon was a curious omission, but as a notice in the *Horticulturist* pointed out, the grounds and buildings had long shown evidence of decay and dilapidation. A dozen additional references to American residences could be found in other sections, mostly in illustration of Downing's ideas on "Rural Architecture."[20]

Among the thirteen in the "Historical Sketches" was Hyde Park, designed by André Parmentier for the prominent physician and botanist Dr. David Hosack (fig. 2.4). This Hudson River estate had been celebrated for many years but lost some of its polish after Hosack's death in 1835. Nevertheless, Downing offered it as one of the finest specimens of the natural style in America. His description of a number of specific plants on the site, including its luxuriant ivy, suggests that he visited Hyde Park.[21]

2.4

View from Hyde Park. (Hudson River.) In N. P. Willis, *American Scenery*, vol. 1 (1840). The Library Company of Philadelphia.

Robert Donaldson's Blithewood, on the east bank of the Hudson River one hundred miles from New York City, commanded such "lovely prospects" and was such "a model of elegant arrangement" that it appeared as the *Treatise* frontispiece. Downing also dedicated his 1842 *Cottage Residences* to Donaldson, labeling this prominent New York City businessman "Arbiter Elegantiarum." Whether Downing provided landscape design services for the estate, described by him as "one of the most tasteful villa residences in the Union," is still debated. Immediately to the south of Blithewood were "one or two" fine places that Downing simply noted as "in the possession of the Livingston family." Livingston holdings along a twenty-mile stretch of the Hudson's eastern shore were impressive; following the War for Independence more than a dozen mansions were built, and Downing could easily have confused them. Although he praised the trees and turf on the

2.5

Thomas Cole, *View of Monte Video, the Seat of Daniel Wadsworth, Esq.* (1828). Wadsworth Atheneum, Hartford, Bequest of Daniel Wadsworth.

grounds at some length, it is likely that his general familiarity with the neighborhood was the source of the description. The two Livingston estates were undoubtedly Montgomery Place (which shared a common border with Blithewood) and Messina. Both received more detailed attention in the *Horticulturist*.[22]

Henry Pratt's Lemon Hill, along the Schuylkill River, was familiar to anyone who visited or lived in Philadelphia. Downing commended its collection of costly exotics, although the gardens, like those at Hyde Park, had reached perfection some ten years earlier. A shipping merchant, the late owner had taken advantage of business opportunities to obtain rare plants, including the lemon trees celebrated in the estate name, as well as oranges, aloes, and pomegranates. This elaborate complex of gardens and grottos was in the geometric style, and Downing could not resist a barb at its "decidedly artificial effect." He mentioned three "elegant country seats of moderate extent" in the suburbs of Boston: "J[ohn] P[erkins] Cushing, Esq. at Watertown, the Hon. John Lowell at Roxbury, and Col. [Thomas Handasyd] Perkins at Brookline." In Perkins's case, a moderate extent was sixty-one acres. Downing's visit to Lowell's home two years earlier was the centerpiece of a moral tale contained in a footnote. Addressed to readers impatient for forest trees to "grow up," the story told of the two men's walk through a fine belt of fully grown trees that Lowell (at the time of the visit "in a green old age") had planted at thirty-two. Another estate, Daniel Wadsworth's Monte Video, Downing commended as "one of the prettiest residences in Connecticut," though it was regrettably cited in the first edition as Daniel Wordsworth's Monte Viedo because of typographical errors (fig. 2.5). Downing briefly referred to the extensive grounds at Bordentown, New Jersey, of the Count de Survilliers, better known as Joseph Bonaparte, the elder brother of Napoleon. Downing's impersonal comments (culled from the *Encyclopedia of Gardening*) about the flat surface varied by plantations were retained for subsequent editions. Readers had to look to *Graham's Magazine* in 1845 for a longer and more accurate description of the fifteen-hundred-acre estate. A favorite resort for picnic parties from Philadelphia, the park had fallen into decay since the count's death. Its situation on a high bank overlooking the Delaware River, with a tower on the estate rising above the thick groves, was shown in an accompanying engraving (fig. 2.6).[23]

The optimistic pronouncement of a "great increase of elegant cottage and villa residences" was supported by only a few specific cases in the *Treatise;* these were, moreover, mostly secondhand reports. However, as Downing began to outline the correct principles of the modern style, he assured his readers that in spite of the many violations of good taste in America, nature herself had done so much that almost every residence in the Union could offer useful hints in landscape gardening.[24]

General Beauty and Picturesque Beauty

The natural scenery with which Americans were so blessed had two distinct "expressions," and Downing informed amateur improvers that, to be successful, they had "to seize at once upon the characteristics of these two species of beauty." For the correct terminology, Downing supposedly turned to "the earliest professors of modern Landscape Gardening" who had generally agreed upon two varieties of beauty: "These are *general or natural,* and *picturesque* beauty: or to speak more definitely, the beauty characterized by simple and

2.6

View of the Delaware near Bordentown. In *Graham's American Monthly* (March 1845). The Library Company of Philadelphia. A tower on the estate of the Count de Survilliers rises above the thick grove of trees on the right side of the river.

flowing forms, and the beauty expressed by striking, irregular, spirited forms." The varieties described were, in fact, the beautiful and the picturesque. In renaming them, Downing tried to avoid terms worn out in old-world debate. He professed a desire not to side "with one or the other of the two schools or parties in Landscape Gardening, which waged battle so fiercely in England": the "Picturesque School," led by Uvedale Price and Richard Payne Knight, and "the more formal school" championed by Capability Brown and Humphry Repton. Nonetheless, Downing's aesthetic categories cannot be understood without reference to the figures involved in setting the nomenclature of eighteenth-century British landscape theory.[25]

The trinity of the sublime, the beautiful, and the picturesque had been the subject of numerous works and often acrimonious quarrels since Edmund Burke's *Philosophical Enquiry into the Origin of our Ideas of the Sublime and Beautiful* (1757) provided the impetus, and Uvedale Price added the third category with his *Essay on the Picturesque, as Compared with the Sublime and the Beautiful* (1794). Price's picturesque was defined not only by its distinction from Burke's aesthetic pair, but also by its difference from the Reverend William Gilpin's "too vague, and too confined" idea, found in his *Essay on Picturesque Beauty* (1794), that the term *picturesque* denoted objects that were "proper subjects for painting."[26]

For Burke, sublimity and beauty in some way depended on qualities in the objects themselves, but he also took into account psychological and physiological origins of the aesthetic experience. His system depended on emotion, with the antithesis of pain and pleasure (both seen as positive qualities) forming its basis. Observing that pain and fear acted upon the body and consisted in "an unnatural tension of the nerves" and that the passion called love was produced by relaxation in the body, Burke concluded that sublimity and beauty acted directly on the nervous system through sense impressions, outside the realm of judgment. The source of the sublime was whatever excited ideas of pain and danger or was in any way terrible; it was productive of the strongest emotion that the mind could experience. Astonishment was the highest degree of passion caused by the great and sublime in nature, and Burke defined it as "that state of the soul, in which all its motions are suspended, with some degree of horror." Qualities of the sublime included obscurity, power, darkness, solitude, silence, infinity, and magnificence.[27]

Burke attacked several established theories on beauty, arguing that it did not consist in certain proportions of parts, or in fitness, or in moral perfection. These were nonaesthetic qualities in his opinion, and their effect partly depended on knowledge and experience. Beauty was "no creature of our reason," Burke insisted, but "some quality in bodies, acting mechanically upon the human mind by the intervention of the senses." Just as the application of ice or fire would produce the ideas of cold or heat, the appearance of beauty would cause some degree of love in a person. Those sensible qualities of beautiful objects that could be "taken in by the eye" included comparative smallness, smoothness, gradual variation, delicacy, and clear, bright, and mild colors.[28]

To support his contention that gradual variation was one of the great constituents of beauty, Burke referred to William Hogarth. Hogarth attempted to show in his *Analysis of Beauty* (1753) "what the principles are in nature, by which we are directed to call the forms of some bodies beautiful, others ugly; some graceful, and others the reverse." He considered line as the element that composed wholes and asserted that there was only one precise line that could properly be called "the line of beauty" (fig. 2.7). His drawing of it showed a waving line neither too straight nor too bulging. In addition, there was only one, serpentine line that he called the "line of grace"; this was illustrated by a horn that varied in three dimensions, twisting and bending at the same time. Downing paired the authors of the *Ideas of the Sublime and Beautiful* and the *Analysis of Beauty* when he described the most beautiful variation in the treatment of ground: "such surfaces are full of the flowing lines, and rounded smoothnesses, which Burke considers characteristic of beauty, or the long undulations exhibit the outlines of Hogarth's favourite line of grace."[29]

Uvedale Price recognized the truth and accuracy of Burke's system in 1794 and claimed it as the foundation of his own *Essay*. Price also acknowledged that he had received "great pleasure and instruction" from William Gilpin, who suggested

2.7
Title page for William Hogarth, *The Analysis of Beauty* (1753), showing the "line of beauty." Kansas State University Libraries.

that the beautiful and the picturesque depended on some special construction of the object. With reference to Burke, Gilpin agreed that smoothness was an important property of beauty and concluded that roughness or ruggedness was the source of the picturesque and the most essential point of difference from its opposite. However, Price basically sought to refute these two authors. He demonstrated that the picturesque had "a character not less separate and distinct than either the sublime or the beautiful" of Burke and disagreed with Gilpin's description of picturesque objects as those that "please from some quality capable of being illustrated by painting," pointing out that painters illustrated grandeur and beauty as well as picturesqueness.[30]

Price wanted to bring the "much less obvious, less generally attractive" character of the picturesque to the attention of landscape improvers and to examine the features of modern gardening according to the general principles of painting. With support from Richard Payne Knight, who attacked contemporary "improvements" in his poem *The Landscape* (1794), Price criticized the affected style of landscape gardener Capability Brown and his imitators, accusing them of substituting a formality of regular curves for the French and Dutch formality of squares and parallelograms. Price looked with disgust at "the eternal smoothness and sameness of a finished place," as did Knight:

—See yon fantastic band,
With charts, pedometers, and rules in hand,
Advance triumphant, and alike lay waste
The forms of nature, and the works of taste!
T'improve, adorn, and polish, they profess;
But shave the goddess, whom they come to dress.

The baldness of the so-called improvements was viewed as a defect because Price judged them

ALMOST EVERYTHING IS YET BEFORE US: *The 1841 Edition*

2.8
Claude Gelée Lorrain, *Landscape with a Piping Shepherd* (1667). The Nelson-Atkins Museum of Art (Nelson Fund).

General Beauty and Picturesque Beauty

2.9

Salvator Rosa, *Mercury, Argus, and Io* (c. 1653–54). The Nelson-Atkins Museum of Art (Nelson Fund).

against picturesque scenery, which was characterized by "intricacy in the disposition, and variety in the forms, the tints, and the lights and shadows of objects." Price and Knight also believed that in nature the picturesque was usually mixed with the beautiful; therefore they considered the Brown school's overly polished beauty—unenlivened by the picturesque—insipid and monotonous.[31]

The standard to which Price referred those interested in improving "real landscape" was the authority of the great painters, for they had studied form and color and had been able to select, combine, and fix them upon the canvas. Price held up Claude Lorrain, the seventeenth-century French painter who had worked in Italy, as "the most ornamented of all the great masters" because his scenes had both the softness and the dressed appearance of the ideal beautiful landscape (fig. 2.8). The Neapolitan artist Salvator Rosa was singled out for the remarkable picturesque effects in his figures and landscapes (fig. 2.9). Much of Price's *Essay* was devoted to the definition of the picturesque as distinct from Burke's beautiful and sublime. The qualities that made objects picturesque were diametrically opposite those of beauty—roughness versus smoothness, irregularity versus symmetry, sudden versus gradual variation, and age and decay versus youth and freshness. The picturesque was equally distinct from the sublime; whereas greatness of dimension was almost essential to the sublime, the picturesque could be found in small objects. The picturesque rendered beauty more captivating, whereas the sublime, by its solemnity, took away from its loveliness. Price stipulated that of the three characters, only the beautiful and the picturesque could be artificially produced; humans could not create the sublime.[32]

Humphry Repton—successor to Capability Brown and therefore drawn into the picturesque controversy—disagreed with Price and Knight on the connection between painting and gardening. Repton argued that the two were "congenial natures" rather than sister arts, and he offered examples of landscape subjects incapable of being painted, such as "the delicious fragrance of a shrubbery, the soul expanding delight of a wide extended prospect, or the grandeur of a view down a steep hill." Repton also emphasized that utility must often take precedence over beauty, and convenience over picturesque effect "in the neighbourhood of man's habitation." In his *Observations on the Theory and Practice of Landscape Gardening* (1803), recommended by Downing, Repton stated that general utility was "the leading feature in the good taste of modern times."[33]

Despite Downing's claim to the contrary, in the 1841 *Treatise* he sided with Price and Knight against Brown and Repton. He repeatedly referred to the *Essay on the Picturesque,* praising the vigor with which Price advocated the picturesque, and published lines from Knight's *Landscape* in support of his own critical commentary on Brown's treatment of water and plantations: "Brown, who was one of the first practitioners of the modern style abroad . . . once disgraced half of the finest places in England with his tame bald pieces of artificial water, and round, formal clumps of trees." In contrast, Downing commended Price for "his unrivalled instructions for the creation of pieces of artificial water" and for the treatment of ground.[34]

Downing's discussion of Repton was more ambiguous. He cited one of his books (*Observations on the Theory and Practice of Landscape Gardening*) and one of his design commissions (Ashridge Park) and quoted his eight rules concerning approach roads. However, Downing judged Repton's style along with Brown's as "verging too much into the rules of an unvarying art." In this regard, Downing was following Loudon, who as a young man had labeled his competitor's work tame and bare. Loudon had been schooled in the beautiful and picturesque of Price and Knight, and until Repton's death in 1818, the two were professional rivals.[35]

In other significant ways, Downing implicitly sided with Price. When he described scenes to illustrate his "two species of beauty" in natural scenery, the landscapes had the distinct qualities of the beautiful and the picturesque. Although not labeled as such, the first scene clearly evoked the beautiful: "Some gently undulating plain covered with emerald turf, partially or entirely encompassed by rich, rolling outlines of forest canopy, its widest expanse here broken occasionally by noble groups of round-headed trees, . . . the shores of [a sylvan lake] jutting out, and receding back, in gently curves lines." The opposing characteristics of the unspecified picturesque were familiar to readers of Price:

Perhaps a romantic valley, half shut in on two or more sides by steep rocky banks partially concealed and overhung by clustering vines and tangled thickets of deep foliage. Against the sky outline, breaks the wild and irregular form of some old half decayed tree near by. . . . If water enliven the scene, we shall hear . . . the cool dashing of the cascade, as it leaps over the rocky barrier.

The artists chosen to exemplify these landscapes were Price's favorites: "To the lover of the fine arts, the name of Claude Lorraine cannot fail to suggest examples of beauty in its purest and most elegant forms," Downing exclaimed. "On the other hand, where shall we find all the elements of the picturesque, more graphically combined, than in the vigorous landscapes of Salvator Rosa!"[36]

Finally, who could doubt Downing's preference between the battling parties in landscape gardening when he devoted a paragraph to explaining how it was "requisite to possess a greater degree of imagination, and perhaps more vigour of mind, termed genius, fully to appreciate the beauty of the more picturesque forms of nature." As did Price—who had opted for the "much less obvious, less generally attractive" character of the picturesque—so did Downing:

Even among artists, while there are many who are able to feel and portray nature in her ordinary developments, how few can make the canvas glow with the expression of her grander and more picturesque beauties! And among mere admirers, it is the multitude, that see and feel the power of beauty in her graceful and flowing forms—but only the imaginative and cultivated few, who appreciate her more free and spirited charms.[37]

Downing did not intend these illustrations of the leading expressions in wild scenery to be understood "in the light of exact models for imitation in Landscape Gardening." He proceeded to explain precisely the relationship between nature and this fine art.[38]

Imitation in the Fine Arts and the Beau Ideal

"In what manner is nature to be imitated in Landscape Gardening?" was at issue, and this question and its answer placed Downing's theory within the tradition of classical idealist aesthetics. He contended that "the principles of imitation common to the other fine arts," including music, poetry, and painting, were to a certain extent equally applicable to landscape gardening.[39]

Theories of imitation or mimesis were formulated in antiquity to define poetry (the most highly respected art) in such works as Aristotle's *Poetics* and Horace's *Ars poetica*. In classical times, poetry, music, dance, painting, and sculpture were considered different forms of imitation, and subsequent efforts were made to invest the others with the dignity of poetry and to draw parallels among the arts. The modern system of the arts assumed definite shape only during the eighteenth century, when the various arts began to be compared and discussed on the basis of common principles such as imitation. The five arts of painting, sculpture, architecture, music, and poetry were generally agreed to form the nucleus; at times gardening was added to the system. The idealist side of the debate in the mimetic arts stressed that art was superior to nature because it selected nature's most beautiful parts for a more perfect, composite work; an alternative view argued that the artist should strive for an exact copy of nature, implying that art could never surpass nature.[40]

Accordingly, in Downing's landscape gardening, nature (in its sense of an object to be imitated in art) could not be "simple," "rude," "unguided," "vulgar," "wild," or "particular." These various terms had been employed by writers on the imitative arts in contradistinction to a concept that Downing adopted and defined in the *Treatise*— namely the beau ideal in nature:

> The *beau ideal* in Landscape Gardening as a fine art, appears to us to be embraced in the creation of scenery expressive of a peculiar kind of beauty, as the elegant or picturesque, the materials of which are, to a certain extent, different from those in wild nature, being composed of the floral and arboricultural riches of *all climates,* as far as possible;—uniting in the same scene a richness and a variety never to be found in any one portion of nature.

Polished scenery was to have the effect "such as we behold in the most captivating passages of general nature." With the use of "beau ideal" and "general nature," Downing linked himself to English, French, and German interpretations of imitation—and forged this connection through Loudon.[41]

In *Le vite de' Pittori, Scultori et Architetti* (1672), Giovanni Pietro Bellori was the first to formulate what French critics in the age of classicism designated *la belle nature*. Retreating from the mimetic theory that called for a faithful and passive imitation, Bellori redefined the "idea" of the artist. For a Platonist, the idea had a metaphysical existence independent of nature; in contrast, the idea for Bellori was an image of beauty derived from a process of selecting the best from nature—as the Greek artist Zeuxis had done when he took the fairest features from the five most beautiful women in his city and composed a likeness of the ideally beautiful Helen. According to this doctrine, nature was to be improved upon, with the means drawn from nature herself.[42]

In eighteenth-century France, Charles Batteux transformed Bellori's thinking into the concept of *la belle nature* in his *Les Beaux Arts réduits à un même principe* (1746), which restated that art was the imitation of a beautiful reality. Following Aristotle and Bellori, Batteux affirmed that to imitate was to copy a model, and nature was to provide this model for the arts. A wise and enlightened imitation did not slavishly copy but selected certain objects and traits and presented them in their perfection; therefore the essence of art was not the *vrai* but the *vraisemblable*. In other words, it was an imitation in which one saw nature not as she was but as she could be—*la belle nature*.[43]

Imitation in the Fine Arts and the Beau Ideal

In 1770, at the stronghold of classicism in England, the Royal Academy, Sir Joshua Reynolds reminded the young painters in his audience that the poets, orators, and rhetoricians of antiquity had continually propounded that all of the arts received their perfection from an ideal beauty, superior to that found in "individual" nature. He noted that every language had adopted terms expressive of this excellence: "The *gusto grande* of the Italians, the *beau idéal* of the French, and 'great style,' 'genius,' and 'taste' among the English." Reynolds was delivering, as president of the academy, the third of his fifteen *Discourses on Art,* in which the primary principle of his aesthetic system was elaborated as an opposition between "particular nature," with its blemishes and defects, and "general nature," which was in a perfect state:

[Painting] ought to be as far removed from the vulgar idea of imitation, as the refined civilized state in which we live, is removed from a gross state of nature.... It seems to me that the object and intention of all the Arts is to supply the natural imperfections of things, and often to gratify the mind by realising and embodying what never existed but in the imagination.

Reynolds applied this principle to gardening as well, asserting that gardening was "a deviation from nature; for if the true taste consists, as many hold, in banishing every appearance of Art, or any traces of the footsteps of man, it would then be no longer a Garden."[44]

Loudon and consequently Downing were influenced by Reynolds and by other champions of the classical ideal. Learning the principles of painting from the *Discourses,* Loudon strove for nature's ideal in landscape gardening rather than for an imitation of its accidental effects. In *Arboretum et Fruticetum Britannicum* (1838), he cited Reynolds to explain that the designer should lay out trees and shrubs so that each could realize its own *ideal* nature under conditions as nearly perfect as possible. Early in the 1830s Loudon also discovered the writings of Antoine Chrysosthôme Quatremère de Quincy, permanent secretary of the Académie Royale des Beaux-Arts. Loudon's *Architectural Magazine* offered nine translated essays from Quatremère beginning with "On the Principles of Taste" in 1835 and running for two years on such subjects as harmony, order, and allegory in architecture. In this same journal and in his *Gardener's Magazine,* Loudon also favorably reviewed Quatremère's *Essai sur la nature, le but et les moyens de l'imitation dans les beaux-arts* (1823), declaring that the work would enable critics to lay down a theory of landscape gardening founded on enduring principles.[45]

Quatremère de Quincy spent his life formulating a coherent philosophical system of the arts; he attempted to establish a general principle that would hold true for all of the fine arts, pointing out "what imitation in the fine arts ought to be, in order to constitute imitation." He stated that artists should strive to create a semblance rather than a copy of reality; therefore, the materials of the work of art had to be in some way different from the materials of the model. For example, the painter reproduced three-dimensional scenes on a two-dimensional canvas; the sculptor modeled his three-dimensional representations of human flesh in clay or stone.[46]

Quatremère devoted a section to the difference between illusion and imitation, for he did not consider them synonymous. He distinguished two sorts of illusion: one deceiving in conformity to rules, the other disregarding rules in order to deceive. Only the first afforded the mind true pleasure, which Quatremère described as the pleasure of a game with the audience half in on the secret. There could be neither illusion nor pleasure when no artifice was suspected; illusion was therefore actually the *effect* of imitation. He accepted that illusion could also be the *end* of imitation, with a certain qualification (the one passage from Quatremère that Downing quoted): "If the end of imitation be . . . to present to the senses and the mind, through the intervention of the fine arts, images which, in all the different forms of imitation, shall furnish an aggregate of perfection and ideal beauty to which particular models afford no equal."[47]

Quatremère ranked the imitative arts according to the amount of pleasure that could be derived by judging the distance that separated the elements of the model from those of the image: poetry took precedence for it was the furthest removed from sensible objects. There followed in order: music, painting, sculpture, architecture, and dance. Landscape gardening was given no place within this system. Although he did not dispute either the gratification yielded by this art or the kind of skill that it required, Quatremère believed that it lacked every element necessary to constitute imitation. What pretended to be an image of nature was nothing more or less than nature herself, especially when the artifice was well concealed in irregular or natural landscapes. Only a pleasure derived from nature—not imitation—could result from viewing such a work; Quatremère found no better illustration of setting the material illusion of the senses above the more immaterial of the mind.[48]

In response to these statements from Quatremère, Loudon formulated his theory of landscape gardening. In 1834 Loudon referred *Gardener's Magazine* readers to Quatremère's *Essai sur l'Imitation,* and announced his intention to publish the work in English for the improvement of young gardeners and architects. He criticized previous writings on the subject for failing to promote landscape gardening as a fine art and for not offering a comprehensive and satisfactory theory for both the ancient and modern styles. While Loudon acknowledged a debt to Whately, Alison, Price, and others for the practical and philosophical foundation of his work as a landscape gardener, Quatremère offered something more. Given Loudon's love of scientific order and system, he was intrigued by the French academician's theory because it embraced all works of art and all styles of gardening.[49]

The title of the 1834 article in which Loudon praised Quatremère's *Essai sur l'Imitation* gave little indication of its subject: "Arboretum Britannicum; or, Portraits from Nature . . . of all the Trees and Shrubs which endure the Open Air in Britain . . . ; and Observations on Their Uses in the Arts, and more especially in Landscape-Gardening." Loudon previewed his forthcoming book, whose object would be "to spread a taste for foreign trees and shrubs." He offered practical incentives to his readers, citing the great number and variety of these exotics, their individual beauties and characteristics, and the rapid growth of many of the species. However, it was the theory that he constructed around the use of these foreign plants that was critical, for it was based on Quatremère's stipulation that the materials of a work of art had to be different from its model's: "There can be no landscape gardening in the natural or irregular style," Loudon stated categorically, "where only the indigenous trees of a country are employed."[50]

Subsumed in that statement was Loudon's desire to change the long-held notion that the object of landscape gardening was to copy nature. Some theorists, he regretted, had carried this principle so far as to recommend the production of facsimiles of wild scenery while others would only employ indigenous plants in order that the scenery would be mistaken for natural: "There is not a single writer . . . from Shenstone to Knight, Price, and Gilpin, who does not adopt the imitation of nature as a principle; and who has not, at the same time, forgotten or failed to see, that, in so far as landscape-gardening is to be considered one of the fine arts, the principle of the imitation of nature must be rendered subordinate to that of the Recognition of Art." Richard Payne Knight, for example, had advocated a clandestine use of art in *The Landscape*:

How best to bid the verdant Landscape rise,
To please the fancy, and delight the eyes;
Its various parts in harmony to join
With art clandestine, and conceal'd design;
T'adorn, arrange;—to sep'rate, and select
With secret skill, and counterfeit neglect.

Loudon, however, believed that art should be discoverable everywhere—in the smoothness of the turf, in the high keeping of the walks, and above all, in the predominance of exotic trees, shrubs, and plants over indigenous ones. The geometric style of landscape gardening easily succeeded in being acknowledged as art, and could be called a fine art because its ground and trees were arranged in artificial surfaces, forms, and lines. The modern or natural style could accomplish this only by employing numerous sorts of foreign plants.[51]

Quatremère's treatise, translated into English by J. C. Kent at Loudon's request, appeared in 1837. In the preface, clearly at Loudon's instigation, Kent lent support to the principle that the recognition of art was necessary to the effect of every art, and he proposed a method of landscape gardening that would meet Quatremère's requirements:

The elements of composition at [landscape gardening's] command, which are *other* than what nature has anywhere associated in one and the same scene, such as trees and shrubs from *all* and *opposite* climates, well kept walks, smooth turf, &c., setting aside the assistance of Architecture and Sculpture, must be so employed as to allow of the presence of Art being at once recognized.

Downing likewise stipulated that the beau ideal in landscape gardening as a fine art called for the use of plants different from those in wild nature—"being composed of the floral and arboricultural riches of *all climates*."[52]

In the *Suburban Gardener* (1838), Loudon's definition of "fine art" revealed the elevated status that this designation held for him and why he wanted to associate it with his profession; the synonyms were "elegant art, art of imagination . . . art of taste, art of design, art of beauty." A work characterized as a fine art undoubtedly had to be created by an artist, but—most importantly in his eyes—it had to be acknowledged as such. Loudon wished to be considered an artist, not a manufacturer or a mechanical repeater, and he looked for "approbation or applause" in recognition of his accomplishments. Like Downing, Loudon relied on proceeds from design commissions and publications. He stated:

To imitate nature in such a way as that the object produced should be mistaken for nature, could never excite much approbation for the artist. . . . On the contrary, when an object is imitated in a totally different material from that in which it appears in nature, and the imitation is successful, the applause of the spectator is great in proportion to the degree of skill displayed.[53]

The *Suburban Gardener* also reinforced his earlier statements concerning the necessary use of exotics. The eighteenth- and nineteenth-century fascination with rare and bizarre foreign plants influenced this stance; as new colonial accessions and overseas trade treaties opened up unknown areas of the world, there was a great influx of new plants into Britain (fig. 2.10). Loudon calculated that in the eighteenth century nearly nine thousand plants were introduced, compared with less than a thousand in the previous century. Status seekers displayed such foreign plants as Pampas, Bamboo, Rhododendrons, and North American conifers. England's Royal Botanic Gardens at Kew displayed these marvelous new imports; one visitor wrote about his enjoyment of the "odours and fantastic beauties of the tropics, the fairy-like vegetation of a clime more favoured in this respect than our own, and such a bewitching sight of exotic loveliness as may nowhere else be obtained." Major portions of Loudon's publications, including his eight-volume *Arboretum et Fruticetum Britannicum,* were devoted to the dissemination of information about these plants and to the encouragement of their use. It is not surprising that this botanical craze was reflected in Loudon's theory.[54]

He developed a new landscape style called the "gardenesque," which combined his fascination with these splendid rare plants, his idealist aesthetics, and the principle of the "recognition of art" based on Quatremère. The gardenesque became one of the two modes of "artistical imitation" defined in the *Suburban Gardener.* The picturesque, borrowed from earlier writers, was the imitation of nature in a wild state; his own gardenesque was the imitation of nature "subjected to a certain degree of cultivation or improvement suitable to the wants and wishes of man." For picturesque effect, no tree or shrub stood isolated but rather each formed a part of a group or mass; therefore the beauty of the individual plant was of little consequence. To produce the gardenesque effect while planting, thinning, and pruning, the designer took into consideration the beauty of every individual tree and shrub—as a single object. New, exotic specimens would in this way be displayed to best advantage. A third landscape type, which Loudon called rustic, indigenous, or facsimile imitation, was considered to have no design merit; therefore

2.10

The Giant Mexican Cactus. The specimen was at the Royal Botanic Gardens at Kew. In *Horticulturist* (November 1846). Author's collection.

it scarcely required the aid of either a landscape gardener or horticulturist.[55]

Another neoclassical architect's philosophy of imitation found voice in Loudon's publications and subsequently in Downing's *Treatise*. Friedrich Weinbrenner had been the principal architect in Karlsruhe, where he built a great number of that city's public and private buildings during the opening decades of the nineteenth century. The third book of his *Architektonisches Lehrbuch* (1810–19), portions of which appeared in Loudon's 1838 *Architectural Magazine,* was meant to furnish the young artist "with an exalted model for a correct judgment of forms and their ornaments." Like Quatremère, Weinbrenner did not consider the end of imitation to be illusion; only horror or disgust resulted if the artist colored human figures, animals, and fruit as they were in nature. Art agreeably deceived, but it did not coarsely cheat the viewer as did a clothed wax figure. Thus, Weinbrenner distinguished between the beauty of nature and the beauty of art. Downing appended this lengthy quotation from Weinbrenner as a footnote to support his explanation of facsimile versus artistical imitation of nature:

> To copy the beauty of nature cannot be called being an artist, in the highest sense of the word, as only a mechanical talent is required for it. The beautiful in art depends on an idea, and therefore the true artist must possess, together with the talent for technical execution, that genial power which revels freely in rich forms, and is capable of producing and animating them. It is by this that the merit of the artist and his productions is to be judged; and these cannot be properly estimated among those barren copyists of nature, which we find so many of our flower, portrait, and landscape painters, &c., to be. But the artist stands much higher in the scale, who, though a copyist of visible nature, is capable of seizing it with poetical feeling, and representing it in its more dignified sense; such, for example, as Raphael, Poussin, Claude Lorraine, &c.

In counseling painters and sculptors to "catch and retain the *beau idéal,* or rather the maximum of perfection in form," in order to insure the beauty of their works, the German architect's theory reflected British as well as French classicism.[56]

The principles of imitation that Loudon adapted from Reynolds, Quatremère, and Weinbrenner reached an American audience with Downing's 1841 *Treatise*. In "Beauties of Landscape Gardening," Downing quoted Quatremère on the end of imitation and concurred that a "fac-simile imitation" of nature in gardening in which only wild trees, shrubs, and plants were employed and which was precisely like wild nature, produced pleasure only as it deceived and appeared to be nature itself. On the other hand, an "artistical imitation" afforded pleasure to the mind, not only by the expressions of natural beauty that could be discovered in it but by the more novel and more choice forms in which they were displayed and "by the tasteful art apparent in the arrangement." Downing illustrated the relative merit of the two with Weinbrenner's comparison of a human figure counterfeited in wax and a marble statue; although both were imitations of nature, the latter was expressive and elegant and could never be mistaken for the original.[57]

As did Loudon, Downing made paramount the necessity of introducing exotic ornamental plants instead of indigenous ones. Other American nurserymen encouraged the taste for imports, as is evident in an 1841 letter to John Jay Smith: "You are partly right and partly wrong in your remarks about or rather attacks upon the gardeners, for keeping *nothing but what is saleable*" (fig. 2.11). He reminded Smith of Robert Buist's nursery in Philadelphia: "Look for example at the Buists who import hundreds of things that they never get a cent

ALMOST EVERYTHING IS YET BEFORE US: *The 1841 Edition*

2.11
View of Robert Buist's City Nursery & Greenhouses, No. 140 South Twelfth St., Philadelphia (1846).
The Library Company of Philadelphia.

for.... A gardener must have zeal, taste, and money to spare, before he can set about leading & improving the popular taste in arboriculture."[58]

Although a section of the *Treatise* entitled "Deciduous Ornamental Trees" enumerates the beauties of native trees such as the American White Oak, White Elm, and White Ash, when Downing offered an example of how one could achieve the tasteful—and necessary—appearance of art, it lay in "the variety of the materials, as foreign trees, plants, &c." A lawn was to be arranged with groups of lindens, horse chestnuts and magnolias, although the native forests were filled with oak and ash trees. It was the broad-leaved European Linden (*Tilia europaea*) that Downing specified in his section on deciduous ornamental trees as "the finest for shade and ornament," and he praised the splendid flowers of the Horse-chestnut (*Aesculus hippocastanum,* a native of Middle Asia), claiming that they surpassed those of almost all native American trees. The Magnolia, although primarily a North American tree, would have been exotic to the majority of readers in the northern states. Downing came to realize, as early as the 1844 edition, that the adoption of Loudon's thinking in this regard was a misjudgment both practically and aesthetically.[59]

To Loudon's picturesque and gardenesque categories, Downing added a third: the beautiful. This was significant because, in differentiating the beautiful from the gardenesque, Downing judged Loudon's style inferior. Although the features of the gardenesque were placed before his readers in a two-page quotation from the *Suburban Gardener,* Downing gave his own opinion that its predominant characteristic was "the exhibition of a highly developed state of cultivation." The gardenesque admitted every species of tree in the same scene, provided it was planted separately; therefore, Downing considered its objective "mainly to produce highly elegant and polished *forms.*" He found this markedly different from beautiful and picturesque imitations of nature, in which trees intrinsically expressive of either of these characters had to predominate, thus achieving the objective of "the *expression* of the whole scene."[60]

When Downing ranked the different modes of landscape gardening on the imitative scale, facsimile was the lowest. Next were the geometric and gardenesque manners, as they depended upon "choice materials arranged in regular and systematic, or in elegant and artistical forms, for the admiration which they elicit." Beautiful and picturesque imitations of nature were the highest, as they joined "to fine forms, and elegance in arrangement, the higher beauty of sentiment or expression."[61]

The Superior Beauty of Expression

Downing informed his readers that recognition of "the beauty of expression" (expression being the power of an object to excite some emotion in an individual's mind) heralded the beginning of "modern" landscape gardening. His account of the progressive stages in the history of gardening allowed no American, keen for civilization and refinement, to doubt the higher order of the modern style. In the infancy of the fine arts, Downing asserted, perceptions of their ultimate capabilities were "crude and imperfect." Thus, people were completely satisfied with "the mere exhibition of *design* or *art.*" The first paintings, for example, were crude attempts to imitate the *form* of a tree. In the art of gardening, the practice had been "to display the skill of the designer in arranging all the materials of nature, in artificial, regular, or symmetrical forms." With advancement, however, came the ability to appreciate "the superior beauty of *expression*."⁶²

The concept of expression was part of the eighteenth-century inquiry into "taste." For such a significant and difficult subject, Downing relied on the authority of the Scottish philosopher Archibald Alison. Downing offered a lengthy quotation from Alison's *Essays on the Nature and Principles of Taste* (1790) in a footnote, revealing his close adherence to Alison on the subject of form versus expression in natural objects:

When the arts have made this progress, circumstances arise which alter in a great measure, the taste of mankind, and introduce a different opinion with regard to the beauty of design. Two causes, more especially, conspire to this: 1st. The discovery, gradually made, that other and much more affecting qualities are capable of being expressed by forms than that of mere design; and 2d, the progress of the arts themselves, which naturally, render comparatively easy, what at first was difficult—and consequently render the production of regularity or uniformity less forcibly the sign of skill than at first.⁶³

Contrary to classical aesthetic dogma, Alison considered that beauty existed in the mind of the individual and was not intrinsic to objects: "The sublimity or beauty of forms arises altogether from the association we connect with them, or the qualities of which they are expressive to us." Certain trains of thought, capable of exciting emotion, were suggested by either beautiful or sublime objects (Alison considered the picturesque a subdivision of the beautiful). For example, the ideas suggested by spring scenery produced the emotions of cheerfulness and tenderness; the view of the ocean in a storm produced emotions related to power, majesty, and terror. Alison labeled "imagination" the power of a given mind to call up the associations; "expression" was the power of an object to evoke them.⁶⁴

These emotions of taste could not be produced without a unity of character in a composition. Alison described the difference between a scene in real nature, which frequently exhibited a confusion of expression, and a scene that had been improved by the art of gardening, which revealed a "purity and harmony" of composition. The artist had the power to remove from the landscape whatever detracted from its character or its effect and thus could awaken "an emotion more full, more simple, and more harmonious" than any that could be received from nature itself.⁶⁵

Alison's interpretation of expression was central to Downing's landscape theory, although Downing did not use the term *association* in the 1841 *Treatise* except in reference to architectural styles. He defined the beautiful and the picturesque as "striking examples of expression in natural scenery" and advised that a landscape was more satisfactory when either one or the other predominated. His description of expression as "the most elevated kind of beauty in landscapes" owed much to Alison: "The highest imitative effects of the art, therefore, consist in arranging the materials, so as to create emotions of grace, elegance, picturesqueness, or grandeur, joined with unity, harmony, and variety, more distinct and more forcible than are suggested by natural scenery." Downing's criticism of Loudon's gardenesque mode of imitation arose out of this belief; his reproof was directed at the gardenesque's mixture of tree species in the same scene regardless of the scene's general expression. In the *Treatise*'s beautiful or picturesque imitations of nature, trees intrinsically expressive of the scene's character predominate.⁶⁶

The Superior Beauty of Expression

Downing described what could be derived from the study of nature if one were blessed with this higher perception of the capacities of landscape gardening—that is, that natural objects had a higher kind of beauty than mere form. Looking around for materials, this new class of artist would observe "the spirit and expression of natural objects, the varied forms of ground and water, and the character of trees individually and in composition." For example, by including oak trees, the landscape artist could introduce an expression of dignity and majesty into a scene; spirited picturesqueness could be evoked by larches.[67]

One would expect Downing's "grand principles," recapitulated at chapter's end, to reflect this forceful argument for "the superior beauty of expression." However, the concept that supposedly heralded the beginning of modern landscape gardening placed third:

1. The Recognition Of Art, founded on the immutability of the true as well as the beautiful: 2. The Production Of A Whole, springing from the necessity in the mind of a unity of sensation: 3. The Imitation Of The Beauty Of Expression, derived from a refined perception of the sentiment of nature: 4. The Production Of Variety, including under this term intricacy and harmony, founded on the ever active desire for new objects of interest.[68]

The "recognition of art," as proposed by Loudon, took precedence in the 1841 edition. "The production of a whole" was a standard principle for all design compositions: the mind could only attend with pleasure and satisfaction to one object or one composite sensation at the same time. "The production of variety" could have been inspired by any number of eighteenth-century writers on aesthetics. In particular, Downing praised Addison for suggesting the philosophical principles of landscape gardening. Addison had commented on the special ability of nature to afford great entertainment: "The Beauties of the most stately Garden or Palace lie in a narrow Compass, the Imagination immediately runs them over, and requires something else to gratify her; but, in the wide Fields of Nature, the Sight wanders up and down without Confinement, and is fed with an infinite variety of Images, without any certain Stint or Number." Variety was similarly presented in the *Treatise* as a fertile source of beauty in landscape gardening: it produced certain contrasts and created in scenery "a thousand points of interest," thus eliciting new beauties through different arrangements and combinations.[69]

This ranking of "grand principles" showed an internal tension in Downing's thinking. Although he accommodated Loudon's theory of imitation in landscape gardening with its concept of an ideal beauty in nature, Downing fell short of his colleague's admiration for order, system, and idealized forms. An example of Loudon's love of scientific order was his adoption of the Jussieuean system in the flower garden; this system, developed by two eighteenth-century French botanists, classified the natural forms of plants rather than their abstract characteristics as had Linnaeus. In addition, Loudon's ideas had much in common with the French academic doctrine of *la belle nature,* which offered a construct of nature subject to rational laws. The garden of Versailles, for example, was based on "general" attributes of nature—symmetry, order, harmony, and proportion. While Loudon was embracing French system, others in England were rejecting it. In the development of "modern" English landscape gardening, it has been suggested that a major influence in the rejection of French system was the new English science of the Royal Society, which opposed

Cartesian a priori theories with an empirical regard for local observations, patient investigations, and histories as opposed to systems. English landscape gardening more flexibly handled the ratio of art to nature.[70]

Downing both rejected and embraced elements of the French system; he explicitly discouraged the odd conceits of the geometric style, castigated the French as despots who achieved their layouts "with but little study or theory upon the subject," and paired the geometric style with Loudon's gardenesque. At the same time, with the adoption of such terms as beau ideal and *general* nature and the incorporation of "the recognition of art" as an essential part of his theory, Downing allied himself with those same conservative academicians whom he so disparagingly described as being satisfied with "mere design or art" and who had little to do with the notion of natural beauty based in modern landscape gardening. The devotees of Downing's preferred modern style offered interpretations radically different from that of the French academy of what constituted "beautiful nature" and the extent to which the artist should mend nature. Rather than abstractly formal compositions such as Versailles, their vision resulted in the freedom and variety of the natural garden.[71]

We can allow Downing this mixture of classical theories and romantic emotions in the *Treatise*'s discussion of beauty in nature and art, given that the French and British academies had been debating "the ideal" versus "the real" since the late eighteenth century. Also, the *Treatise*'s premier ranking of Loudon's fundamental principle despite Downing's disagreement with certain of his ideas seems reasonable in context. Loudon was, after all, "the most distinguished gardening author" of standard works then in use in the United States. A strong professional relationship bound the younger American to his renowned British colleague. The two shared a determination to bring landscape gardening into the ranks of the fine arts as well as a fascination with horticultural matters. Loudon had pondered and reworked his theory over a period of nearly forty years, with the advantage of extensive journeys through Britain, continental Europe, and Russia. It was not until 1837, however, that he found his comprehensive theory, declaring himself "more indebted to [Quatremère's *Essay*] than to all the other works on landscape gardening, or the fine arts, put together." Downing, in contrast, was just beginning his study of such authors as Price, Knight, Whately, Alison, and Repton; his travels were limited; and his professional landscape gardening career at its start. With time, he too would revise his theory.[72]

3

ON HIS NATIVE HEATHER

The 1844 Edition

More than three years passed before Downing was able to bring out the second edition of the *Treatise* in the late summer of 1844, although, on the advice of his publishers, he had begun almost immediately to gather material for the revision. Delays in the publication were reported in a series of letters to his friend John Jay Smith of Philadelphia (fig. 3.1). The postponement ultimately proved beneficial, for the correspondence also reveals experiences that helped to shape Downing's understanding of his country's particular needs and landscape resources as he explored a number of American estates and expanded his professional landscape gardening practice.[1]

In November 1841, Downing asked Smith to suggest a few Philadelphia residences to include in the new edition and told him of his own travels in search of the finest Hudson River places. Downing had been busy "giving designs for laying out grounds both in the neighborhood of Boston and New York," and he was optimistic about the growing opportunities in the profession (fig. 3.2). The following month, Downing thanked Smith for his recommendations: "I want very much to look at some of the noble places you describe"; he planned to expand the first section of the *Treatise* in order to give it "a national or American interest":

> I had intended as I wrote you to issue a second edition in the spring according to the desire of my booksellers: but as I look around the subject opens and the material accumulate[s] so fast that I think of delaying if possible the publication. . . . I wish to add a brief notice of all the most interesting places in the Union and some sketches or engravings of several of them and I wish to add so much to the work as is possible to be able to publish a large edition

The 1844 Edition

and make it the standard work on the subject for this country.[2]

Downing had just returned from Albany, New York, where he saw the new country seat of William P. Van Rensselaer, and he confessed to Smith that he found it "deficient in that *comfortable, home-like* look which ought to be the *beau ideal* of a country house." At that time Downing was thinking about what should constitute a country house, for he was also preparing material for a volume (at first called "Model Cottages and Gardens") that would be published in the summer of 1842 under the title *Cottage Residences*. This was Downing's "practical" book, addressed to Americans with small parcels of ground; a reminder was added to the new edition of the *Treatise* that "Landscape Gardening, in its proper sense, [could] not be applied to the embellishment of the smallest cottage residences."[3]

October 1842 found Downing in the midst of an "absorbing season"; he was thoroughly occupied with business matters both at home and on landscape gardening journeys in Massachusetts, New York, Connecticut, and New Jersey. He also had recently inspected the improvements at another Van Rensselaer family mansion in Albany. At the new year, Downing reported to Smith that he had been "perfectly charmed" with the country seat of George Sheaff, one of the Philadelphia places recommended by his friend, and he promised to do it ample justice in the coming edition. In April 1843, although the *Treatise* had been out of print for three months, Downing wrote that the new edition would be kept back for "prudential reasons . . . so as to come out in time for the early fall sales." His most trusted engraver became engaged on another project, however, and yet another postponement was announced that fall.

3.1

Portrait of John Jay Smith. The Library Company of Philadelphia.

But Downing was able to boast to Smith that the book was "constantly in demand," and he felt the unsatisfied want would result in "a better receipt of the new edition."[4]

Loudon died in December 1843, and Downing commented to Smith on the circumstances of his last year: "How singular that poor Loudon should have died just as he had completed his little work on *cemeteries*. Do you know it gave me quite a melancholy forboding—knowing his infirm health—to see the directions about interment and the cut

ON HIS NATIVE HEATHER

BOTANIC GARDEN AND NURSERIES.
NEWBURGH, N.Y. 3d Dec 1841

My dear Sir

I have perused several times your last and my interesting letter in which you kindly offer some suggestions towards my second edition. The account of the places near Phila interest me deeply and is precisely what I wanted. I had intended to enlarge very greatly my section of Historical Notices, and to take in as much as possible that could [have] id a national or American interest; and what you have written me shall be duly worked up and incorporated into that section of my work together with anything else usefully interesting that you may be able to collect for me. I had intended as I wrote you to [issue] a second edition in the Spring according to the desire of my publisher; but as I look around the subject opens

3.2

First page of letter from A. J. Downing to John Jay Smith, 3 December 1841, Smith Manuscript Collection at the Library Company of Philadelphia on deposit at the Historical Society of Pennsylvania, Philadelphia. The Library Company of Philadelphia.

The 1844 Edition

of the bier at the conclusion of that little book." With the death of his mentor, Downing acquired a different perspective on Loudon's work, and the changes made for the second edition included a reappraisal of his landscape designs and theory. In fact, a collection of Repton's writings published by Loudon undoubtedly influenced Downing's treatment of the former rivals.[5]

Downing's own maturation in terms of broadening experience and knowledge also affected the revisions. As the *Treatise* was finally going through the press in February 1844, he explained to Smith how determined he had been to have it reprinted with great improvements, although the publishers received orders every day and quarreled about the delay. Downing seemed to be following his own advice from the 1841 edition: "In examining such [tasteful country seats], the mind is at a single view more fully impressed with the beauties of the art and its capabilities, than by ten times the amount of time spent in investigating the theory without any such practical illustrations." This sentence was dropped from the *Treatise,* and Downing gave less emphasis to the theory of imitation in landscape gardening and offered twenty-five more descriptions of American estates.[6]

He also raised to first place the principle of the "Beauty of Expression," relegating Loudon's "Recognition of Art" to second. Associated with these changes was the absence of a strong statement concerning the necessity for exotic plants. He observed that his countrymen were beginning to prefer the picturesque over what he labeled the graceful school. Downing himself was newly intrigued with the picturesque, as is indicated by his citation of Sir Thomas Dick Lauder's 1842 edition of Uvedale Price (fig. 3.3). This book also reacquainted Downing with Archibald Alison, who

3.3

Title page for Thomas Dick Lauder, *Sir Uvedale Price on the Picturesque* (1842). Special Collections, Weigel Library, Kansas State University.

was quoted at length in Lauder's introduction. These revisions indicate the 1844 *Treatise*'s general shift toward the more individual sensibilities and emotions central to the experience of "expressive" American landscapes.⁷

The Reading of the Past

"In the present [second] edition," Downing announced in the August 1844 preface, "a large part of the first portion of the work has been rewritten, —some modification of the principles of the art have been introduced, —considerable new matter has been added, —[and] the whole has been revised, and newly and more copiously illustrated, from examples now existing in this country." Section 1 retained its heading of "Historical Sketches" and the outline from the previous edition, but in expanding his discussion of the "two distinct and widely differing modes of the art," Downing provided even more abundant proof than was offered earlier that in the infancy of the fine arts, mankind was completely satisfied with "the mere exhibition of *design* or *art*." His new retrospective "glance at the history and progress of the art of tasteful gardening" was addressed to "the enquiring reader," and Downing explained that to be fair, classical gardens—"however artificial"—had to be included. Downing meant to make this second edition the standard work on the subject; therefore, he provided the more detailed historical background that American readers previously had found in Loudon's *Encylopedia of Gardening*. Downing later had cause to regret the expediency of simply copying the greatest portion of this information from Loudon's book.⁸

In the 1841 *Treatise,* Downing had dismissed the geometric style in Europe from antiquity to 1700 in one sentence and described the extravagance of Versailles in one paragraph. In contrast, eight pages in the 1844 edition were devoted to this mode, including the hanging gardens of Babylon, the gardens of Epicurus and Plato, Isola Bella, and Versailles. The Dutch school was the most severely criticized as a "double distilled compound of laboured symmetry, regularity, and stiffness which seems to convey to the quiet owners so much pleasure, and the tasteful traveller and critic so much despair!" An extract from Alexander Pope's satire in the *Guardian* offered readers a better idea of the Dutch notions in vogue in the opening years of the eighteenth century, when a "virtuoso gardener" carved Adam and Eve in yew and St. George in box.⁹

Downing gave more space as well to the main actors in the "glorious revolution" in public taste known as the modern style. Downing added a reference to Pope's "Epistle to Lord Burlington," suggesting that it offered "sound principles for the new art; —the study of nature; the genius of the place; *and never to lose sight of good sense*." Downing did not actually quote Pope's well-known lines:

   Consult the Genius of the Place in all;
That tells the Waters or to rise, or fall,
Or helps th'ambitious Hill the heav'ns to scale,
Or scoops in circling theatres the Vale,
Calls in the Country, catches opening glades,
Joins willing woods, and varies shades from shades,
Now breaks, or now directs, th'intending Lines;
Paints as you plant, and, as you work, designs.
   Still follow Sense, of ev'ry Art the Soul.

Urging readers to "follow Sense," Downing directed his advice toward "ambitious, would-be men of taste" and their "discordant abortions." The partners George London (mistakenly spelled "Loudon") and Henry Wise, and the Leasowes's proprietor William Shenstone were introduced into this revised edition, and William Kent was newly described as "undoubtedly, the first professional landscape gardener in the modern style."[10]

Downing abandoned his avowed neutral position concerning the two schools of landscape gardening that had waged battle in eighteenth-century England and criticized Capability Brown while lauding Uvedale Price and Richard Payne Knight. Brown had "so little true sympathy with nature, as to be made the jest of every succeeding generation" because his mind had been furnished with but one model, consisting of a round lake, a smooth bare lawn, a clump of trees, and a boundary belt. Downing contrasted this so-called mannerism with Price's celebrated *Essay on the Picturesque*. In 1841, this book was listed in the midst of other recommended readings, but Price's *Essay* took precedence in 1844. Downing described it as "a series of elegant and masterly essays, [which] pointed out the faults and follies of this Brown and his imitators, analyzed the beautiful and picturesque in nature and art, and founded a new school, more spirited and free in its aim, deriving its principles directly from nature and painting." Knight's poem *The Landscape* was awarded standing with Price's work and those of William Mason and Thomas Whately for having "established the new style firmly in the public mind."[11]

Downing's intense admiration for the English landscape garden remained undiminished; while conceding the Chinese taste as "the nearest previous approach to the modern style," he stood by his former statement and denied that the English were indebted to the "curious ingenuity" of the Chinese. However, he did soften his condemnation of the geometric style with the addition of a qualifying word. Rather than dismiss it as requiring "but little study or theory," he conceded that it "usually involved little or no theory." Nonetheless, Addison's mocking words about "the Mark of the Scissars upon every Plant and Bush" could have been the caption for the new illustration of a geometric-style garden (fig. 3.4). Having spelled out the worst excesses of the mode, Downing added a paragraph describing the special cases in which it might be introduced with good effect. These included public squares and gardens where a highly artificial character was desirable and very small gardens where variety and irregularity were not possible. Those with a taste for an "old and quaint style of residence" would perhaps prefer a symmetrical and knotted garden; in this case, "pleached alleys, and sheared trees, would be admired, like old armour, as curious specimens of antique taste and custom." Even with these changes, a British review criticized Downing's treatment of geometric gardening: "Our American friend is totally unacquainted with the numerous princely

3.4

The Geometric Style, from an Old Print. In *Treatise* (1844). Kansas State University Libraries.

examples of the purest kind [of geometric gardening] existing in England, neither does he appear to have read her best authors on this subject; if he has, it must have been through his *modern* spectacles."[12]

Downing's half-hearted attempt to recognize the alternative mode was perhaps a belated acknowledgment of Loudon's preference for the geometric style for public squares and small gardens bordered by straight lines and his censure of those blindly "captivated by the novelty of the irregular style." Downing's tempered remarks concerning Chinese taste in gardening also moved closer to Loudon's treatment of the subject. With these modifications and in the new pairing with Humphry Repton as "the most distinguished English Landscape Gardeners of more recent date," Loudon seemed to be elevated to a more visible place of honor in the 1844 *Treatise*. But in reality, Loudon lost ground to his former competitor, for Repton's stature was even more greatly enhanced in the revised edition.[13]

Downing no longer linked Repton with Brown as the misguided champions of the more formal school. Downing praised Repton's taste in landscape gardening as "cultivated and elegant"; many of the finest parks and pleasure grounds of England bore witness to "the skill and harmony of his designs." Repton's published works were full of instructive hints, Downing reported, and this knowledge was directly attributable to Loudon, whose one-volume collection *The Landscape Gardening and Landscape Architecture of the Late Humphry Repton* (1840) made his books newly available and affordable. Downing evidently did not read this book until after the completion of his 1841 *Treatise;* and considering the cost of the original Repton works, published separately in one folio and three quarto volumes between 1795 and 1816, it is unlikely that Downing was familiar with them. Loudon announced the forthcoming edition in the fall of 1838, telling readers of the *Gardener's Magazine* that he had purchased the unexpired copyrights of Repton's works in order to publish them at a price that would enable every gardener to own the collection.[14]

After the reference to the instructive Repton works, Downing turned to Loudon's "writings and labours in tasteful gardening," noting that they were so well known in the United States that he had only to allude to them. He mourned the loss of his friend in a footnote: "While we are revising this edition, we regret deeply to learn the death of Mr. Loudon. His herculean labours as an author, have at last destroyed him; and in his death we lose one who has done more than any other person that ever lived to popularise, and render universal, a taste for Gardening and Domestic Architecture." Downing made a point of qualifying his admiration, however: "[Loudon] is, as it seems to us, somewhat deficient as an artist, in imagination."[15]

Downing reiterated this judgment while brashly admitting a debt to Loudon's work, in response to a critique of the 1844 *Treatise* by the English botanist and horticulturist John Lindley. The latter wrote: "There is much error in the reading of the past; there is a slavish admiration of the late Mr. Loudon. . . . As to his 'Historical Sketches,' of the science in this country, the less said the better. It is done clumsily, and abounds in errors as to fact." Indeed, the supposedly erroneous information—those numerous pages on the history and progress of the art added to section 1—had been culled from Loudon's *Encyclopedia of Gardening*. Downing handily replied that he regretted that his "Historical Sketches" of landscape gardening in Britain were not satisfactory in the eyes of Lindley. "Luckily for our reputation," he added, "it is the portion of our work which has no claim to originality, and as it was entirely compiled from standard English works, the 'errors as to fact' must be sent elsewhere for correction." He also countered Lindley's accusation of a slavish admiration: "Mr. Loudon's taste was by no means perfect in landscape gardening or architecture. (It would be difficult to say whose is.)" Downing defended him as "the most philosophical writer on the subject that any country has produced" and in the same breath reminded Lindley that in the *Treatise* he had expressly pointed out Loudon's deficiency of imagination as an artist. In the 1844 *Treatise,* Downing began to distance himself from an old-world apprenticeship.[16]

Comparatively Little Having Yet Been Done

John Lindley, reviewing the second edition, noted the negative aspects of Downing's dependence on Loudon but praised the material arising from the author's own experience: "It is when 'his foot is on his native heather,' that he shakes off every such encumbrance, and speaks out plainly and well." Downing included twenty-five more notices and many new engravings of American estates in the 1844 edition. His visits to such places as the Manor of Livingston (Mrs. Mary Livingston's seat near the town of Hudson, New York) and to a number of suburban residences in the vicinity of Boston were evident in the *Treatise* accounts, for the descriptions seemed to be phrased to point out his personal inspection. Although newly featuring several small estates, Downing bluntly cautioned: "We should convey a false impression, were we to state that [landscape gardening] may be applied with equal success to residences of every class and size."[17]

Certain "old and celebrated" Livingston country residences on the Hudson River were mentioned in the 1841 edition, but Downing admitted to Smith that he had never visited the Manor of Livingston before, and he exclaimed at its beauty: "The eye from the terrace sweeps over half a million of dollars worth of the proprietor[']s domain & the park filled with noble trees." He also noted that the thirty-year-old house built of marble was in elegant condition. The 1844 *Treatise* carried an illustration and a revised description (fig. 3.5). Readers learned that the park, because of its upkeep and "noble simplicity" of character, was the most remarkable in America: "The turf is, every-where, short and velvet-like, the gravel-roads scrupulously firm and smooth, and near the house are the largest and most superb evergreens. The mansion is one of the chastest specimens of the Grecian style, and there is an air of great dignity and grace about the whole demesne."[18]

3.5

The Manor of Livingston. In *Treatise* (1844). Kansas State University Libraries.

In the winter of 1841, upon viewing William P. Van Rensselaer's Beaverwyck, north of Albany, New York, Downing discovered it to be "quite the palace of America costing about $100 000" but not living up to his beau ideal of a country home. However, in his letter to Smith, he admired the extensive grounds, which had "a good deal of natural fine wood." Neither the frightfully high cost nor any hint of criticism appeared in print: "The mansion . . . is perhaps the most splendid in the Union. The grounds are yet newly laid out, but with much judgment; and six or seven miles of winding gravelled roads and walks have been formed. . . . The drives thus afforded, are almost unrivalled in extent and variety."[19]

Within a year after Smith sent a letter regarding interesting places near Philadelphia, Downing inspected at least two of them, and he added new accounts and illustrations of the country seat of George Sheaff and the cottage of Mrs. William M. Camac. The *Treatise* distinguished the Sheaff estate as "one of the most remarkable in Pennsyl-

3.7

Mrs. Camac's Residence. In *Treatise* (1844). Kansas State University Libraries.

vania" and a "striking example of science, skill and taste." At Downing's request, Smith asked one of the young ladies in the family to make a sketch of the house with a few of its most characteristic trees, and the engraving done for the new edition featured "the conspicuous ornament of the grounds"—a magnificent White Oak of enormous size (fig. 3.6).[20]

Elizabeth Markoe Camac's residence four or five miles outside Philadelphia provided an example of a "picturesque cottage, in the rural gothic style, with very charming and appropriate pleasure grounds" (fig. 3.7). The diarist Sidney George Fisher was acquainted with this "young & handsome widow," and an entry referred to Mrs. Camac's circumstances—on her husband's death in 1842, she was left "a splendid estate." In the summer of 1843, Fisher attended a ball at the cottage and described the elegant establishment: though it was June, the weather was so cold that "the best part of the entertainment could not be enjoyed—the grounds, the garden, the greenhouse & grapery, which were all lit up." Perhaps Downing was

3.6

The Seat of Geo. Sheaff, Esq. In *Treatise* (1844). Kansas State University Libraries.

a guest at one of Mrs. Camac's fancy balls, for he remarked that the conservatory attached to the house was the most tasteful and elegant that he remembered having seen. In an 1846 *Horticulturist* editorial, Downing commended the cottage's lawn as "a gem of neatness and high keeping."[21]

Older and more celebrated Philadelphia country residences were also highlighted in the revised edition; the large specimen trees, both exotic and native, found on the extensive grounds of the Woodlands and Belmont were deemed especially remarkable (figs. 3.8, 3.9). Downing was fascinated with the Japanese Ginkgo, a "curious tree" that the late William Hamilton had brought to the Woodlands from England in 1784; two had flourished and grown to a height of nearly sixty feet. Downing further praised Hamilton's Ginkgos in the *Treatise*'s section on deciduous ornamental trees, telling readers that the tree was "so singularly beautiful when clad with its fern-like foliage, that it is strikingly adapted to add ornament and interest to the pleasure-ground" (fig. 3.10). The rare trees at Belmont, the Schuylkill River home of the late Judge Richard Peters, included a chestnut planted by George Washington and a grand old avenue of ninety-foot-tall hemlocks.[22]

3.8

Woodlands, the Seat of Mr. Wm. Hamilton, Pennsylva. In *Birch Country Seats* (n.d.). The Library Company of Philadelphia.

Downing was able to explore the Boston area also, for beginning in the fall of 1841 numerous business trips to that city occupied his time. The new edition offered seemingly firsthand descriptions of seven country seats in the city environs, although they were still lacking in detail. The Brookline retreat of the wealthy Boston merchant Thomas Handasyd Perkins, Downing noted, abounded in "exquisite trees, finely disposed; among them, some larches and Norway firs." Through worldwide commercial ties (his fortune was made in rum, slaves, and opium), Perkins collected rare and valuable plants that he generously shared with other interested horticulturists. He may have been one of the private individuals praised in Downing's 1852 *Horticulturist* editorial where the author suggested that giving away spare plants to neighbors was the "readiest method of diffusing a knowledge of beautiful trees and plants, and thereby bettering our homes and country." T. H. Perkins's nephew was the John Perkins Cushing of Belmont illustrated in the *Treatise* (fig. 3.11). Downing commended the high culture of Cushing's gardens, although an essay by a Boston correspondent published eight years later in the journal was harshly critical: "The grounds . . . seem to have been done without any obvious leading principle, other than that suggested by the

3.9

View from Belmont, Pennsyla., the Seat of Judge Peters. In *Birch Country Seats* (n.d.). The Library Company of Philadelphia.

Comparatively Little Having Yet Been Done

3.10
The Ginkgo Tree. In *Garden and Forest* (June 1888). Kansas State University Libraries.

3.11

Belmont Place, near Boston, the seat of J. P. Cushing, Esq. In *Treatise* (1844). Kansas State University Libraries.

idea of filling the ground with trees, and letting them grow till they destroy each other." Thomas Lee was a member of another horticultural clan, and Downing's most laudatory comments were reserved for his cottage on the border of Jamaica Pond in Brookline. Native and foreign rhododendrons, kalmias, and other rare shrubs and a fine English Oak made it an instructive place for the naturalist and plant lover. The grounds possessed as much variety and interest as Downing had ever seen in "so moderate a compass—about 20 acres." The environs of Boston abounded in this class of residence and, according to Downing, this type of suburban cottage was likely to become more numerous than any other in the United States. Professional engagements in Hartford, Connecticut, resulted in additional reports of places in that state. A curious notice concerned a Mr. Gardiner's "remarkable seat" in Gardiner, Maine. There were several possible sources for Downing's knowledge of Robert Hallowell Gardiner's Oaklands on the Kennebec River. The Gardiner family had Boston connections, and the architect for the Gothic revival house built in 1835–36 was Richard Upjohn, whose Trinity Church in New York Downing greatly admired.[23]

Downing thus honored his country's recent achievements in tasteful gardening, albeit in a circumscribed area of the Union. His northeastern regional bias, especially for his native Hudson River Valley, remained steady. Also, a negative assessment of the South appeared: "At the south are many extensive country residences remarkable for trees of unusual grandeur and beauty, among which the live oak is very conspicuous; but they are, in general, wanting in that high keeping and care, which is so essential to the charm of a landscape garden."[24]

The greatly expanded section on American estates was offset by the equally expanded European retrospective, and Downing balanced his nationalist statements with comparisons to old-world accomplishments: "Landscape Gardening, in America, combined and working in harmony as it is with our fine scenery, is already beginning to give us results scarcely less beautiful than those produced by its finest efforts abroad." Downing admitted, however: "Almost every thing is yet before us, comparatively little having yet been done."[25]

Expression: The Master Key

In section 2—with the heading changed from "Beauties of Landscape Gardening" to "Beauties and Principles of the Art"—Downing turned to expression as the "master key to the heart, in all landscapes" and declared that the art's highest imitative sphere was an arrangement that awakened emotions more distinct than those suggested by natural scenery. Landscape gardening was to be understood as "not only an imitation, in the grounds of a country residence, of the general forms of nature, but *an expressive, harmonious, and refined imitation*." Emphasis thus shifted away from Quatremère's and Loudon's theory of an "artistical imitation," which appealed to "the senses and the mind" and not to the heart and its attendant emotions, toward Archibald Alison's concept of expression as set forth in his *Essays on Taste* (1790). In the laying out of grounds, Alison looked for a general expression to provide the imagination with "the *key* of the scene": "The art of gardening has gradually ascended from the pursuit of general beauty . . . to create a scenery *more pure, more harmonious, and more expressive,* than any that is to be found in nature itself."[26]

By qualifying imitation as "expressive," Downing diffused the connection with the academic beau ideal. Quatremère's statement linking the end of imitation to images furnishing "an aggregate of perfection and ideal beauty" was omitted in 1844, as was any reference to him, and the description of the beau ideal in landscape gardening was relegated to a footnote. However, Downing did not abandon the distinction between the beauty of nature and the beauty of art. While newly conceding that "an agreeable effect" would result from following "the simplest hints derived from the free and luxuriant forms of nature," he still maintained that this "easy assemblage of sylvan scenery [was] scarcely Landscape Gardening in the true sense of the word." The 1844 *Treatise* defined the aim of Landscape Gardening not in terms of "artistical imitation" but in terms of the expressive potential "more or less pervading every attractive portion of nature."[27]

Downing directed his American readers "to separate the accidental, and extraneous in nature, and to preserve only the spirit, or essence." By eliciting or heightening this expression, they could give their landscape gardens a higher charm than the polish of art could bestow. On one hand, Downing still acknowledged the aesthetic system that opposed the blemishes and defects of "particular nature" to the idealized "general nature." On the other, he retreated from the old-world standard of perfection and ideal beauty; consequently, aspiring improvers could more readily meet the challenge set before them.[28]

Perhaps his more extensive experience of rich and various American landscapes brought Downing to the realization that a scene's spirit or essence lay partly in its indigenous plants, for in the 1844 *Treatise* he no longer insisted upon the introduction of exotics. What previously had been a necessity became merely a suggestion that "among the trees and shrubs [in the more polished scene], should be conspicuous the finest foreign sorts." He indicated that "firm gravel walks near the house, and a general air of neatness in that quarter [could] properly evince the recognition of art in all Landscape Gardening." The diminished importance of the polish of art became even more apparent when Downing recapitulated his grand principles, for the ranking had changed: [1] "The Imitation Of The Beauty Of Expression, derived from a refined perception of the sentiment of nature: [2] The Recognition Of Art, founded on the immutability of the true, as well as the beautiful: [3] And The Production Of Unity, Harmony, And Variety, in order to render complete, and continuous, our enjoyment of any artistical work."[29]

Although Downing's concept of expression was based on Alison's *Essays on Taste,* he cited a secondary interpretation of this Scottish philosopher in 1844. Sir Thomas Dick Lauder had edited *Price on the Picturesque* (1842) partly to supply the proper associative foundation for Price's theories, and Lauder's introductory "Essay on the Origin of Taste" was a version of Alison (fig. 3.12). The opening pages were devoted to "an exposition of . . . the true Theory of the process by which the human mind is affected by emotions of beauty, of sublimity, or of the picturesque." This edition of Price reinforced for Downing the connection between the theory of association and the picturesque. He was able to note with satisfaction that within the previous five years Americans had begun to prefer the picturesque. Furthermore, he coached his readers that persons of imagination in possession of certain artistlike feeling could not help but be affected by "the peculiar beauty of wild nature, combined with the advantages of a suitable convenience for habitation"—assuming, as did the 1844 *Treatise,* that they recognized the beauty of expression to be the most important principle.[30]

The Graceful and the Picturesque

Other than the picturesque, a "striking example of expression in natural scenery" was, of course, the beautiful—however, as before, Downing avoided the traditional term. Remarking that each of the leading styles had its admirers, Downing announced that *he* would "distinguish them as the Graceful, and the Picturesque." The section previously taken up with a discussion about landscape gardening as an art of imitation and with the lengthy quotation from Loudon on the gardenesque was reorganized and included new pages devoted to a detailed examination of these "schools," which were illustrated with new engravings (figs. 3.13, 3.14). Downing also added a warning that although grand and sublime characters abounded in nature, they were beyond the capacities of the landscape improver.[31]

3.12

Frontispiece in Thomas Dick Lauder, *Sir Uvedale Price on the Picturesque* (1842). Special Collections, Weigel Library, Kansas State University.

In a lengthy footnote Downing explained his decision to differentiate his interpretation and nomenclature from the European tradition. He claimed America as a "new starting ground" for landscape gardening, and stated with bravado that he felt "fairly at liberty to define, and clear up, the confused and cloudy views of the end and aim of imitation, pervading most European authors." Having established his view that the art's highest imitative sphere lay in expression, Downing proceeded to outline his version of the different schools of the modern style:

Price, whose work on the Picturesque (see late edition of Sir. T. Lauder,) is most full and complete, we consider the master, and able exponent of the Picturesque school. Repton, who advocates in his works a more polished and cultivated style, (see Loudon's edition of Repton,) we hold to be the first authority in the Graceful School. Mr. Loudon's *Gardenesque* style, is but another word for what we term the Graceful school; except that we consider the latter exemplified in all flowing, luxuriantly developed forms; while Mr. Loudon, who prefers mere artistical beauty to that of expression, properly limits the *gardenesque* to artificial planting only. The distinction between the *picturesque,* and the *beautiful,* is perhaps open to some difference of opinion, and all Landscape Gardening aims at the produc-

The Graceful and the Picturesque

3.13

Landscape Gardening, in the Graceful School. In *Treatise* (1844). Kansas State University Libraries.

3.14

Landscape Gardening, in the Picturesque School. In *Treatise* (1844). Kansas State University Libraries.

tion of the beautiful. But in the graceful outlines of highly cultivated forms of trees, and beautiful curves of surface and walks, in highly polished scenes, lies so different a kind of beauty from that of the irregular ground, trees, etc., of picturesque landscape, that we conceive the two terms will be found, at least for the moderate scale of the art with us, at once precise and significant.

The selection of Uvedale Price to represent the picturesque school was predictable, especially with the recent republication of the *Essay on the Picturesque*. The fresh enthusiasm for this "elegant and masterly" work suggests either that Downing was particularly enlightened by Lauder's introductory essay and editorial notes or that he read Price only after this edition appeared in 1842.[32]

Although in the 1841 *Treatise* Downing was enthusiastic about the picturesque, in the revision his partiality was even more pronounced—for aesthetic and practical reasons. The importance of only a small "annual tax on the purse" to carry out landscape improvements would become increasingly clear to him as his practice grew, and when he noted the circumstances "which must exert a controlling influence over amateurs" in the United States, he included "fixed locality, [and] expense." He spelled out the advantages of the picturesque in a suitable location—such as the naturally wild and bold character of his own native Hudson Highlands (fig. 3.15). The raw materials of wood, water, and surface could be appropriated with much effect and little art—in other words, economically. Readers learned that in the picturesque mode they could be less careful in maintaining the landscape—the lawn less frequently mown, the edges of the walks less carefully trimmed. In areas more removed from the house, the walk could even sink into "a mere footpath without gravel, and the lawn change into the forest glade or meadow." Who could doubt the

American preference for this money-saving and low-maintenance mode?³³

Nonetheless, the improver who purchased "a bit of scenery naturally flowing and beautiful in its outlines"—that is, graceful—was obligated under the *Treatise*'s precepts to "heighten that expression by the refinements of care and culture." The most polished maintenance was necessary: "grass mown into a softness like velvet, gravel walks scrupulously firm, dry, and clean, and the most perfect order and neatness." Downing allowed that in a landscape of this character, the finest foreign sorts of trees and shrubs should be conspicuous. Owners of a graceful landscape could look to a new appendix in the 1844 edition; "Note on the treatment of Lawns" detailed requisite soil conditions, the best mixture and amount of seeds, and the proper kind of scythe.³⁴

Downing cited Repton as the authority for the graceful school, and Loudon's new edition of *The Landscape Gardening of Humphry Repton* caused Downing to reevaluate his contribution. Following Loudon's lead, Downing recognized a "Repton School," which he chose to label "the

3.15

Hudson Highlands, From Bull-Hill. In N. P. Willis, *American Scenery*, vol. 1 (1840). The Library Company of Philadelphia.

Graceful." As presented by Downing, the school aimed at the production of a landscape that would have been designated as the beautiful by Burke and Price, with its gradual undulations, soft surfaces, smooth-stemmed and symmetrically headed trees, and curvilinear brooks and lakes. Repton, in Loudon's anthology, did not use the term *graceful* to characterize his design aesthetic, although he mentioned Brown's partiality for the Hogarth-inspired "serpentine or graceful curve." Repton too applied "grace" to Brown's style when describing his own position as a compromise between his two famous predecessors: "I do not profess to follow either Le Nôtre or Brown, but, selecting beauties from the style of each, to adopt so much of the grandeur of the former as may accord with a palace, and so much of the grace of the latter as may call forth the charms of natural landscape." Repton specified that landscape gardeners should not adopt nature's rules for "spontaneous plantations"; rather they should look to the models of *la belle nature* or "those occasional effects of extraordinary beauty, which nature furnishes." This stance, of course, was similar to Downing's in spite of his retreat from French academic doctrine in the 1844 *Treatise*.[35]

However, other aspects of Repton's theory were in direct contradiction to Downing's. The two differed on the shapes of trees appropriate for certain styles of architecture. Repton suggested that "the lines of Gothic buildings are contrasted with round-headed trees . . . and those of the Grecian will accord either with round or conic trees; but, if the base be hid, the contrast of the latter will be most pleasing." For Downing, the house in the picturesque landscape was to be a Gothic mansion, an old English cottage, or a Swiss chalet, and the trees pines and larches—that is, conic trees;

the house in a graceful scene was to belong to one of the classical modes, with rounded trees for complement (fig. 3.16). Furthermore, Repton's requisites for "the perfection of Landscape Gardening" included the condition that "it must studiously conceal every interference of art, however expensive, by which the scenery is improved." In contrast, Downing noted in 1844: "The recognition of art, as Loudon justly observes, is a first principle in Landscape Gardening, as in all other arts. . . . [It is] always apparent in both modes. The evidences are indeed stronger, and more multiplied, in the careful polish of the Graceful school." Thus, the selection of Repton to exemplify this school was curious; apparently outweighing any theoretical conflicts was Downing's expressed admiration for the skill and harmony of Repton's executed designs.[36]

Downing feared that the graceful school would be acknowledged as "the most beautiful and perfect" for inappropriate reasons. Persons who mistakenly assumed that the recognition of art was the most important principle were too impressed by pol-

3.16

Swiss Cottage. In *Horticulturist* (February 1847). Author's collection.

ished effects, and those whose only standard was cost and expense tended to make this error. Downing moved the statement concerning the beau ideal in landscape gardening to a footnote in this section, evidently to explain the proper reason for admiring the graceful school. If, as Downing professed, the principle of the beauty of expression was primary, one would relish the picturesque: "The improver who unites with pleasing forms, an expression of sentiment, will affect not only the common eye, but, much more powerfully, the imagination, and the refined and delicate taste." He was disappointed that improvers who admired the smoothness, softness, and flowing outlines predominant in the lawn and pleasure grounds seemed to far outnumber those who preferred a cottage in a highly irregular and picturesque valley or a castle on a rocky crag. This issue of "mere artistical beauty" versus expression constituted Downing's major criticism of the gardenesque. The 1841 *Treatise* had been more accommodating to Loudon's style; although judged inferior to both beautiful and picturesque imitations, Loudon's description of the gardenesque received a significant amount of space. In the 1844 edition, Downing essentially dismissed the gardenesque as only another word for the graceful school and omitted Loudon's lengthy explanation of its characteristics, replacing it with a curt statement that the gardenesque was limited "to artificial planting only."[37]

Downing hoped that this interpretation of the two distinct schools would be found "at once precise and significant." It was not; one of the major changes to the 1849 *Treatise* was to be his adoption of the traditional nomenclature of eighteenth-century landscape theory—the beautiful and the picturesque.[38]

4

LET THE PRINCIPLES BE PRESERVED

The 1849 Edition

An enlarged, revised, and newly illustrated *Treatise* appeared at the beginning of 1849 and was presented to the public as the fourth edition. There is no known copy of a third, which suggests that Downing and his publisher were attempting to give an exaggerated impression of its popularity. Downing claimed to be assured by the call for a fourth edition that his own "imperfect labors" to promote tasteful rural embellishment were "most kindly appreciated." In fact, there was no need to exaggerate Downing's accomplishments during the four and a half years since the second edition of the *Treatise*. In June 1845 the publication of Downing's *Fruits and Fruit-Trees of America* met with immediate acclaim; the *Cultivator,* for example, praised the six-hundred-page volume as "an honor alike to its author and his country" that demonstrated an "indefatigable research and untiring industry." Downing described the work in a letter to Smith, explaining that it was comprised of "digested descriptions of fruits." He added: "Everything hitherto issued on the subject here is full of errors & as the subject is one that interests every one having a garden I flatter myself that I shall be able to offer an interesting volume." His self-esteem proved well-founded; he boasted to Smith two years after publication: "It has been on the whole the most popular gardening book ever written. I am now correcting for the *8th ed.*" Downing also took on the editorship of the monthly *Horticulturist* in the summer of 1846 and, deciding soon after to devote himself "to literary pursuits," officially retired from the nursery business in February 1847. By December, he was "busy with 'Downing's New Cottages & Villas' with interiors[,] furniture etc.," which was published in 1850 as *The Architecture of Country Houses*.[1]

Due to his new editorial responsibilities, Downing had two and a half years of compulsory monthly meditations on the rural arts while he deliberated on what would be (for him) the final revisions of the *Treatise*. He began a campaign in the March 1847 *Horticulturist* to convince readers to use indigenous ornamental trees, and the 1849 *Treatise* reflected this attention to native plants. However, a concern increasingly addressed after July 1848 in the journal—namely, that the majority of Americans had small incomes—did not effect a corresponding change in the *Treatise*. Those persons with "neither room, time, nor income" who were advised in 1844 to attempt "only the simple and the natural" once again were given limited attention and essentially the same advice. Readers could have expected otherwise as, the summer before the new edition appeared, Downing expounded upon the wisdom of moderation and simplicity in rural improvement. Nevertheless, the *Treatise* firmly held to its exalted aspirations and its audience of country gentlemen, even as Downing marked out a different path for American landscape gardening in the *Horticulturist*.[2]

As the new preface promised, some portions of the 1849 *Treatise* contained "considerable alterations and amendments." Downing's fame as an author, editor, and practitioner had enabled him to gain access to America's hidden "rural gems," and he shared his experiences of these notable estates. In this edition Downing finally adopted "the beautiful" and "the picturesque" to describe the "two most forcible and complete expressions" in natural scenery. This change and other more minor ones were in response to John Lindley's series of articles that appeared in 1847–48 in the respected English horticultural periodical that he edited, the *Gardeners' Chronicle*. The most significant influence on the revised *Treatise* came from a book published in America in 1848—John Ruskin's *Modern Painters II*. In Ruskin's theory of "Typical Beauty," Downing discovered an alternative to the beau ideal. As a result of his decision to define a beautiful living form as one in which the individual specimen was "a harmonised and well balanced development of a fine type," Downing could take advantage of the expressive potential in native landscape plants such as the American Elm, and improvers could use these common trees to realize landscape gardening in the highest sense of the term.[3]

American Rural Gems

A few notable changes appeared in the 1849 "Historical Sketches" section. Not content with the earlier tripling of the retrospective view, Downing added more pages on the subject of "the early condition of the art in Great Britain" to reinforce his point that "modern landscape gardening owes its existence almost entirely to the English." He took the material, spanning from William the Conqueror to William and Mary, nearly verbatim from Loudon's *Encyclopedia of Gardening*. More significant additions to the chapter were two new exemplars of landscape gardening from Downing's home state of New York: Montgomery Place and Geneseo.[4]

Montgomery Place, located on the Hudson River one hundred miles from New York City, was mentioned in the 1844 *Treatise;* however, since 1845 Downing had become increasingly involved with the landscape improvements being carried out there by owner Louise Davezac Livingston and her daughter Cora Livingston Barton (fig. 4.1).

LET THE PRINCIPLES BE PRESERVED: *The 1849 Edition*

4.1
Montgomery Place, Seat of Mrs. Edward Livingston. In Horticulturist (October 1847) and Treatise (1849). Author's collection.

Although not acting in a professional capacity, Downing provided friendly advice during visits and in letters. The October 1847 *Horticulturist* editorial was devoted to chronicling the charms of Montgomery Place, and its opening paragraph bemoaned the ignorance of most Americans concerning "those rural gems that embroider the landscape here and there, in the older and wealthier parts of the country." Downing himself was only beginning to extend his knowledge:

There are few persons, among what may be called the travelling class, who know the beauty of the finest American country seats. . . . Held in the retirement of private life, they are rarely visited, except by those who enjoy the friendship of their possessors. The annual tourist by the railroad and steamboat, who moves through wood and meadow and river and hill, with the celerity of a rocket, and then fancies he knows the country, is in a state of total ignorance of their many attractions.[5]

The 1849 description of Montgomery Place abridged the earlier *Horticulturist* editorial. Two of the estate's most interesting features—"one of the most perfect flower gardens in the country" and an arboretum—were discussed in Downing's correspondence with the family. In 1845 Downing suggested design changes for the flower garden when it became necessary to diminish its size, while assuring Mrs. Livingston that he had "the greatest confidence" in her judgment and taste. A year later he expressed his delight that the great charms of Montgomery Place were to be enhanced by an arboretum: "How few persons there are yet in this country who know any thing of the individual beauty of even our own forest trees!"[6]

Geneseo had been mentioned in both of the earlier editions, but the Wadsworth family seat on the Genesee River, New York, received a longer notice and a new illustration in 1849 (fig. 4.2). The previous accounts suffered from the fact that Downing had never been to Geneseo; after the visit he conveyed his delight in superlatives in a letter to Smith dated August 1846:

We were the guests of Mr. [James] Wadsworth & were truly charmed with the most beautiful inland country— & finest agricultural country that I ever beheld. Imagine a thousand acres lying before his door of the most beautiful meadow that you ever beheld sprinkled & grouped with three or four thousand of *specimen oaks* developed on every side—such trees as you have only seen one or two of your life in America & you have some notion of the beautiful natural Park that I feasted my eye upon. . . . I was truly proud of this country & especially of the taste of the late Mr. Wadsworth whose fine perceptions led him to preserve these trees.

A three-page illustrated account of Geneseo in the October 1848 *Horticulturist* captured these vivid memories (fig. 4.3). The arboreal wonders of the estate inspired one of Downing's few references to a contemporary American artist as he praised the extensive stands of oaks: "such oaks as you may have dreamed of, (if you love trees,) or, perhaps,

4.2

Residence of James S. Wadsworth, Geneseo. In Henry Greenleaf Pearson, *James S. Wadsworth of Geneseo* (1913). The Library Company of Philadelphia.

4.3

View in the Meadow Park at Geneseo. Frontispiece in *Horticulturist* (October 1848) and figure in *Treatise* (1849). Author's collection.

have seen in pictures by Claude Lorraine, or our own [Asher B.] Durand." The description of Geneseo in the 1849 *Treatise* was a much abbreviated version of this notice but included the reference to Durand.[7]

Downing's pairing of the French classical painter with Durand, then president of the National Academy of Design, indicated his equivocal position toward two camps of thought—one that remained attached to established European tradition, the other holding that art in America should be stimulated only by native resources. In both the *Horticulturist* and the 1849 *Treatise* Downing started to move toward Durand's view; the latter was one of the first American artists to advocate direct painting of landscape scenes out-of-doors and to insist that the work be done at home: "Go not abroad then in search of material for the exercise of your pencil. . . . Many are the flowers in our untrodden wilds that have blushed too long unseen" (fig. 4.4). The other American artists whom Downing cited shared this nationalist bias; Durand portrayed the pair, his fellow Hudson River School artist Thomas Cole and the poet William Cullen Bryant, in *Kindred Spirits* (1849). Downing praised Cole, who had died in 1848, as "the greatest of our landscape painters" (fig. 4.5), and in every edition of the *Treatise* he quoted Bryant's poems to sing the praises of the native plane, birch, and pine trees. Significantly, both Montgomery Place and Geneseo owed a good portion of their beauty to *native* wood.[8]

The Beautiful and the Picturesque

While the 1849 *Treatise* drew increasing inspiration from America's own resources, in this edition Downing finally adopted the traditional terms of eighteenth-century landscape theory—the beautiful and the picturesque. He admitted in the preface that "the difference among critics regarding natural expression and its reproduction in Landscape Gardening" had led him to examine this subject more carefully. Downing was alluding to a sharply critical letter to the *Gardeners' Chronicle* and the response from John Lindley, which had appeared early in 1848. "The truth is," a "Professor of Taste in Landscape Gardening" asserted, "that a more clumsily composed and compiled work it has not often been my lot to see." The correspondent reserved particular scorn for what he labeled an "obscure passage"—Downing's statement concerning the "two species of beauty, of which the art is capable . . . *general,* and *picturesque* beauty." Lindley defended Downing and responded with his own interpretation of this passage after remarking that "certainly, at first sight, the phrases *general* and *picturesque* do not seem to answer the purposes of definition very clearly." In the 1849 *Treatise,* Downing sought "the clearest and most definite manner" to present these ideas.[9]

The earlier confusion of categories within the word *beauty* disappeared; the offending sentence was changed to: "two variations, of which the art is capable . . . the *beautiful* and the *picturesque.*" The descriptions of the distinctive features of the beautiful and the picturesque simply repeated the 1844 examination of the graceful and the picturesque. However, this information was prefaced by extensive new material because, as Downing explained, it was necessary to "attach some definite meaning to terms which we shall be continually obliged to employ," most particularly because of "the vague and conflicting opinions of most preceding writers." On one point at least, Downing's own understanding of the picturesque controversy

LET THE PRINCIPLES BE PRESERVED: *The 1849 Edition*

4.4

Student at Work, Point Pleasant. In John Moran, albumen prints 1860–61. The Library Company of Philadelphia.

The Beautiful and the Picturesque

4.5
Schroon Lake, by Thomas Cole. In *Home Book of the Picturesque* (1852). The Library Company of Philadelphia.

was faulty; he opposed Repton to Price, stating that the former viewed the beautiful and the picturesque as identical while the latter found them widely different. In fact, Repton had written to Price: "I was . . . peculiarly interested and gratified by your ingenious distinction betwixt the *beautiful* and the *picturesque;* but I cannot admit the propriety of its application to landscape gardening; because *beauty,* and not '*picturesqueness,*' is the chief object of modern improvement."[10]

As had Price, Downing criticized as "vague" Gilpin's definition of picturesque objects: "those which please from some quality capable of being illustrated in painting." In explanation, he pointed out the difference between Claude's beautiful landscapes and Rosa's picturesque scenes; as before, he turned to these traditionally cited painters. Downing's description of Claude was subtly less eulogistic than in the 1844 edition. Perhaps he had been swayed by John Ruskin, who claimed in *Modern Painters I* (1843) that Joseph Turner was more true to nature than the established masters Claude and Rosa: "There is no evidence of their ever having gone to Nature with any thirst, or received from her such emotions as could make them even for an instant lose sight of themselves."[11]

After distinguishing between the beautiful and the picturesque, Downing reminded readers that even though it was possible to combine them in the same landscape, as was often seen in nature, landscape gardening was rarely attempted on such a large scale. He advised that improvers would be more successful directing their efforts toward the "production of a *leading* character or expression." Downing more clearly articulated his views on this subject in the 1849 edition, again in response to one of Lindley's questions: "Assuming Downing's definition of General and Picturesque Beauty in Landscape Gardening to be correct, is his assertion that the one or the other should predominate in any created scene [within grounds of *moderate extent*] equally correct?" Downing now specified the design approaches only for small and large places: the smaller scale permitted only "a single phase of natural expression," and one had clearly to aim either for the beautiful or the picturesque. A large estate, however, allowed the landscape gardener to "give to each separate scene its most fitting character"; a skillful artist would be able to create "great variety both of beautiful and picturesque expression" and give "a higher proof of his power, viz. by uniting all those scenes into one whole, by bringing them into harmony." Downing here allied landscape gardening with its sister fine art, painting: "that in proportion to the limited nature of the subject should simplicity and unity of expression be remembered."[12]

He then set forth several subordinate expressions of the beautiful: simplicity, dignity, grace, elegance, gaiety, and chasteness. Gaiety, for example, could be conveyed by "a great abundance of bright climbers and gay, flowering shrubs and plants." However, Downing cautioned that to create "these more delicate shades of expression," the would-be designer had to be "a profound student both of nature and art" and be able "by his own original powers, to seize the subtle essence, the half disclosed idea involved in the finest parts of nature." Evidently, amateurs would do better to seek out a professional landscape gardener for artistic guidance—especially on these rather elusive aspects of the beautiful and the picturesque.[13]

The Finest Form of a Fine Type

Downing offered a choice of explanations to help readers distinguish between the beautiful and the picturesque—the first, an esoteric reference to an Italian and a Dutch painter; the second, more easily understood. Those who could not discern that the beautiful female heads of Carlo Dolci were different from those of the picturesque peasant girls of Gerard Douw were probably familiar with the native trees of the other example: "A symmetrical American elm, with its wide head drooping with garlands of graceful foliage, is very different in expression from the wild and twisted larch or pine tree, which we find on the steep sides of a mountain." Downing was preparing the ground to introduce the concept of "type," choosing images to demonstrate that there was "a widely different idea hidden under these two types, in material form." This concept—adapted from John Ruskin's *Modern Painters II*—was new to the 1849 *Treatise*, and Downing devoted a significant amount of space to this shift from beau ideal to type.[14]

Downing avoided the association with classical idealist aesthetics that accompanied the term *general nature;* he changed the definition of landscape gardening as "an imitation of the general forms of nature" to "an imitation of the agreeable forms of nature." Consequently, native American plants (albeit only in their most pleasing forms) could be accommodated because they were recognized by the Creator—the highest authority. "Beauty, *in all natural objects,"* Downing stressed, "arises from their expression of those attributes of the Creator—infinity, unity, symmetry, proportion, etc.—which he has stamped more or less visibly *on all his works.*" For this statement, Downing owed much to Ruskin's theory of Typical Beauty, the "symbolizing of Divine attributes in matter."

For Ruskin the term *typical* meant "any character in material things by which they convey an idea of immaterial ones." He related the various qualities of beauty to aspects of the Divine will and plan: for example, the quality of "Unity" was related to the Type of Divine Comprehensiveness, and "Symmetry" to the Type of Divine Justice. Ruskin defined symmetry as "the *opposition* of *equal* quantities to each other," exemplified by a tree sending out equal boughs on opposite sides. Downing adopted Ruskin's notion and specified a beautiful American Elm as the tree that realized "the finest form of a fine type or species." Grown under the most favorable influences, it would have "the most complete and perfect balance of all its parts."[15]

For Downing, the concept of type included the picturesque. He saw "on all sides evidences of nature struggling with opposing forces" and wanted to recognize the animal and vegetable life that did not manifest itself in complete and perfect forms but instead labored to express its ultimate character: "The Beautiful is nature or art obeying the universal laws of perfect existence (i.e. Beauty), easily, freely, harmoniously, and without the *display* of power. The Picturesque is nature or art obeying the same laws rudely, violently, irregularly, and often displaying power only." Hence, Downing found all beautiful forms characterized by curved and flowing lines to express infinity, grace, and willing obedience, and all picturesque forms characterized by irregular and broken lines to express violence, abrupt action, and partial disobedience. In further explanation of "the curve," he made his first and only reference in the *Treatise* to Ruskin: "Hogarth called the curve the line of beauty, and all artists have felt instinctively its power, but Mr. Ruskin (in Modern Painters) was,

LET THE PRINCIPLES BE PRESERVED: *The 1849 Edition*

we believe, the first to suggest the cause of that power—that it expresses in its varying tendencies, the infinite." A chapter of *Modern Painters II* was devoted to "Infinity, or the Type of Divine Incomprehensibility," and Ruskin asserted that "a curve of any kind is more beautiful than a right line." This agreeableness was due to the fact that "every curve divides itself infinitely by its changes of direction." A representation of "Infinity" had a power over the human heart because it suggested something "the farthest withdrawn from the earth prison-house, the most typical of the nature of God."[16]

Ruskin found this subtlety and constancy of curvature in all natural forms except freshly broken ground, which nature had not yet modeled. He also observed that "curves vanish, and violently opposed or broken and unmeaning lines take their place" in instances of convulsion, ruin, and disease. Ruskin did not label these lines as picturesque and in fact would not explain his conception of the "noble picturesque" until 1856 in *Modern Painters IV*. However, Downing's 1849 *Treatise* couched both the beautiful and the picturesque in Ruskinian language: "The Beautiful is an idea of beauty calmly and harmoniously expressed; the Picturesque an idea of beauty or power strongly and irregularly expressed." Recognizing the need to provide more explicit images, Downing offered a number of examples of the beautiful and the picturesque in sculpture, painting, architecture, and nature—opposing the *Apollo* of the Vatican to the *Laocoön*, Raphael's angels to Murillo's beggar boys, the Temple of Jupiter Olympus as known by the Greeks to its modern-day ruin, and a finely formed elm to a pine on a rocky crag.[17]

Although Downing's summary of grand principles remained unchanged, type (an aesthetic order from moral laws) took precedence even over the beauty of expression, with its emotional appeal to the heart. Downing omitted both the declaration that "*Expression* [is] the master key to the heart" and the statement, "Assuming the principle of *beauty of expression* to be the higher, many imaginative persons will prefer the picturesque school." In 1849 the beautiful was the more perfect species of landscape simply because it displayed "the most beautiful and perfect ideas in its outlines, the forms of its trees, and all that enters into its composition."[18]

Also with reference to type, Downing explained that the picturesque was so much more attractive "owing partly to the imperfection of our natures, by which most of us sympathize more with that in which the struggle between spirit and matter is most apparent, than with that in which the union is harmonious and complete. . . . The manifestation of power is to many minds far more captivating than that of beauty." Using terms that previously had been applied only in opposition to the sought-after beau ideal, Downing represented the class of admirers who relished landscape gardening's picturesque charms as those who enjoyed most "a certain wild and incomplete harmony between the idea and the forms in which it is expressed." How appropriate was this American preference for the picturesque: a person could lay claim to an obedience of universal laws but do so rudely and violently.[19]

Despite these concessions to the peculiarly "wild and incomplete" aspect of the country—including the American people and scenery—the *Treatise* remained the source of "leading principles" on the elegant art of landscape gardening. While professing to suggest "practicable methods" of embellishing the rural residences of American landholders "on a scale commensurate to [their] views and means," Downing maintained that the end and aim of landscape gardening were to embody the "*ideal* of a rural home." In an 1870 book dedicated to Downing's memory, Frank J. Scott agreed with the *Treatise*'s distinction: "The term landscape-gardening is misapplied when used in connection with the improvement of a few roods of suburban ground." Scott disavowed any claim that his own work on "the arts of *suburban-home* embellishment" treated landscape gardening on the large scale or in the thorough manner in which it had been handled by the masters of the art in England and by Downing in the United States.[20]

Downing seemingly took to heart the advice of a critic who wrote about the necessity for both purity and practicality: "Let the principles . . . be preserved and insisted on in their purity, at all hazards. Real artists must guide and sway, or there will be no lofty attainments. . . . But practicability must be considered. Common builders, all through the land, need instruction, instruction that they will heed, feel to be reasonable, and follow. A spirit of Art must be enkindled among the people." The "new starting ground" for American landscape gardening claimed in the 1844 *Treatise* rested more truly in the *Horticulturist,* where Downing instructed the common builder yet upheld the spirit of art. Here he reached a harmony between the real and the ideal: the nation's existing natural resources and the economic situation of most Americans in balance with the lofty principles inherent in a fine art.[21]

PART II

LANDSCAPE GARDENING AS A
HARMONY BETWEEN THE
REAL AND THE IDEAL

The 1846–52 Horticulturist *Editorials*

In July 1846 publisher Luther Tucker presented Americans with a new journal under the editorship of A. J. Downing. *The Horticulturist and Journal of Rural Art and Rural Taste. Devoted to Horticulture, Landscape Gardening, Rural Architecture, Botany, Pomology, Entomology, Rural Economy, &c.* was offered "to the thousands" who had made Downing's popular volumes part of their household libraries, and the new editor cheerfully noted that a large number of readers were "already congenial and familiar spirits" (fig. 5.1). Tucker, as proprietor of the New York agricultural journal the *Cultivator,* could appreciate Downing's stature, and he boasted of having secured his services; the *Treatise, Cottage Residences,* and *Fruits and Fruit-Trees of America* had given Downing "a rank among the first writers of the age." Although the *Cultivator* had criticized the linguistic pretensions of the *Treatise* fifteen months earlier, on the whole the reviewer was extremely complimentary, noting that the book was "an admirable work [to be] hailed with pleasure by every friend of rural improvement." The *Horticulturist* was equally well received. From New Orleans came the comment: "Every one at all ambitious of keeping pace with the improvements of the day in gardening, should subscribe." And from Albany, New York: "Mr. Downing unites in a rare degree, qualities as a writer and practical designer and horticulturist, which cannot fail at once to give character and value to this new periodical."[1]

As the full title indicated, a great percentage of the *Horticulturist* was devoted to practical subjects. Downing was a renowned expert on pomology, and much space was given to the discussion and illustration of hundreds of new and improved va-

5.1
Masthead for the *Horticulturist*. Author's collection.

rieties of fruit, pomological reform, and related topics such as the best manures for fruit trees. Downing also wrote about rural architecture, lightning conductors, agriculture, safe methods of home heating, and under the pseudonym "An Old Digger" offered hints on such things as how to cook peas and how to use tobacco water as an insecticide. In addition, he reviewed books, added editorial comments to contributors' essays, and responded to subscribers' letters. One-quarter of the seventy-four editorials that Downing penned between July 1846 and July 1852 specifically addressed landscape gardening, and many more did so peripherally. The monthly format offered Downing the opportunity to articulate his thoughts in a timelier manner than in his books and to answer the multitude of complaints, inquiries, and suggestions from his wide readership. Forty-four of these editorials were written after the 1849 *Treatise* and before Downing's death in a steamboat accident on July 28, 1852, and these later essays are an essential addendum to the *Treatise*'s ideas on the theory and practice of landscape gardening.[2]

Downing embarked on his first and only trip abroad on July 6, 1850. Although too late to influence the *Treatise,* these travel experiences benefited the *Horticulturist* because he acquired a firsthand knowledge of England and a fresh understanding of his own country's worth. Within days of the publication of *The Architecture of Country Houses,* as he informed his friend Samuel G. Ward, Downing took the steamer *Pacific* to Liverpool, "for a little summer trip of a month or two by way of recreation . . . [and] to look into the state of architecture & rural arts in that country." Downing assured Luther Tucker that he would "try to pick up [wood]cuts" for the journal while abroad. He also had plans to find a partner, and after visiting the Architectural Association Exhibition in London asked the secretary of the association to introduce him to Calvert Vaux, whose drawings had impressed Downing. He and the

English architect exchanged references, and according to Vaux their subsequent affiliation was "an instance of the confidence he could always inspire"; Downing convinced him the following day to return with him to America where they arrived on the steamer *Canada* on September 16.³

That month, with the series "Mr. Downing's Letters from England," journal readers began to share vicariously in his travels. Downing took every opportunity to compare England and America, and the New World's natural features frequently won out. Writing first from Warwick Castle, he found the English Elm "wanting in grace"; its predominance rendered the roadside landscape one of less sylvan beauty than scenery of like character in the United States, which exhibited a greater variety of foliage. The mile-long arboretum at Chatsworth, the celebrated seat of the Duke of Devonshire, was planted with "the rarest trees," and Downing proudly reported that two of the most striking and superb specimens—the Douglas Fir and the Noble Fir—were from California and Oregon. A sixty-two foot Douglas Fir was one of the finest trees in the pinetum at Dropmore as well (fig. 5.2). Other imported treasures were discovered in the "American garden" at Woburn Abbey, where Downing saw rich masses of rhododendrons, azaleas, and kalmias. Finally, from London he complained about the repulsive, dingy look of almost all of the buildings; they were a particular shock to his "American eye, accustomed to the clear, pure, transatlantic atmosphere."⁴

On the other hand, British artistic and social refinements greatly impressed Downing. The Emperor Fountain at Chatsworth elicited a distinctly unpatriotic comparison to Niagara Falls; this new-world natural feature was frequently cited and illustrated at midcentury as uniquely impressive and,

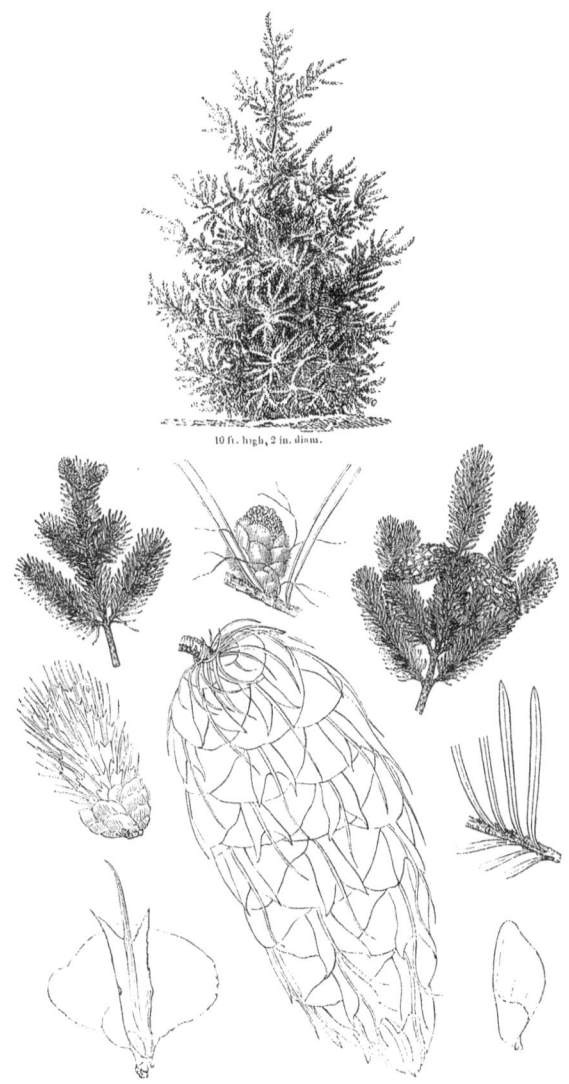

5.2

Douglas's Fir. In J. C. Loudon, *Arboretum et Fruticetum Britannicum* (1838). Library, Pennsylvania Horticultural Society, Philadelphia.

LANDSCAPE GARDENING AS A HARMONY BETWEEN THE REAL AND THE IDEAL

5.3

Emperor Fountain, Chatsworth, Derbyshire. Author's photo.

most importantly, having no old-world counterpart (figs. 5.3, 5.4). Nothing in America, however, could compare to the grand parks of London; Downing described the "noble breathing-places" of Hyde, Regent's, St. James', and Green parks and chided his audience: "Every American who visits . . . feels mortified that no city in the United States has a public park" (fig. 5.5). He also regretted that the Royal Botanic Gardens at Kew, "the finest public botanic garden in Europe," had no counterpart in America. In addition, he discovered that English roads were finished to a degree unknown back home; the grades were covered with well-kept turf, and the division between the

5.4

Niagara Falls from the Ferry. In N. P. Willis, *American Scenery,* vol. 1 (1840). The Library Company of Philadelphia.

road and adjoining lands made by neatly trimmed hedges (fig. 5.6).⁵

As he visited Wimpole, the Earl and Countess of Hardwicke's 37,000-acre seat, those differences that made the English books on landscape gardening "worse than useless" due to societal and climatic differences became vividly apparent to Downing. Unlike American ladies, English women of rank did not lead a life of drawing-room languor but one full of active duties. He was struck by his hostess's involvement in estate matters: every improvement and embellishment was planned under her special direction. He realized, however, that the cool English summers were more inviting to outdoor exercise than the sultry atmosphere at home.⁶

Although the perfection of English country life impressed Downing, other contributing social and political factors could not be replicated in republican America: a long enjoyment of hereditary right and a division of labor that provided access to domestic services. In general, Downing found that the great wealth of the English landed aristocracy and the enormous size of their establishments raised houses and gardens to a scale far above those in America, and he cautioned his readers that they were not directly or practically instructive:

5.5

View in St. James Park, London. In *Vick's Magazine* (January 1881). The Library Company of Philadelphia.

LANDSCAPE GARDENING AS A HARMONY BETWEEN THE REAL AND THE IDEAL

5.6

English Country Road. In *Vick's Magazine* (November 1881). The Library Company of Philadelphia.

The 1846–52 Horticulturist Editorials

For this reason, one who can only learn by seeing the thing done to a scale that he can easily measure, should come to the Isle of Wight to study how to get the most for his money—rather than to Chatsworth or Eaton Hall. And it is this kind of rural beauty, the tasteful embellishment of small places, for which the United States will, I am confident, become celebrated in fifty years more.[7]

The many insights resulting from this trip abroad effected a change in the *Horticulturist*. The editorials show that while encouraging Americans to live a life refined by the rural arts, Downing increasingly advocated republican simplicity and frugality linked with making the best use of the country's existing natural landscape—most particularly its native vegetation. Downing spun a dream of the ideal country residence in the *Treatise* only to realize that it was unattainable for all but a few Americans. The journal, in contrast, set its sights on more modest establishments; Downing sought to imbue his readers with a concept of landscape gardening shaped by the American economy—specifically the limited means of the majority of his readers and the high cost of labor. In the *Horticulturist* Downing also elaborated on the moral improvement of individuals, families, communities, and the nation as a direct benefit of beautiful surroundings. The *Treatise,* on the other hand, referred only briefly in the 1841 preface to the domestic and social happiness arising from country life and the pursuit of the rural arts. To encourage these tastes, Downing consistently challenged his *Horticulturist* readers with the best exemplars in landscape gardening, rural architecture, and numerous other improvements, working the competitive spirit that he saw at the bottom of the American character and that would not allow a Yankee to be outdone by his neighbors.

5

THE *HORTICULTURIST*

Aspirations and Audience

Moderation, simplicity, and the moral effects of the fine arts—reflecting the "republican" way of life—were elaborated month by month in the *Horticulturist*. The readership did not consist primarily of country gentlemen but of male and female "citizens" with a wide range of aspirations and monetary resources. Many were of course novices in the rural arts, and as Downing's professional stature and experience grew, he repeatedly warned them about the perils of improving without expert guidance. Significantly, both the theoretical and practical aspects of Downing's writing on landscape gardening came to be conveyed to this expanded American public in a colloquial rather than a foreign idiom.

Moderate Establishments

The *Horticulturist*'s first editorial of July 1846 promised to honor "all fruitful and luxuriant grounds" and to give attention to "the humblest cottage kitchen garden, as well as the most extended pleasure ground." In a declamatory style worthy of the occasion, Downing set forth his all-encompassing aspirations: "If it is a laudable ambition to 'make two blades of grass grow where only one grew before,' we shall hope for the encouragement and assistance and sympathy of all those who would see our vast territory made smiling with gardens, and rich in all that makes one's country worth living and dying for."[1]

During the first year and a half, the *Horticulturist*'s examples of tasteful landscape gardening did indeed encompass a rural cottage, an extensive American pleasure ground, and Chatsworth. Downing tried to counteract any envy aroused by

Moderate Establishments

Chatsworth, maintained by the greatest ducal income in Great Britain, with a comparison of the satisfaction that a wealthy nobleman and a humble cultivator found in their shared hobby of gardening. He suggested that the latter would be better compensated by the few fruits and flowers carefully watched and reared by his own hands because a strong personal interest gladdened the heart of "the possessor of a small, dearly-prized garden" (fig. 5.7).[2]

Only one American country seat warranted an entire editorial, and this was early in Downing's six-year tenure. In October 1847 readers of the *Horticulturist* were taken on "A Visit to Montgomery Place." The estate's Hudson River setting, with the Catskill Mountains as background, was remarkably beautiful, and owners from Janet Livingston Montgomery to Louise Davezac Livingston had been improving the property since 1802. Its four hundred acres were fully capable of displaying what the *Treatise* distinguished as the art of landscape gardening in its proper sense, and an abridgement of this editorial was later added to the 1849 edition. A large part of the estate was devoted to pleasure grounds and ornamental purposes, and Downing reported "numberless lessons" for the landscape gardener within its boundaries. Montgomery Place exhibited an exemplary combination of a naturally wooded location, a varied surface, and the owners' artful addition of garden structures and vegetation (fig. 5.8). Downing again recognized Montgomery Place in the July 1848 *Horticulturist,* recommending the most interesting American residences for study. He listed the property among several Hudson River estates for those who wished to view landscape gardening on a larger scale.[3]

Beginning with this editorial, however, Downing presented not the grander, more extensive seats such as Montgomery Place but the smaller suburban residences of five to twenty acres around Boston as better models for the general public. Downing had come to see them as "more expressive of the means and character of the majority." The aspirations for a refined country life in America as opposed to aristocratic Europe henceforth became a constant refrain in the *Horticulturist.* Downing stipulated that no more should be attempted than could be done well and in perfect harmony with the country's "habits, mode of life, and domestic institutions." Whether the improvers were wealthy or only moderately so, the main instruction given in this editorial, entitled "Hints to Rural Improvers," was that everyone needed more convincing lessons in landscape gardening than could be found in Downing's written advice and descriptions. He admonished amateurs to visit and carefully examine up to twenty good examples of residences; if they did so, America's number of specimens of bad taste would be "astonishingly diminished." Downing was quick to point out that

5.7
Chatsworth. In *Garden and Forest* (October 1889). Kansas State University Libraries.

107

5.8

The Conservatory and Flower Garden at Montgomery Place. In *Horticulturist* (October 1847) and *Treatise* (1849). Author's collection.

it was far better for Americans to study at home rather than in Europe because successful examples in the United States were based upon "republican modes of life, enjoyment, and expenditure."[4]

After this, Downing's advice on landscape gardening in the *Horticulturist* increasingly became concerned with the majority of Americans with limited means; however, this concern in the journal was not reflected in the 1849 *Treatise*. The editorial "On the Mistakes of Citizens in Country Life" and the preface to the *Treatise*'s fourth edition, both dated January 1849, delivered different messages. The *Horticulturist* remarked on the continual distribution of fortunes in America due to the almost total absence of primogeniture and reported on the folly of extravagant improvements under these conditions. As a cautionary measure, Downing offered a half-dozen examples of one- and two-hundred-thousand-dollar country residences that were no longer enjoyed by those who had constructed them. It was ironic that Downing, who lionized the builders of great estates in the *Treatise,* regretfully observed that his countrymen had "as much fascination in the idea of a large landed estate as in the eye of a serpent" and scolded wealthy men, "ambitious of taste," who believed that only by great expenditure on large places could "the problem of rural beauty and enjoyment be solved."[5]

The editorial expanded the call for a republican mode of life that Downing had made earlier in the journal when he proposed "the true philosophy of living in America" to be "moderate desires, a moderate establishment, and moderate expenditures." Reporting that he had seen many more examples of success in residences of moderate size or less, Downing was tempted to adopt a line from the English poet Abraham Cowley: "a little cheerful house, a little company, and a very little feast." The editor who just two years earlier had enticed his audience with a contributor's impressions of Chatsworth and visions of "the enjoyment of great estates, grand palaces . . . [and] stately gardens" now urged his readers "to be content with simplicity!" Americans reading this editorial and the latest *Treatise* could be perplexed. The section of the *Treatise* defining landscape gardening "in its proper sense" was unchanged from 1844. Both editions attempted to convince readers that most of the beauty and all of the charms of landscape gardening could be enjoyed in ten to twenty acres and that the principles of the art could help even the proprietor with three trees, but these statements were essentially asides. The central message was that landscape gardening found a complete manifestation only in large estates. Devotees who aspired to be considered persons of taste could be forgiven their desire for those fifty- to five-hundred-acre country residences surrounded by groves and gardens that Downing so eloquently described.[6]

Surely it was no coincidence that in January 1849, as Downing put the finishing touch to the new edition of the *Treatise,* he also took the opportunity in the *Horticulturist* to counteract the book's more grandiose suggestion that Americans seek through the fine art of landscape gardening their "*ideal* of a rural home." The journal, in contrast, argued that the so-called beau ideal of retirement to the country did not always produce the fondly imagined Elysium. Although Downing seemed determined to hold up the *Treatise* as evidence of prosperity and taste in America, from this point on the *Horticulturist* would be the vehicle for his growing convictions concerning moderation and restraint.[7]

Republican Simplicity

Simplicity was an essential aspect of the republican ideology that Downing advocated in the *Horticulturist,* for he felt that show, magnificence, and luxury were incompatible with the American way of life. When Downing declared "We are *republican*," he was taking for granted a shared characteristic with his American readers, and this statement covered a wealth of beliefs and duties. While "republican" referred in general to the constitutional form of government in which supreme power resided in a body of citizens entitled to vote, there was also a republican ideology. In this sense, Downing opposed the term to all that was decayed and corrupt in monarchical and aristocratic Europe. Even Pomona, the goddess of fruit trees, had republican tendencies: Downing asserted that she had always been "rather republican in her taste, [hating] above all things, the fashion in aristocratic countries of tying her up to walls, and confining her under glass." Pomona, like Downing and his countrymen, preferred "the open air, and the free breath of orchards."[8]

The strongest expression of Downing's vision of the "new-world republic" corresponded with the bloody "June Days" of 1848 in Paris, when workers erected barricades throughout the city. A series of insurrections had begun early that year because of dissatisfaction with the French Second Republic, and that summer in the *Horticulturist* Downing contrasted the fortunate position of the United States to the troubles in Europe, where the Old World's monarchical institutions were falling to pieces: "Abroad, the sovereign springs from a privileged class, and holds his position by the force of the army. His state and government are supported by heavy taxes, wrung from the laboring classes, often entirely without their consent." At home, Downing continued, the people were the sovereign power, and taxes paid for the maintenance of public order and to create public works were wisely and justly distributed throughout all classes of society.[9]

Later that year Downing praised the American agriculturist Henry Colman for his sensible attitude toward the luxury and civilization of the Old World. Colman, who had just returned from a trip abroad, purported to prefer linsey-woolsey to fine purple linen; the coarse sturdy material covered the bodies of free, healthy men while the royally hued fabric clothed "forms of lifeless majesty." Other American authors joined in to proclaim "the beauty and excellence of simplicity." Susan Fenimore Cooper regretted that simplicity was too little valued or understood in the United States but hoped that with progress in civilization, people would come to see that "a large shady tree in a door-yard is much more desirable than the most expensive mahogany and velvet sofa in the parlor." A writer for the *New-York Mirror* was vociferous in his objections to old-world "gew-gaws" and the "frippery of monarchical government" but qualified the definition of republican simplicity. Americans should not be called upon to discard the refinements of life:

We would not exchange the elegant simplicity of our forms for all the ornamental frivolity of the east; but, we are not so shockingly obstinate in our democracy—so peevishly republican—that it "strikes to the stomach" to see a beautiful object formed by republican skill and ingenuity. . . . We never supposed that "republican simplicity" meant "in puris naturalibus". . . . Republican simplicity is not the naked nature of the savage.[10]

For Downing, too, simplicity was not of the savage sort. Essentially, he wanted every rural dwelling in America to manifest civilized and cultivated aspirations—with a fitting, appropriate, and beautiful form. He assured readers that a "simple and fit manner" for dwellings did not mean that the country's more humble cottages would be left "bald and tasteless." Downing carefully detailed which type of house and grounds was appropriate for each class. From the industrious workingman to the wealthy proprietor, life and habits differed in America. It was not fitting, Downing advised, for the humble cottage to wear the decorations of a superior one, any more than the plain workingman should wear the diamonds that represented the wealth of his neighbor. He thus reinforced the warning added to the 1844 *Treatise,* where he had charged the cottage owner with one acre to embellish with propriety.[11]

Downing articulated this subject further in the October 1846 *Horticulturist,* assuring a Boston country gentleman who had written to him that it was "perfectly allowable for the man of wealth and leisure to indulge his taste in a dwelling of any style" as long as it was becoming to its location. However, a residence and its grounds had to correspond; a richly decorated country house with a poorly planted and ill-kept landscape, Downing cautioned, would be "a sight as painful as that of a man of learning and accomplishments starving in the midst of a rude and barbarous people." Downing also applied the rule of propriety to America's farmers, whom he saw as "dignified and free, yet plain and simple." Their buildings were to be simple in character and unambitious in style, with neat and quiet grounds. There could be no doubt of Downing's conviction that a distinctive beauty belonged to each class of dwelling when he preached again: "Let the cottage be a cottage—the farm-house a farm-house—the villa a villa, and the mansion a mansion." In April 1848 he supplied a plan and exterior view for a small cottage that could be built for four hundred to six hundred dollars in areas where timber was abundant (fig. 5.9).[12]

Downing became less tolerant of the wealthy indulgences that he had allowed his Boston correspondent. By January 1849 Downing was directing even the rich toward an understanding of "the charm of grace and beauty in their simple dress." He devoted a scathingly critical editorial, published later that year, to the topic of wealthy men from the city who retired to the country to rusticate, not because they had any taste for it but because it was fashionable to do so. These so-called cockneys were dangerous, for their country neighbors might take it for granted that wealth and taste went together and try to imitate the city splendor. In general, simplicity and modesty were the laws of taste that belonged to the country, and Downing was fearful lest a quiet country neighborhood be "tainted with the malaria of cockneyism." Different laws belonged to the country and the city; therefore a person wishing to build a country seat needed to forget all that was considered the standard of excellence in town houses, furniture, and gardens. Although Downing professed to admire what was excellent in town, he obviously viewed wealthy urbanites as unrepublican: they lived in prodigiously fine houses, drove in coaches with liveried servants, and paid thousands for the transfer of "little scraps of paper" called stocks.[13]

In the July 1850 *Horticulturist* Downing returned to the subject of propriety in country houses. The editorial referred to the just published *Architecture of Country Houses,* which elaborated the belief that the entirely satisfactory country house possessed not only "pretty forms and details" but "some meaning in its beauty, considered in relation to [people's] own positions, character and daily lives." Downing continued to press the point of the superior charm of simplicity when, the following summer, he responded to criticism of the simple farmhouses illustrated in *Country Houses*. One western paper asked why farmers "should not be allowed to live in as handsome houses . . . as any other class of our citizens, if they can afford it." Unshakable, Downing answered that the simplest expression of beauty that grew out of a man's life ranked higher than the most elaborate one borrowed from another's life or circumstances. He ultimately stated in 1852 that only millionaires did not have to follow his advice concerning moderation and simplicity in country residences. Persons without the income of the late American capitalist John Jacob Astor could adopt the creed:

Man wants but little land below,
Nor wants that little dear.[14]

Moderation and simplicity as expressions of the republican mode of life and in the interest of econ-

SMALL COTTAGE.

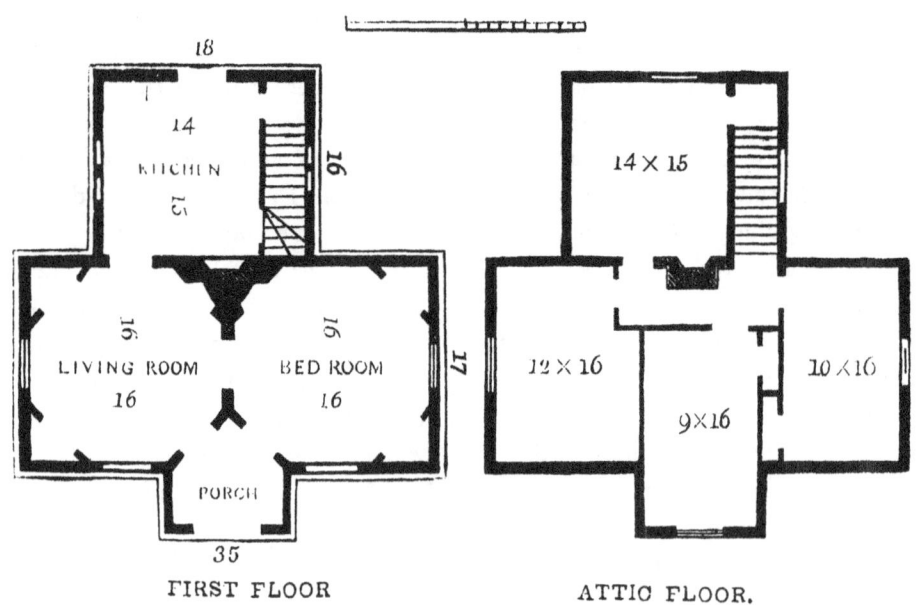

5.9
Design for a small cottage. In *Horticulturist* (April 1848). Author's collection.

omy thus became Downing's landscape gardening creed in the *Horticulturist*. In addition to contact with an increasing number of people through his extensive editorial correspondence, Downing's expanding design practice shaped his convictions. Calvert Vaux, the English architect who became his partner in 1850, recorded that Downing tried to conduct his practice with American conditions in mind, preferring to design villas of moderate, though handsome, dimensions to villas of more pretension. After his partner's death, Vaux wrote about Downing's belief concerning the effects of the country's inheritance laws; readers of both the *Treatise* and the *Horticulturist* were familiar with this position:

> The whole working of American Institutions was averse to this mode of laying out very large sums of money because altho one man might be amply rich enough to build such a house and live in it liberally with an appropriate establishment, at his death the right of primogeniture being most justly abolished the property would in all probability be an unmanageable and difficult one to divide among the family.[15]

In a letter written at the end of 1850, the Swedish author Fredrika Bremer similarly commended Downing for a devotion to "the great Idea" of the American people. Bremer felt that Downing was happily carrying out his part, "building the homes of great and small in the noble and chaste style of republican beauty, and according to the republican idea," which she carefully articulated as "not the idea of humanity in its extravagances but humanity in its harmony and beautiful proportions." Downing's participation in this great American idea, however, went beyond a concern for homes. He envisioned a role for landscape gardening at every scale: in the improvement of the individual, family, community, and nation through the beneficent effects of beautiful cottages, lovely gardens, cheerful schoolhouses, spacious parks, and orderly villages.[16]

The Moral Effects of the Fine Arts

In the *Horticulturist* Downing vigorously held forth on what he called "the moral effects of the fine arts," the blessings from those rural arts listed in the journal's subtitle. He claimed that a political as well as a moral influence (vastly more important than the mere gratification of the senses) could be had from improvements in the culture of flowers, fruits, and vegetables. Horticulture and its kindred art of landscape gardening were capable of elevating the character of the whole population. According to Sir Joshua Reynolds, concern with such moral ends raised the history painter's status from the craft level; perhaps Downing believed that these lofty aspirations could have a similar effect on landscape gardening.[17]

Downing shared with his contemporaries the belief that individual embellishment efforts could have a salutary effect on their immediate neighborhoods, spread benefits throughout towns, and strengthen the nation in general. The New York educator Theodore Dwight enumerated the advantages that accrued from landscape improvements: the planting of trees on private grounds, for example, often contributed to the gratification of neighbors and to the beauty of a town. Dwight extended this notion, stating: "The laying out and decorating of public squares . . . might easily be rendered subservient to the improvement of public taste, intelligence, and morality." Downing concurred with this view. He was not interested simply in beautiful habitation as an end in itself but as a means to secure a higher moral and social good: "We have firm faith in the *moral* effects of the fine arts. We believe in the bettering influence of beautiful cottages and country houses—in the improvement of human nature necessarily resulting to all *classes,* from the possession of lovely gardens and fruitful orchards." Downing promised the reader who gave to the public "a more beautiful and tasteful model of a habitation than his neighbors" that he would be "a benefactor to the cause of morality, good order, and the improvement of society" in his community.[18]

For support on this particular subject, Downing turned to a well-known work by Timothy Dwight, an American clergyman who had been president of Yale. Dwight's *Travels* (1821) commended a style of building and living that was neat, tidy, and convenient, for he found that persons surrounded by these accompaniments tended to be virtuous in every way (fig. 5.10). He preached that taste in building (or the want of it) powerfully operated on the human mind. Downing quoted at length Dwight's dark vision of a society without taste:

The *perception* of beauty and deformity, of refinement and grossness, of decency and vulgarity, of propriety and indecorum, is the first thing which influences man to attempt an escape from a grovelling, brutish character; *a character in which morality is chilled or absolutely frozen.* In most persons, this perception is awakened by what may be called the *exterior* of society, particularly by the mode of building. Uncouth, mean, ragged, dirty houses, constituting the body of any town, will regularly be accompanied by coarse, grovelling manners. . . . Of morals, except in the coarsest form, and that which has the least influence on the heart, they will scarcely have any apprehensions.

The home environment was critical for the development of children who, some believed, were open to impressions from everything they saw. Theodore Dwight advised society to think about

5.10

Progress and Improvement. In *Vick's Magazine* (February 1880). The Library Company of Philadelphia.

the benefits to children in planning and furnishing a house. On a similar note, American theologian Horace Bushnell warned mothers that young children had no powers of resistance and selectivity; whichever type of home a mother created—a den of disorder and filth or a showplace of finery and fashion—would imbue her children with its particular spirit.[19]

Architectural requirements for schoolhouses were equally important, and writers competed in sketching out the most idyllic setting. Downing, of course, joined in and described his ideal of "that primary nursery of the intellect and sensations": every good and ennobling influence would be concentrated around these "little nests of verdure and beauty." These "embryo arcadias" would act as "play-grounds for the memory" long after everything else in childhood was forgotten and would beget an adult taste for lovely gardens, neat houses, and well-cultivated lands. American author Lydia Sigourney made a plea for every schoolhouse to be "as an Attic Temple, on whose exterior the occupant may study the principles of symmetry and of grace." An open and well-ventilated interior would keep young children from associating education with taskwork and discomfort. Furthermore, these temples were to be erected on fine, airy sites, overshadowed with trees, and embellished with shrubbery, for teachers claimed that it was easier to enforce neatness and order among tasteful and valuable objects worthy of care.[20]

Henry Barnard, who helped stimulate the American revival of popular education in the mid-nineteenth century, similarly described the ideal schoolroom and grounds. In *Practical Illustrations of School Architecture* (1851), he acknowledged Downing's help in providing woodcuts of a national school near Brentwood, England, which he hoped would offer a pleasing alternative to "the everlasting sameness of our rural school architecture" (fig. 5.11). Barnard emphasized that a playground—"the uncovered school-room"—was the best place to teach children manners and personal habits; the site was to be secluded and dry, with flower borders, shrubbery, and shade trees that the children would be taught to love and respect. Other essential requirements included equipment such as a rope-climbing stand, parallel bars, and wooden swings (fig. 5.12). Barnard believed that the "right education of early childhood," which regulated the hours of play and study, could correct the evils of society in large cities and manufacturing towns.[21]

The same reasoning that saw a direct and beneficial influence of beautiful surroundings on schoolchildren deduced that spacious parks—offering cleanliness, fresh air, and opportunity for relaxation—were essential to the morals and health of city dwellers (fig. 5.13). Downing's editorials in favor of public parks began in October 1848 with "A Talk About Public Parks and Gardens." In the form of a dialogue between the "Editor" and an anonymous "Traveller," the talk offered what were, in fact, Henry Colman's impressions of parks in Paris, The Hague, Munich, and Frankfurt. Colman had just returned from a five-year agricultural study tour of Great Britain and the continent, and his experience of the crowded, wretched parts of London had convinced him that there was "a connection not to be overlooked between condition and character . . . between outward filth and impurity of mind, neglect of person and neglect of morals." He argued that the social enjoyment of public parks—"those salubrious and wholesome breathing places . . . full of really

THE HORTICULTURIST: Aspirations and Audience

We are indebted to A. J. Downing, Esq. for the reduced cuts of a plan by J. Kendal, for a National School near Brentwood, in England. It affords accommodation for sixty children. The door is sheltered by a porch, and on the other side is a covered waiting-place for the children coming before school-hours. The cost, with the belfry, was $750. A house in this old English domestic character would give a pleasing variety to the everlasting sameness of our rural school architecture.

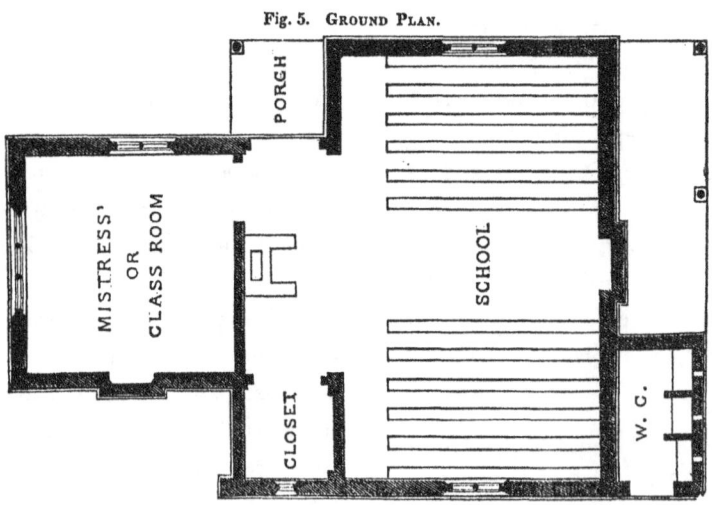

5.11

View and ground plan of a National School near Brentwood, England. In Henry Barnard, *Practical Illustrations of the Principles of School Architecture* (1851). The Library Company of Philadelphia.

5.12

Play-Ground for an Infant or Primary School. In Henry Barnard, *Practical Illustrations of the Principles of School Architecture* (1851). The Library Company of Philadelphia.

grand and beautiful trees, fresh grass, [and] fountains"—was even more important than the intellectual luxuries of public art museums and libraries. Americans, who had a reputation for being obsessed with the feverish activity of business, were meant to be allayed by the pleasure ground. Colman predicted to Downing that the value and influence of beauty, no less than the true and the good, would better the condition of the people "as good citizens, patriots, men."[22]

Downing encouraged the design and maintenance of orderly, neat, and tasteful villages for the similar benefits that would accrue. A Mississippi reader of the *Horticulturist* noted that "those born and raised in one of those sweet villages was [sic] too proud to remain poor, or to do a mean act." Downing expanded on this idea of "the true rural faith"; in a June 1849 editorial he accused people who did not care about the appearance of their homes and villages of having dulled affections and blunted domestic virtues. Only in a village shaded by avenues of trees and "made tasteful by the affection of its inhabitants" did order, good character, and virtuous deportment adorn the lives and daily conduct of its people (fig. 5.14).[23]

Downing complained even more vigorously the following summer: where there was no poverty or ignorance, he considered it immoral and uncivilized to live in mean and uncouth villages. Massachusetts was one of the only states in the union

THE *HORTICULTURIST: Aspirations and Audience*

5.13

Life Scenes in Park. In A. Kollner, *Bits of Nature and Some Art Products in Fairmount Park at Philadelphia, Pennsylvania* (1878). The Library Company of Philadelphia.

that exhibited better citizens, better laws, and higher civilization. The moral and social advantages that Downing believed would result from improvements in the outward life and appearance of rural towns were significant for the nation at large: the laws would be respected, homes would be dearer and more sacred, and domestic life and the enjoyment of property more truly estimated. The reactions of nineteenth-century English travelers to the less prosperous settlements in America echoed these sentiments; to them, the slovenly unkempt appearance implied a less caring society. Therefore, another positive result not mentioned by Downing would be an enhanced status in the eyes of the civilized world.[24]

Downing offered a simple explanation of what he wanted to accomplish: to counteract the ignorance or prejudice of readers who would think "a cow-shed good enough to live in, if only their wants were concerned," he sought to raise their ideas "above the level of their own accustomed

The Spirit of Emulation

vision." His vision included beautiful houses, gardens, schoolhouses, parks, and villages; these would become serious matters to Americans once their eyes were open to what Downing and others recognized as "the value and importance of external objects on the mind—on the heart—on the manners—on the life of all human beings."[25]

The Spirit of Emulation

In the quest to instill these ideas of beauty and fitness, Downing refused to be discouraged by any display of "lukewarmness and opposition"; he had faith in a trait at the core of the American national character that he labeled "imitation." He meant imitation in the sense of emulation, and he described it as the goad that "never allow[ed] a Yankee to be outdone by his neighbors." John Adams defined emulation as "imitation and something more—a desire not only to equal or resemble but to excel." Downing understood that his countrymen had a great deal of national pride and sensitivity and saw these two characteristics as the warp and woof out of which the stuff of national improvement was woven.[26]

"There is much to be hoped for from the spirit of emulation amongst us," the *North American Review* proclaimed in 1841. The reviewer felt that this spirit had done wonders for the country's internal improvements and public works and was certain

5.14

Park-Like Avenue. In *Vick's Magazine* (January 1882). The Library Company of Philadelphia.

that its influence would be "equally happy in the peaceful rivalry of the arts." Downing likewise invoked the "spirit of emulation" in an editorial that enumerated the beneficial effects of the great horticultural shows in the United States. Just as "in the olden times an uncontrollable passion for wealth was begotten by the occasional exhibition of the treasures of gold and silver, made to poor mortals by the genii of the mountains," people would be "fairly astonished into the enjoyments of gardening, by having the wealth of the soil displayed under their eyes." There were others, he suggested, who could be roused into becoming good cultivators by viewing their neighbors' delicious fruits and improved vegetables. The extremes of the analogy—from gold and silver to fruits and vegetables—were appropriate; throughout his tenure as editor, Downing shrewdly challenged Americans to aspire to the highest possible attainment from social refinements to practical improvements. In the editorial "A Reform Needed," Downing criticized the supposedly civilized city of New York for allowing barnyard animals to run at large in the streets, reporting: "Hardly a month passes by that newspapers do not record accidents to women and children—gored and trampled upon" (fig. 5.15). Downing searched for examples that would inspire emulation in such various areas

5.15

Runaway Pig (n.d.). The Library Company of Philadelphia.

The Spirit of Emulation

5.16

The Park of Brussels. In *Boston Miscellany of Literature & Fashion* (January–July 1842). The Library Company of Philadelphia.

as rural life, tree planting, laying out flower gardens, rural architecture, horticulture, landscape gardening, and public parks. His audience repeatedly heard that the English held the key "to the poetry of rural life." From the perfection of their landscape gardening and their spacious London parks to the selection of quiet and harmonious colors for their country dwellings, the English put Americans to shame.[27]

France and Germany, although not republican in the political sense, also offered Downing good republican examples in their public amenities. These countries provided, at public cost, enjoyments open to all classes of people while the "professedly democratic" United States did not. This particularly irksome point was often emphasized in the mid-nineteenth-century campaign for urban parks: "Shame upon our republican compatriots," Downing scolded in 1851, "who so little understand the elevating influences of the beautiful in nature and art, when enjoyed in common by thousands and hundred of thousands of all classes, without distinction." Colman found it humiliating that while under monarchical and despotic governments the most liberal provision was made for public health and recreation, in a republican country like the United States, "where the people have all the power in their hands," nothing comparable was accomplished (fig. 5.16). Some European practices, however, were deemed inappropriate for the new nation. In parts of Germany, Downing reported, the government made it a duty for every landholder to plant trees along the highway in front of his property. Downing recognized that Americans did not like to be "over-governed, or compelled into doing even beautiful things"; he therefore recommended an innovative idea in tasteful improvement from New England. An Ornamental Tree Society, organized by the citizens of Northampton, Massachusetts, had been working to encourage tree planting; neighbors, stimulated into action by the zeal of the society, set the example for others—the spirit of emulation at work (fig. 5.17).[28]

In the *Horticulturist* editorials Downing consistently turned to New England for his American exemplars; he observed that the whole population of the region enjoyed the advantages of education and its more spirited and intelligent citizens tried to rouse their communities. Downing felt that these two conditions—an educated populace and zealous individuals willing to set an example—were critical to public improvements. He strongly believed in this "force of fashion," finding it "a more powerful teacher of the multitude than the press or the schools." Downing thus acknowledged that he needed apostles in order to raise the

5.17

Northampton, Mass. In N. P. Willis, *American Scenery*, vol. 2 (1840). The Library Company of Philadelphia.

The Spirit of Emulation

ideas of Americans above the level of their own accustomed vision: "Many a man who would never be led to make any progress in mental, moral, or social culture, for the intrinsic value of these things in themselves, is induced to do so because he finds others considering them essential. The powerful, original, inventive minds lead; the merely imitative and dull are content to follow." James Hillhouse of New Haven, Connecticut, served as a model for Downing to refute those who believed that it was impossible to accomplish anything by themselves. New Haven was known as "the City of Elms," and Hillhouse had planted the majority of its trees. This inventive mind determined the town's character because his example was followed in every street (fig. 5.18).[29]

Others wrote of emulation and its stimulus for improvement. In his *Travels,* Timothy Dwight suggested that only sensible objects made any considerable impression on coarse minds, therefore the sight of good houses could start a coarse society on the path to improvement. Having similar expectations, a Reverend Choules on a visit to Saratoga, New York, in 1845 was agreeably impressed by the trees and flowers that marked the

5.18

The Gothic Church, New Haven. In N. P. Willis, *American Scenery,* vol. 2 (1840). The Library Company of Philadelphia. Willis noted that "the trees in the magnificent avenue in front of these churches were planted by a single individual."

resort: "It is not easy to measure the influence which a few individuals in any town or neighborhood may exercise in disseminating a partiality for such adornments." The reverend praised Downing for encouraging and enlightening the public taste in landscape gardening—for doing in the United States "what was done with less existing necessity for England" by Repton, Price, and Loudon. Downing had achieved recognition as an apostle of taste.[30]

A review appearing that same year commended Downing's writings for fostering and enlarging America's aesthetic culture. The *Democratic Review* argued that the American tendency toward emulation turned the creation of a house into a serious act with far-reaching consequences:

Whoever orders and superintends the erection of a human home, places that upon the earth which must, in the ordinary course of things, stand there and speak and exert its share of influence, for good or for evil, in moulding the preference and guiding the future methods of more than one generation. Whoever builds an ill-proportioned, unsightly house, insults the community, wrongs his neighbors, perhaps lowers the standard of taste and detracts from the common weal.

As Downing professed, taste once formed became contagious, and he devoted himself to molding the country's taste.[31]

Citizens Turning Country-Folk

Although country gentlemen of leisure retained a place in Downing's *Horticulturist* readership, the Americans whom he now addressed could best be described as "citizens turning country-folk": retired statesmen, professional men, merchants, traders, and mechanics. Even ladies were included. When Downing directed an editorial to this group, he took into consideration a wide range of aspirations and resources in the landowning population:

If you wish to be prudent, lay out your little estate in a simple way, with grass and trees, and a few walks, and a single man may take care of it. If you wish to indulge your taste, you may fill it with shrubberies, and arboretums, and conservatories, and flower gardens, till every tree and plant and fruit in the whole vegetable kingdom, of really superior beauty and interest, is in your collection.[32]

Downing made an effort to enlist into the ranks of improvers not only the "poets, or lovers of nature" but also "the earnest, practical, working owners of the soil"—and everyone in between. His editorials spoke to those artists and naturalists who selected a country residence for its grand and beautiful scenery, as well as to farmers whose income and taste called for simple houses with neat and quiet grounds. Downing observed in his opening editorial that America's fortunate range of climate and easily acquired and fertile land tempted "persons even of little means and leisure into the delights of gardening." Fredrika Bremer commented about the extent and diversity of his audience: "Nobody, whether he be rich or poor, builds a house or lays out a garden without consulting Downing's works. Every young couple who sets up housekeeping buys them."[33]

In the *Horticulturist* Downing expressly courted the female half of American couples who valued the house and garden. The ultimate female virtues were portrayed in numerous works of fiction and nonfiction as piety, purity, submissiveness, and most of all, domesticity. Thus, in the mid-nineteenth century, "the voice of home"—with its powerful associations of stability and order—was feminine, and Downing made an effort to recognize what he called the hegemony of women.

5.19

May Flowers. In *Graham's American Monthly* (September 1843). The Library Company of Philadelphia.

Charles Downing remembered his brother's concern for the development of women's minds, and his friend Bremer felt that his interest in the elevation of women's culture and social influence marked Downing "as a true American man." Many women shared his view that home was the best place for them; Susan Fenimore Cooper asserted that a woman's "labors, pleasures, and interests, should all centre there, whatever be her sphere of life." Downing spoke with great satisfaction of Miss Cooper's work and hoped that the women of America would cultivate the taste for rural science and occupations.[34]

Although Downing cited two residences with female proprietors in November 1846, it was not until his "Talk With Flora and Pomona," almost a year later, that he directly acknowledged the women in his audience. Flora, the deity of the garden, shared her wisdom with Downing and counseled that floral designs were best performed under the direction "of the more tasteful eyes of ladies." He was not the only one to expect ladies to take care of "the realm of flowers"; other male writers concurred that without flowers and female smiles, men were indeed but savages. Downing begged "the assistance of the fairer half of humanity" in February 1849 and offered an opinion in his own voice, rather than Flora's. All that was most graceful and charming in the art of embellishment owed its existence to female hands, he asserted: "Over the heavy exterior of man's handiwork, they weave a fairy-like web of enchantment." The editorial had been written "especially for the eyes of the ladies" because Downing wanted their aid in dressing and decorating the outsides of the country's cottages and country homes with vines. He promised stability to his fair readers if they would wreath their houses about with fragrant verdure; their husbands and brothers would no more think of giving up such adorned houses than they would of abandoning them "to the misery of solitude on a desolate island."[35]

Only two months later, another lengthy editorial was devoted to the topic of feminine taste in rural affairs, as Downing tried to persuade his countrywomen to work more often in their gardens. He assured them that there was nothing rustic, unfeminine, or unrefined about an interest in country out-of-door matters. To convince skeptics, he related a story of a young unmarried lady—mistress of herself, a mansion, and thousands of acres—who personally examined the crops, projected improvements, and directed repairs. Despite these activities, Downing added, she was still the most gentle, retiring, and refined of her sex when in the drawing room. Continuing to flatter his female readers the following spring, he contrasted their poetic sensibilities with those of his sober and practical male readers: "However stupid the rest of creation may be, [you], at least, see and understand that those early gifts of the year, yes, and the very spring itself, are types of fairer and better things" (fig. 5.19). Downing professed to believe in "the powerful influence of woman, in any question touching the improvement of our social and home education." It was she, he declared in 1852, who silently directed, controlled, and governed the whole social machine in America. Downing was carrying out his initial pledge to seek "the encouragement and assistance and sympathy of *all* those who would see our vast territory made smiling with gardens."[36]

Novices, Amateurs, and Professionals

With the *Horticulturist,* Downing wanted to imbue the greatest number of his countrymen and countrywomen with the taste to improve their houses and grounds and to teach them the basic skills for this task. On both sides of the Alleghenies, Downing reckoned in his opening editorial, were "friends rapidly turning the fertile soil into luxuriant gardens, and crying out loudly for more light, and more knowledge." Faced with this diversity of readers, he gave markedly different appraisals of their artistic and practical competence. "Novices" held the lowest rank; Downing addressed them in his best professional voice with the parenthetical reminder "(as we know from experience)," for they tended to make innumerable and costly mistakes. "Amateurs" occupied a middle ground; at times Downing was generous in his portrayal of their accomplishments, for he acknowledged a number of American amateurs with taste and genius. "Professionals"—the highest level—had attained a hard-won expertise that combined refined taste and creative genius with experience; needless to say, both novices and amateurs could benefit from their advice. Downing, without directly claiming genius, presented himself as a professional landscape gardener.[37]

Successful amateur efforts received recognition early in Downing's *Horticulturist* tenure when he described two estates designed by their proprietors. The first, a residence at Nahant, east of Boston, had "one of the most remarkable gardens in existence," which owed its luxuriance and beauty not to a landscape gardener but to Frederic Tudor, a gentleman renowned in the ice-shipping business. The second was Montgomery Place in Dutchess County, New York; its outstanding natural beauty had been elicited and heightened by its owners in "a tasteful and judicious manner." Downing was quick to warn admirers of the Nahant garden that few individuals had the desire and the means and still fewer the courage to plan and carry out such improvements. Indeed, he soon seemed to run out of encouraging examples.[38]

Downing began to question the ability of citizens, recently retired from urban occupations, to understand the difficulties in forming a country residence, and he offered them advice as an "experienced landscape gardener." He counseled that improvers could get "fresh hints" from nature if they would first cultivate their eyes and taste. A perception of the beautiful could only be brought out "by a certain process of refining and mental culture, as the lapidary brings out, by polishing, all the rich play of colours in a stone that one passes by as a common pebble." Downing found proof in the lamentable "treatment of nature's best features, by her untutored children" that most of his readers were still novices in need of polishing.[39]

Downing continued to enumerate the pitfalls of uninformed improvements. In a February 1848 editorial concerning domestic architecture, he singled out a want of propriety as "the rock on which all novices split" in striving after architectural beauty. Not all Americans, Downing sadly remarked, had moved beyond "utter indifference, or puerile fancy" toward good taste. That summer, in "Hints to Rural Improvers," he presented readers with cases in which novices spent large sums of money—"unwisely and injudiciously"—on tasteless rural improvements. Good taste was not a natural gift, Downing lectured, and he advised "beginners" to visit a dozen to twenty of the finest residences: "The study of the best productions in the fine arts is not more necessary to the success of the young painter and sculptor than that of building and grounds to the amateur or professional improver, who desires to improve a country residence well and tastefully." But good taste was insufficient to turn out an extensive, complete work in architecture or landscape gardening. To be successful "in the highest degree," one had to possess not only taste to appreciate the beautiful but genius to produce it. Downing conceded to knowing amateurs among his countrymen who united taste with genius; however, the editorial left no doubt that these faculties were hard-won.[40]

Building and planting without the advice of an experienced person of taste and genius—that is, a professional—was one of "The Mistakes of Citizens in Country Life" enumerated in the January 1849 *Horticulturist*. Recalling Sir Joshua Reynolds's definition of a genius as the artist who ascended "the celestial regions to furnish his mind with [a] perfect idea of beauty," Downing rendered his profession more difficult than the practice of law: "One may plead his own case in law . . . with more chance of success than he will have in realizing, in solid walls, the perfect model of beauty and convenience that floats dimly in his head." In Britain, the Provincial Law Association recently had been created to improve standards and the social prestige of solicitors; Downing was trying to do the same for his young profession on both aesthetic and practical grounds. He claimed that not only would the architect and landscape gardener have a clear artistic vision, they would know what the proposed improvements would cost—within 20 percent. Most amateurs, much less novices, tended to correct and revise their work while the house was in progress and inevitably had "the mortification of paying twice as much."[41]

The following summer Downing excused his countrymen's inexperience, declaring that "a perfect taste in the arts is no more to be expected in a young nation, mainly occupied with the practical wants of life, than a knowledge of geometry is in an infant school." Downing was willing to step in; he proposed that Americans required not so much the impulse to improve but the "right direction." He was positive that with a little direction the popular taste could develop itself; Downing, of course, suggested his recently published *Architecture of Country Houses* as a guide to the deeper meaning of rural architecture. Returning to the subject of popular versus high taste in June 1851, Downing discussed the difficulties of achieving "a pure and correct taste" in domestic architecture. He was disdainful of the many private fancies and personal vanities manifested in houses. Numerous persons set about building their own houses without the aid of an architect while they would not think of being their own lawyers. Downing admitted that both professions demanded equal study and skill. He did not deny that a man could often build his own house and plead his own rights to justice satisfactorily, but he must do both in the simplest and most straightforward manner: "If he attempts to go into the discussion of Blackstone on the one hand, or the mysteries of Vitruvius and Pugin on the other, he is sure to get speedily swamped."[42]

Five months later Downing again offered hints on the best and purest taste to the "rising generation of planters." He reported that the great mistake made by most novices wanting to embellish their places was that they studied "gardens too much, and nature too little." Were these the same novices who busily had been visiting a score of America's finest residences after Downing told them to do so in the summer of 1848? Perhaps the explanation for these conflicting messages could be found in his latest description of the country's state of ornamental gardening. Downing found American gardens in general to be "stiff and graceless," strongly marked by "certain poorer sorts of foreign trees," with an almost total neglect of the finer native plants. He therefore felt it more instructive to turn to the fields and woods, reiterating even earlier advice from December 1847, when he had directed the improver to get "fresh hints" from nature. In order to do this, the planting public had to cultivate its eyes and taste; the task of selecting from the finest sylvan features of nature and recomposing these materials was not for the novice.[43]

Later that winter "new beginners" retiring to the country were reminded of Downing's professional experience: "As [I am] daily brought into contact with precisely this class of citizens, seeking for and building country places, [I] should be glad to be able to offer some useful hints to those who are not too wise to find them of value." Adding yet another cautionary story, Downing reported on a man who built a house "with his own ignorance instead of architect and master builder" and was roundly cheated by those kind of people who take advantage of ignorance "in the matter of bricks and mortar." With more than a decade of practice in landscape gardening and an active architectural office since Calvert Vaux had joined him in 1850, Downing could knowledgeably relate such a tale, and he had a strong vested interest in promoting professionalization. Throughout the pages of the *Horticulturist* he thus constructed a case like a proficient lawyer, arguing that to go beyond the simplest improvements either in building or grounds, most amateurs and certainly all novices needed expert guidance. This direction could be gleaned either from the *Horticulturist* or from paying a professional fee. Those who favored the do-it-yourself advice in the journal were to understand that a "perfect model of beauty and convenience" could be realized only by a professional.[44]

Wisdom Conveyed in Pleasant and Familiar Words

The lessons in the *Horticulturist,* whether for self-help or for the promotion of the professions of landscape gardening and architecture, were less studied and polished than those of the *Treatise.* Why Downing considered this shift advisable can be deduced from his comments in an 1847 review of Henry Colman's *European Agriculture.* Downing predicted that the book would be better understood and appreciated in the United States in another ten years; the practice and principles presented were too advanced for readers' present knowledge. Some American farmers were "little accustomed to solid treatises," and Downing feared that they would consider Colman's work too heavy or profound. He explained a deep-rooted conviction that evidently shaped his own editorial writing:

When practical men are just commencing the study of the science which should direct their daily labors, they must not be treated as patient and trained students, eager to explore the whole temple of science, but rather like cautious and somewhat unwilling candidates, who must be lured into its outer vestibules, by wisdom, conveyed in pleasant and familiar words.[45]

This method of instruction would be successful with Downing's *Horticulturist* readers, for many were novices just beginning to study the rural arts. Downing was alive to the importance of using a vernacular language appropriate to an American expression of landscape gardening. Although he would label as absurd the story of an Englishman requesting a Yankee "to do them the favor to put on his savage dress and talk a little American," Downing nonetheless made the *Horticulturist* talk American. He thus demonstrated the particular talent for which the clergyman William Ellery Channing had called when pondering the question of a national literature for America; Channing praised the author who could embody a people's "own character and feelings" and speak in the voice of a friend. Downing's friendly voice was evident, for example, in his July 1847 editorial, in which he explained how horticulture contributed to the development of local attachments and counteracted the spirit of unrest that caused so many Americans to lead socially and physically uncertain lives—like trees transplanted from place to place and shifted to a new soil every season. He first described a "son of Ishmael" whose ties to one spot were no stronger that the cords that confined his tent to the sandy desert floor. Realizing the foreignness of this image, Downing then related—in American—the familiar case of the western emigrant: "He emigrates, he 'squats,' he 'locates,' but before he can be fairly said to have a fixed home, the spirit of unrest besets him; he sells his 'diggins' to some less adventurous pioneer, and *tackling* the wagon of the wilderness, migrates once more." Homely figures of speech emphasized the difference in cost between a highly embellished place and simple improvements added to a place already blessed by nature with a good patrimony:

> Open walks must be scrupulously neat, and broad sunshine and rich soil make weeds grow, faster than a new city in the best "western diggins". . . . On the other hand, woodland walks are swept and repaired in the spring, and like some of those gifted individuals, "born neat," they require no more attention than the rainbow, to remain fresh and bright till the autumn leaves begin to drop again.[46]

Downing ruminated about the makeup of the American people, recognizing that education had to be "adapted to the character of our people"; he believed this character to be distinct from that of all other nationalities. He well understood how to increase his own effectiveness: "Class-books, text-books, essays and treatises, written in clearer terms, and illustrated with a more captivating style, rob learning of half its terrors to the beginner, and fairly allure those who do not come willingly into the charmed circle of educated minds." With his remarks intended for the "uninitiated," Downing followed his own advice in the opening words of the November 1848 editorial: "We must have a little familiar conversation this month, on the subject of transplanting trees." With American prose rather than foreign poetry he began the new year with resolutions, urging his rural readers to live economically. Exotic dishes needed to be replaced with a more prosaic diet: "*Patés de foie gras,* or *perigord pies,* must be given up for boiled mutton and turnips," Downing lectured.[47]

Downing cleverly portrayed the American distrust of anything smacking of "foreign airs" in a humorous editorial that had Downing attending a mass meeting of all the fruits in America. Pears, mostly of French origin, sat next to the numerous Apple family, evidently of the Teutonic race; Peaches, Apricots, Nectarines, Plums, Strawberries, and Grapes were similarly personified. The business of the day concerned the passing of an alien law by which all foreigners settling in America would be obliged to have their names translated into "plain English." Fruit cultivators were described as plain, honest countrymen who did not get on well with foreign names: "They found them to stick in their throats to such a degree that they could not make good bargains over such gibberish." The Belle et Bonne, a type of apple illustrated in the *Horticulturist,* was not even French; it was a native variety, so named by the French when their troops were stationed in East Hartford, Connecticut, during the Revolutionary War (fig. 5.20).[48]

5.20

The Belle et Bonne Apple Tree, at East Hartford, Conn. In *Horticulturist* (January 1849). Author's collection.

The fruity discussion echoed the debate then raging over an American national literature. Should things be called by names that "sounded real" or by names that had "a foreign, fictitious and romantic air"? A Newtown Pippin, an apple that gloried in being a native New Yorker, thought it time for Americans to assert their nationality and hoped that foreigners would have the courtesy to drop their airs and come down to "plain Yankee comprehension." He claimed that a Pippin—in plain English—was worth as much in the market as "the finest French title that was ever lisped in the Faubourg St. Germain." This speech produced a great commotion, especially among the pears; the Poire Episcopal declared that "the man who could utter such sentiments was a radical, and dangerous to the peace of established institutions."[49]

While it is difficult to single out Downing's sentiments among the broad range of opinions offered by the fruits, the remarks by the lady pear Duchesse d'Angoulême appear to be his:

She added it was impossible to live in America without mixing with the people; and it was impossible to mix with the people, if one's very name could not be understood. It was very distressing to her feelings to find, as she did, that French was not taught in the common schools; and she hoped if an agricultural college was established, the scholars would be taught that language which was synonymous with everything elegant and refined.... If republicans preferred to call her simply the Duchess of Angouleme, she saw nothing amiss in it.

A blunt, sturdy Red Streak Apple from New Jersey neatly summarized the issue: "Boil it down to a little pure, plain English essence, if there was any substance in it; if not, throw the lingo to the dogs." Downing, however, did not abandon his habit of sprinkling his writing with foreign words and phrases—most often French, with a few in Italian and Latin. As noted by the lady pear, French was synonymous with everything elegant and refined, and for certain editorial subjects Downing found the foreign cachet appropriate.[50]

The following month Downing again tried to lure readers in clear terms rather than in elegant language. He posed the question "How to lay out a country place?" and mused about bridging the distance between editorial rhetoric and a friendly chat: "That is a question about which we and our readers might have many a long conversation, if we could be brought on familiar terms, colloquially speaking, with all parts of the Union where rural improvements are going on." In an exchange of neighborly advice Downing recommended a wire fence used by his friend Henry Winthrop Sargent, who lived across the Hudson River at Wodenethe. He also described in informal terms the benefits of planting for seclusion and privacy: "This will enable you to feel at home all over your place, and to indulge your individual taste in walking, riding, reciting your next speech or sermon, or wearing any peculiarly rustic costume, without being suspected of being a 'queer fellow' by any of your neighbors."[51]

In the May 1850 editorial, appropriately entitled "A Spring Gossip," Downing turned to the American poet James Russell Lowell to express the season's charm. This was significant, for although Downing increasingly used an American prose style, he typically quoted English poets and dramatists in the *Horticulturist*. When discussing such topics as lawns, hedges, the color of country houses, and flowers, he incorporated lines of poetry by Matthew Prior, Alexander Pope, Geoffrey Chaucer, Edmund Spenser, Leigh Hunt, and Beaumont and Fletcher. Downing venerated this poetic tradition because he believed that the deep and instinctive love of natural beauty revealed in the poetry explained the superiority of English taste in rural embellishments. In spite of this deep-seated Anglophilia, Downing's admiration for his countrymen's poetry grew, and he sought to widen the appreciative audience for American poems. When the Swedish Bremer visited the Downing's home in the fall of 1849, they made an effort to show her the genius of America's writers. Bremer recorded that Downing and his wife read her "passages from their most esteemed American poets"; she thus became acquainted with the works of Lowell, Bryant, and Emerson and came to see them as representative of life in the New World.[52]

Bremer's proposed visit to Boston prompted Downing to write a letter of introduction to Lowell, asking the Cambridge poet to "endeavour to know her" as she deserved. Downing described the delight with which she had read and reread some of Lowell's poems; both he and Bremer "recognized in them the highest poetry based on that right understanding of this country's mission and the significance of the age which to her mind (as well as my own) places you above all our poets."

Lowell sent Downing a new edition of his poems several months later, and in the May 1850 "Spring Gossip" Downing quoted six lines from Lowell's "The Vision of Sir Launfal" and tried to convince his sober, practical readers: "You, too, are a little of a poet in spite of yourself." Lowell's humorous poem "The Rural Cot of Mr. Knott" was appended to the end of a later editorial, where Downing labeled Lowell "one of the wittiest and cleverest of American poets." These were the only times a native poet was so distinguished in the *Horticulturist* editorials.[53]

The horticulturists in Downing's audience may have begun to acquire a taste for poetry, but they were essentially realists, and Downing's editorial style was shaped by this awareness. In September 1850 the subject of fruit once again gave Downing a chance obliquely to address methods of instruction. He found the horticultural show's method of displaying fruit "deaf and dumb." Amateurs had to rely solely on their eyes for information, and every good cultivator knew that among the carefully arranged and labeled varieties of fruit there would be "optical delusions, phantasmagorias, and painted cheats." Downing's criticism of this way of conveying information revealed much about his own methods: "This severe abstract address to the eye and the imagination, may do for poets and artists, but not for such *realists* and practical demonstrators as most horticulturists are." He charged the horticultural societies to disseminate useful knowledge in addition to mounting their usual displays if they wished for a wider and deeper utility in the United States.[54]

Downing continued to explore the ramifications of America's uniqueness, finding the nation "indeed, too distinct in its institutions, and too vast in its territorial and social destinies, not to shape out for itself a great national type of character, manners and art." He used a lively metaphor to address American architecture that could well have described the development of a national literature or landscape gardening:

It is a fermentation that shows clearly there is no apathy in the public mind, and we feel as much confidence as the vintner who walks through the wine cellar in full activity, that the froth of foreign affectations will work off, and the impurities of vulgar taste settle down, leaving us the pure spirit of a better national taste at last.[55]

In the final months before his death, the tone of Downing's editorials became increasingly nationalist. "No two languages can be more different than the gardening tongues of England and America," Downing stated, and the opening to the June 1852 *Horticulturist* proclaimed his resolve to have American landscape gardening "live in the new world":

When a man goes into a country without understanding its language—merely as a traveller—he is likely to comprehend little of the real character of that country; when he settles in it, and persists in not understanding its language, manners, or customs—and stubbornly adheres to his own, there is little probability of his ever being a contented or successful citizen. In such a country as this, its very spirit of liberty and progress, its freedom from old prejudices, and the boundless life and energy that make the pulses of its true citizens—either native or adopted—beat with health and exultation, only serve to vex and chafe that alien in a strange land, who vainly tries to live in the new world, with all his old-world prejudices and customs.

The gardening tongues of the editorial referred to practices founded upon opposite climates: the bad words of English gardening included "damp" and "want of sunshine," those of America, "drouth" and "hot sunshine." But they could also be understood in another sense: to write about a landscape gardening different from England's, Downing needed to use a language different from English—a vernacular American that spoke directly to his audience in familiar words.[56]

The editorial that appeared a few days after Downing's death brilliantly evoked the vernacular as it encouraged Americans to plant the finer native forest trees in spite of the difficulties in transplanting them. Downing had consistently preached in the pages of the *Horticulturist* about the skills and preparation essential for all types of rural improvements and had written eloquently about the rich personal and societal rewards that would be gained from beautiful surroundings. He was never so convincing, however, as when he descended from the pulpit and challenged the "true sportsmen" among his audience in a language that they could understand and on a subject that was close to their hearts: "Any body can catch 'suckers' in a still pond, but a trout must be tickled with dainty bait. Yet true sportsmen do not, for this reason, prefer angling with worms about the margin of stagnant pools, when they can whip the gold spangled beauties out of swift streams with a little skill and preparation."[57]

Downing gained confidence in his American voice and national standing, and during the last two years of his editorship noticeably decreased citations from European and American authorities. The only person to whom Downing made more than a passing reference in his last year was Major Marsena Rudolph Patrick, a retired soldier who had taken up scientific agriculture. Downing devoted more than half of his editorial space in January 1852 to the text of Patrick's speech to the New York Agricultural Society on home education in rural districts. Significantly, this address referred to Downing's *Treatise;* Patrick assured his audience that this work, "laid one year upon that centre table, will show its effect to every passer-by, for with books and studies like these, a purer taste is born, and grows most vigorously." Downing added as his editorial comment: "[or the *Horticulturist,*]" after Patrick's citation of the *Treatise,* as a reminder that his journal also was meant to have this salutary effect.[58]

Thus in January 1852, eleven years after the publication of the *Treatise* and after almost six years as editor of the *Horticulturist,* Downing could record that his own name was being invoked as a revered authority. It was no longer appropriate or necessary to rely on European learning; both Patrick and Downing had come to the same realization as the publisher Luther Tucker, who wrote a month after Downing's death: "Our tastes and wants are peculiarly our own, and must be fostered with American talent and research." Downing cited the "peculiar wants of [this country's] inhabitants" in the 1841 preface to the *Treatise* as the rationale behind his intended changes to old-world landscape gardening. In the pages of the *Horticulturist,* however, Downing explored the different motives that inspired Americans to beautify their country. Tucker summarized these inducements as he eulogized his former editor: "We want the ornamental and useful together,—we require facts as well as theories,—we build houses to live in as well as for effect,—we cultivate gardens for profit, as well as beauty. There is, then, a broad field for the student of Horticulture, and a widening sphere for the taste of the amateur." Moderation, simplicity, and the moral effects of the fine arts became woven into Downing's adapted theory and practice of landscape gardening in the *Horticulturist*. In the journal he sought to achieve "a harmony between the real and the ideal."[59]

6

A THEORY AND PRACTICE ADAPTED

How did Downing adapt his theory and practice of landscape gardening—already spelled out in three editions of the Treatise—for the *Horticulturist?* The January 1849 editorial indicated a course of moderation and simplicity and the more fervent nationalism to come, as Downing welcomed journal readers who brought "hearts capable of understanding the lessons of truth and beauty, which the Good Creator has written so legibly on all his works." The changes to the 1849 Treatise included a similar Ruskinian exhortation that "beauty, in all natural objects . . . arises from their expression of those attributes of the Creator . . . which he has stamped more or less visibly on all his works." However, the *Horticulturist* diverged on a critical point. The Treatise was not content with "an easy assemblage of sylvan scenery," but the journal found the highest and most expressive (and parenthetically least expensive) rural beauty in "a pretty little natural glen, filled with old trees, and made alive by a clear perennial stream." Although Downing refined his definition of landscape gardening over the next three years, the basic points of his mature position could be discerned: first, the American national identity was manifested in the natural style of landscape gardening; second, the country's rich patrimony from nature permitted economy in gardening; third, America's indigenous plants had been shamefully neglected; and fourth, true art in landscape gardening lay in the truth and freshness of the American landscape.[1]

Downing addressed country-place layout in the March 1850 *Horticulturist,* strikingly departing from the *Treatise's* declaration that "the development of the Beautiful is the end and aim of Landscape Gardening." He now ranked the three cardinal points of consideration—convenience, comfort, and beauty—and explicitly warned against reversing this order. If beauty were placed first ("as, intellectually considered, it deserves to be," Downing added), the country place would lack "a harmony between the real and the ideal." His contemporaries in the Hudson River School of painting were also questioning academic precedent, as the critic Henry T. Tuckerman observed: "Time was when a landscape was painted by a kind of mathematical formula; rules of composition, far more than observation of fact, formed the basis of the work." Old-world formulas were beginning to seem restrictive for literature and architecture, but in landscape gardening the idea of a national art rooted in native soil found a literal manifestation.[2]

Downing's vision of an American landscape gardening focused on the country's existing patrimony of rich natural features in landforms and woods. The ideal of a velvetlike lawn remained an essential component of a rural home; however, Downing offered more practical ways of achieving it. The concept of type-form allowed the use of native trees—in an idealized situation. Seemingly, the switch from beau ideal to type-form was simply a semantic sleight of hand; but the former was inextricably tied to the French and English academic doctrine of "general" nature while the ideal in the guise of type-form could accommodate America's "particular" nature.

In the *Horticulturist,* Luther Tucker believed, Downing demonstrated "the peculiar fitness of his talents to educate the popular taste for the beautiful in nature and art." As Downing's editorship of the journal ultimately established:

It was not his aim to build castles too grand and lofty for human realization, or to show the power of his intellect by forming conceptions, which imagination only could give being to. The great question with him, was, how much of the really beautiful can be made subservient to the public good? how far can elegance and utility be combined?[3]

A National Taste in Gardening

American "national taste in gardening" implicitly meant the "natural style" in the pages of the *Horticulturist.* The "more exquisite beauty of natural forms" received a theoretical basis in the *Treatise,* and with these arguments Downing did his best to prove the superiority of the natural over the geometric style. This strong bias carried over into the journal, and readers were offered quasi-scientific, aesthetic, and economic reasons to adopt this particular mode. Downing also blessed the natural style with the Ruskinian authority of divine right.

Downing adroitly coupled his concern with shaping a national identity in landscape gardening with his often stated and somewhat contradictory contention that England ranked above all other countries in the perfection of the favored natural style. Downing claimed that Americans shared ancestral bonds with the British, and he went to great lengths to convince his countrymen and countrywomen that they were predisposed toward the same taste in gardening and outdoor employments as their reputed ancestors. His July 1848 declaration was typical: "Along with other traits of the Anglo-Saxon mind, we [Americans] have by no means failed in our inheritance of that fine appreciation of rural beauty, and the power of developing it, which the English have so long possessed." Other inherited traits that were consistently mentioned included a love of country life and a love of nature. The existence of different cultural strains in the American population was barely recognized; only once did Downing allow that the English had "almost as mixed an origin as ourselves." Downing's Anglo-Saxon bias appeared when he criticized American women's inclination to "love gardens as the French love them—for the results." Downing generalized that French women knew none of the enjoyment of planning, creating, and watching the daily growth of their gardens and speculated about why American wives and daughters emulated them: "As it is plain, from our love of the country, that we are not French at heart, this manifestation that we complain of, must come from our natural tendency to copy the social manners of the most polished nation in the world." He urged the females in his audience to be like the English and personally participate in the development of their gardens.[4]

"The Philosophy of Rural Taste," published in August 1849, was the first editorial devoted to landscape gardening after the final *Treatise* appeared, and Downing again deferred to England's "unrivalled" taste in the art with an allusion to Ruskin's *Modern Painters II*. While making a token effort to recognize the admirable qualities of southern European gardens, Downing left no doubt about his true opinion: "The surroundings of the superb villas of Florence and Rome, are fine examples of a species of scenery as distinct and striking as any to be found in the world; but which, however splendid, fall as far below the English gardens in interesting the imagination, as a level plain does below the finest mountain valley in Switzerland." The art-to-nature ratio of the two opposing styles concerned Downing, and he interpreted their essential differences. In the English landscape garden one could see and feel the spirit of nature everywhere, only softened and refined by art. In the French or Italian garden, one could see and feel only the effects of art, slightly assisted by nature. In the former, the free and luxuriant growth of ev-

6.1

Italian Style of Gardening. In *Vick's Magazine* (April 1879). The Library Company of Philadelphia.

ery tree and shrub and the widening and curving of every walk suggested a higher ideal of nature: "a miniature of a primal paradise, as we would imagine it to have been by divine right." As in Ruskin's theory of Typical Beauty, the character of the garden material conveyed something immaterial—some aspect of the Divine will. For Ruskin, the curve, as a representation of infinity, suggested something "the farthest withdrawn from the earth prison-house—in other words, a primal paradise. In contrast, Downing considered the French or Italian garden to be like a statue gallery in the open air—an accompaniment to the architecture of the mansion, rather than any "pure or natural ideas of landscape beauty."(fig. 6.1).[5]

The striking difference in national tastes in gardening was attributed to the fact that people of northern and southern Europe inherently differed because of the physical and moral effects of their climates. Downing felt compelled to prove the northern or Anglo-Saxon love of nature and of the natural style (the one invariably accompanied the other) because he was convinced that "the larger part" of his American audience had inherited this sensibility. For credibility he turned to contemporary theories of climatic causality. Europeans in the mid-nineteenth century, including the German explorer and natural historian Alexander von Humboldt and the Swiss-born American geographer Arnold Guyot, proposed that the races of man were determined by climate, and their ideas quickly found acceptance in America. For example, a contributor to *Godey's* was fascinated with "how far human character is modified and moulded by the aspects of external nature." As he considered the many changes "in the countenance of great Nature" and how the climate and characters of various nations coincided, the author concluded that the influence was great. John Bull (the prototypical Englishman) was a blustering fellow just like his winds and as moody as his climate was fickle; the soft and transparent atmosphere of France with its uniform and genial temperature was strikingly reflected in French manners. Downing drew similar conclusions, describing the influence of "the most delicious climate in the world" on a native of the Sandwich Islands: he slept away the best part of his life in "that happy state which the pleasure-loving Italians call *'dolce far niente,'* (sweet do nothing)."[6]

In the August 1849 *Horticulturist* Downing used these theories to validate his ideas on national tastes in gardening; to do so, he misrepresented Humboldt's *Cosmos,* which had been published in America earlier that year. Through selective quotations Downing gave a false impression of Humboldt's thesis. Referring to the section of *Cosmos* entitled "Incitements to the Study of Nature," Downing reported that Humboldt demonstrated "very conclusively, that certain races of mankind, however great in other gifts, are deficient in their perceptions of natural beauty; that northern nations possess the love of nature much more strongly than those of the south." Downing could make this unequivocal statement because he did not define his terms. His Anglophilia prompted him to link "natural beauty" with the English style of landscape gardening, and his logic was colored by his belief that a nation that did not prefer the beauty of this particular style was generally deficient in its perceptions of natural beauty and, furthermore, that this same nation would possess a less developed overall love of nature.[7]

Contrary to Downing's account, Humboldt clearly stated in the introduction to *Cosmos* that there were different degrees of enjoyment in the contemplation of nature. The first was a sensation common to everyone and wholly independent of the particular character of the surrounding region:

Mere communion with nature, mere contact with the free air, exercise a soothing yet strengthening influence on the wearied spirit, calm the storm of passion, and soften the heart when shaken by sorrow to its inmost depths. Every where, in every region of the globe, in every stage of intellectual culture, the same sources of enjoyment are alike vouchsafed to man.

According to Humboldt, the other source of enjoyment that awakened vivid impressions came from the contemplation of individual landscape characteristics and the shape of the land in distinct regions of the earth. From his own extensive travels, Humboldt recalled a variety of charming sensations arising from different scenes; these ranged from a sense of the grandeur of nature to a softer emotion excited by the contemplation of rich harvests.[8]

The section of Humboldt's study that Downing specifically cited investigated the causes that had "by the active medium of the imagination so powerfully encouraged the study of nature and the predilection for distant travels." Humboldt identified three kinds of inducements that promoted such contemplation of nature: poetic descriptions of nature, landscape painting, and the cultivation of exotic plants. He intended to show "how differently the aspect of nature has acted on the intellect and feelings of different nations at different epochs." In Downing's attempt to demonstrate the superior Anglo-Saxon love of nature, he quoted from this section of *Cosmos,* but his excerpts gave a distorted picture of Humboldt's conclusions. For example, Downing cited Humboldt on the Greeks: "In Grecian art all is made to concentrate within the sphere of human life and feeling. The description of nature, in her manifold diversity, as a distinct branch of poetic literature, was altogether foreign to the ideas of the Greeks." Downing omitted the accompanying sentence: "Occasionally, however, even in the writings of their tragic poets, a deep sense of the beauty of nature breaks forth in animated descriptions of scenery." Downing also paraphrased Humboldt's judgment of the Romans: "The Romans, tried in the alembic of the great German *savan,* are found still colder in their love of nature's charms than the Greeks." Humboldt's own words were as follows: "That which we miss in the works of the Greeks, I will not say from their want of susceptibility to the beauties of nature, but from the direction assumed by their literature, is still more rarely to be met with among the Romans."[9]

Downing thus constructed his own argument out of bits and pieces from the revered natural scientist's *Cosmos*. This selective rendering of Humboldt's discussion of the classical world and its literature diminished Greek and Roman (i.e., "southern") accomplishments and aesthetic sensibilities and effectively inflated those of the "north" (i.e., England). Downing claimed a distinctive place for English poetry; its exhibition of a deep and instinctive love for nature explained "the riddle of the superiority of English taste in rural embellishment." He falsely drew a corollary from Humboldt's investigation that upheld his own belief: "As success, in 'the art of composing a landscape' . . . depends on appreciation of nature, the taste of an individual as well as that of a nation, will be in direct proportion to the profound sensibility with which he perceives the Beautiful in natural scenery." Downing linked the preference for the natural style of landscape gardening to the "peculiar" character of the majority of Americans who had inherited the rarest and best English traits. Although Downing declared that it was not part of his philosophy to urge his countrymen "to war against their organization"—meaning that they were certainly free to exercise their opinions—who among his readers would care to admit a preference for the second-class taste: that "symmetric taste, based on a perception of the Beautiful, as embodied in works of art." For this supposed minority, the classic villa with its vases and statues would be more pleasurable than "the most varied and seductive gardens, laid out with all the witchery of nature's own handiwork."[10]

Downing wanted to ensure that his *Horticulturist* audience formed the correct taste of the beautiful in natural scenery. Therefore, he devoted editorials to the aesthetics of trees and ground to instruct his readers on the proper handling—in the national/natural style—of these basic elements in landscape gardening. In "The Beautiful in a Tree," Downing renewed his battle against the geometric garden's "tedious and distasteful constraint" and against the class of improver that believed that a tree "in a state of nature" was no more respectable than "an untamed savage." Echoing Addison's *Spectator* essay of 139 years earlier, Downing's was a stinging critique of pruning shears and of the mind that wielded them: "To [the pruner's] mind, there is nothing comparable to the satisfaction of trimming a tree. . . . It is running to waste with leaves and branches, and has none of the look of civilization about it. Only let him use his saw for a short time . . . and you shall see how he will improve its appearance." A tall, naked stem would show that the tree had been "trained and educated into a look of respectability." Downing surmised that the pleasure of pruning was based on the feeling that trees growing naturally were capable of "some amelioration by art." Champions of the pruning saw (heartless as "young surgeons in hospitals") would see a pollarded willow as a model of beauty. Downing suggested that the finest parallels in "the art of mending nature's proportions for the sake of beauty" lay in the flattened heads of a certain tribe of Indians and the deformed feet of Chinese women.[11]

One year later Downing took on another despoiler of natural beauty—the so-called leveler. "The Beautiful in Ground" paid homage to "the mere surface of the ground" where the earth was composed of curved lines and one undulation melted gradually and insensibly into another. He opposed this loving description of a natural surface to a level line—chiefly of value because it evinced art and was "interesting" as an expression of power. Just as Downing had conceded with scarcely concealed aversion the good qualities of artfully contrived French and Italian gardens, he admitted that many considered a flat or level surface beautiful. Believing that there were a thousand men who valued power for every one who could feel beauty, Downing clearly opted for the more rarified sentiment: "We see all ignorant persons, who set about embellishing their pleasure-grounds, or even the site for a home, immediately commence *levelling* the surface. Once brought to this level, improvement can go no further, according [to] their views, since to subjugate or level, is the whole aim of man's ambition." Americans, not wishing to be classified ignorant, sided with Downing's and supposedly the nation's taste for ground in an unsubjugated natural state.[12]

With regard to "improving" the surface of ground or the proportions of trees, Downing reinforced his aesthetic argument against these practices with an economic one. If his readers did not care to consider the question "In what does natural beauty really consist?", he challenged them to ask whether they were wasting money. The *Horticulturist* increasingly addressed these practical concerns in landscape improvement: *art,* not nature, cost money. The natural style, adopted as the national taste, would accommodate "economy" in gardening in all senses of the term: frugality, or the wise management of time and expense, and the efficient use of available resources—most particularly the country's existing natural landscape.[13]

Economy in Gardening

Not until December 1847 did Downing introduce the ideas on economy that would become typical of his landscape gardening advice in the *Horticulturist.* By this date perhaps a sufficient number of budget-minded clients and correspondents and his own practical experience had converted him. Recognizing the generally moderate means of his audience and the high cost of labor in America yet maintaining a regard for his art's essential elements of trees and lawn, Downing began to emphasize that improvers without sufficient patience, time, or money should begin with the advantage of "a good patrimony from nature": a site where nature generously offered existing wood and a surface that had the capability to be a fine lawn.[14]

A THEORY AND PRACTICE ADAPTED

Downing's eventual modification in the spring of 1849 of a costly and labor-intensive aspect of landscape gardening—namely, the lawn—is one of the best examples of his attempt to achieve a balance between new-world realities and his vision of an ideal rural home. Just one year earlier in his tenure as editor Downing had shown little concern for economy as he extolled the beauty of American lawns. He considered grass, idealized in the lawn, as one of the most enduring sources of beauty in a country residence. Its highest form was manifested in "a perfect wonder of tufted freshness and verdure"; he referred not to the grass of cattle fodder allowed to grow into "tall meadows, or wild bog tussocks" but to the "refined and graceful" grass of the well-kept scythed lawn. Downing was more poetic than practical when he first discussed in an early number of the *Horticulturist* "the soft turf which, beneath the flickering shadows of scattered trees, is thrown like a smooth natural carpet over the swelling outline of the smiling earth." He admitted that the sunny American summer did not, like the moist and humid conditions of Britain, favor fine lawns; nevertheless, Downing offered the perpetual softness and verdure of the English lawn as the ideal. He claimed to have witnessed over and over again admirable lawns "in all the northern half of the Union"—wherever they had been properly treated. According to Downing, the necessary conditions were simple: deep soil, the correct kinds of grasses, and frequent mowing; both preparation and maintenance, needless to say, required a great deal of labor. Downing also specified that the mowing could be done only with an English lawn scythe with a broad blade "of the most perfect temper and quality" (fig. 6.2).[15]

6.2

Page from 1852 "Catalogue of Agricultural and Horticultural Implements, &c, sold by David Landreth, at His Warehouse, No. 65 Chestnut Street, Philadelphia." Library, Pennsylvania Horticultural Society, Philadelphia.

As a model for the American lawn, Downing directed readers in November 1846 to Livingston Manor, the seat of Mrs. Mary Livingston near Hudson, New York; he promised that surprisingly few men were needed to keep so large a surface in the highest order. But in a letter to a friend Downing revealed the details of the labor force required for maintenance, which, if published, would have made his audience skeptical of the practicality of this ideal lawn: "The *park* filled with noble trees . . . is kept in such perfect order by 10 men that even the carriage tracks are *rolled out* every day." Downing editorialized: "Though it may seem a heavy tax to some, yet no expenditure in ornamental gardening is, to our mind, productive of so much beauty as that incurred in producing a well kept lawn."[16]

The following winter Downing implicitly confessed that he had underrated the difficulty and cost of laying the groundwork for a rural residence. His professional practice was flourishing, and as a self-proclaimed "experienced landscape gardener," he recognized that the best advice that he could give America's would-be proprietors of country seats was to start with the advantage of "a good patrimony from nature." Downing acknowledged that these retired businessmen had not had the opportunity "to become familiar with the difficulties to be encountered in making a new place." The phrasing provokes speculation that Downing, in a professional capacity, had recently suffered through such difficulties, for he now sought to convince novices that "labor and patience must be added to taste, time and money before a bare site can be turned into smooth lawns and complete pleasure grounds." Entitled "How to Choose a Site for a Country Seat," this editorial strongly advised readers to examine what mother Earth had to offer "in her choicest nooks"; without this base, all of the elements required for landscape gardening had to be created from naught—neither a cheap nor a rapid process. Downing questioned how many would be willing to wait for ten or twenty summers' growth for groves of weeping elms and overshadowing oaks. He believed that in nine cases out of ten the choice of a poor location—that is, one not naturally well wooded—was due to prejudice or ignorance rather than necessity.[17]

One prejudice that Downing fought was his countrymen's long-standing aversion to trees. He struggled to convince readers that to destroy their land's rich forest cover made little sense in terms of economy, comfort, or aesthetics, but this American "taste for nakedness" seemed endemic. The *North American Review* explained: "They are as unwilling to veil [a house's] beauties by a single tree, as were our fathers, in the day when a grove, or a single trunk, might serve as a stalking-horse for an Indian marksman." In 1832 a man who had emigrated to the western slope of Pennsylvania's Allegheny Mountains wrote to Loudon concerning his experiences after he started to gather trees and shrubs from the woods to put around his house:

I did not receive much encouragement. My neighbours viewed it quite as an act of supererogation: that an Englishman should take the trouble to come and plant trees, when all other men employed themselves to cut down, was beyond all comprehension; was out of all custom and precedent, among a race whose habits and associations lead them to view as the greatest of natural beauties a naked "clearing," surrounded by a "worm fence" of split rails.

Charles Lyell, the Scottish geologist who explored North America in 1841, related a similar story about new settlers living in the midst of a clearing filled with blackened stumps: "When we admired the forest, the settler's wife was pleased, but said, sighing, that she could not get her children to see any beauty in trees." Downing saw the lamentable treatment of nature's best features (that is, trees) as proof of a deficiency in uncultivated persons; for some inexplicable reason, their "perception of the Beautiful" was clouded over.[18]

Downing likewise recounted tales of settlers, pioneers, and squatters who girdled trees and made clearings "in a centennial forest, perhaps one of the grandest that ever God planted, with no more remorse than we have in brushing away dusty cobwebs." In March 1847, reviling this "principle of destructiveness" that tended to accompany progress in America, Downing claimed his business to be the task of bringing men back to their better feelings. "Woodman, spare that tree" became an often repeated plea in the *Horticulturist* as Downing tried to instill a respect for the old trees that he believed could teach lessons of antiquity as instructive and poetic as ruins of a past age. In the December 1847 *Horticulturist,* as a reminder of what the spirit of destruction had brought about in England, where the woodman and ploughman had obliterated the original landscape, Downing quoted from one of Lindley's *Gardeners' Chronicle* essays. Lindley compared his own country's design process to America's: the task of the English landscape gardener was more arduous because he had to create an almost entirely new scene. However, in the New World one could erect a villa on the bank of some magnificent river or on the edge of some equally noble forest, surrounded by native plants and flowers. Assuming that the natural landscape wisely was left intact, "the first skill to be shown [was] not in Creation—but in Removal, in clearing away superfluous objects, and so making the views on all sides marked by Unity, Harmony and Variety."[19]

To dissuade those inclined to thoughtless destruction and needless waste, Downing offered a fanciful analogy in that same month's editorial: the beautiful native American scenery was a strong, rich, and permanent warp upon which the improver could embroider "all the gold threads of fruit and floral embellishment." He accepted no excuses for unfinished and meager grounds; one could erect a house on a site where nature had lavished treasures of wood, water, and undulating surfaces. Placing the finishing touches on such a property was made to seem a simple task: the existing masses of trees easily could be broken into groups that immediately had the effect of old plantations, and the minor details of shrubbery, walks, and flower and fruit gardens would fall gracefully into their proper positions. In grim contrast, Downing painted a picture of the man who paid a high price for a middling site:

Weary with the labor and expense of levelling earth, opening roads and walks, and clothing a naked place with new plantations, all of which he finds far less easily accomplished than building brick walls in the city, the once sanguine improver often abates his energy, and loses his interest in the embellishment of his grounds, before his plans are half perfected.

Downing conceded that many persons settling in the country were concerned that "the production of picturesque effect, [and] the working out a realm of beauty" not make serious inroads into their incomes. Although the 1844 *Treatise* added an acknowledgment of the controlling influence of expense, this concern certainly was not a factor in Downing's November 1846 "Chapter on Lawns." A more practical assessment of his readers' capabilities was starting to emerge, and a remark in December 1847 sounded suspiciously like it might have been recalled from a frank discussion with a client: "One's private walks and parterres, unluckily, cannot be had at the cost of one's daily bread and butter." He could not resist adding, however, that "the Beautiful overtops the useful, as stars outshine farthing candles."[20]

The next summer, following up on this new theme of economy, Downing told novice rural improvers that through careful planning they might attain a more agreeable and satisfactory result "at one-half the cost." He had the difficult task of convincing these proprietors to spend time and money in order to save time and money: ten days devoted to examining what had already been done at the best specimens of building and gardening in the country could prevent them from making their places "absolutely hideous, and throwing away ten, twenty, or thirty thousand dollars." As an added dividend, through the study and comparison of tasteful examples the improver could also cultivate a "sensibility to the Beautiful," the faculty that Downing found so sadly missing among his tree-felling countrymen. He evidently realized that the economic argument for the instructional visits would be understood more readily than the philosophical one. As in an earlier editorial, however, Downing was determined to coax his readers into an elevated consciousness; interwoven with the assurances about saving "much unnecessary outlay" was a discourse on taste, the beautiful in nature, and genius, with a quotation from the French philosopher Victor Cousin.[21]

Continuing to address the economic side of landscape gardening, Downing identified one of "The Mistakes of Citizens in Country Life" as "undertaking too much" while underestimating the cost of building and improving. Everything, Downing stressed, called for "a mint of money," because labor was always costly in America. Consequently, a large fortune did not produce the same amount of enjoyment that it could abroad: "Large estates, large houses, large establishments, only make slaves of their possessors; for the service, to be done daily by those who must hold aloft this dazzling canopy of wealth, is so indifferently performed, servants are so time-serving and unworthy in this country, where intelligent labor finds independent channels for itself." Downing gave notice that the person seduced into expenditures *en grand seigneur* (the foreign phrase was an extra warning to his republican readers) would find himself perpetually nervous about money and constantly obliged to maintain a mansion that gave "no more real pleasure than a residence on a small scale." He offered an alternative to beautiful parks, pleasure grounds, or flower gardens ("the most *expensive*" kinds of rural beauty) that did not require thousands of dollars: "a cottage embosomed in shrubbery, a little park filled with a few fine trees, a lawn kept short by a flock of favorite sheep." In that same number of the *Horticulturist,* a contributor from Toledo, Ohio, noted that the majority of those who built houses in the United States spent from nine hundred to two thousand dollars on construction.[22]

Another contributing writer, this time from Terre Haute, Indiana, asked Downing to tell "the masses" with small incomes how much natural beauty they might appropriate and enjoy at almost no cost at all. "Make [them] understand that there is a bank, whose funds are exhaustless, upon which [they] may draw." The next month, Downing devoted an editorial to "Economy in Gardening"—yet another cautionary essay about "the unsuspected cost of country pleasures." Labor was the main topic of concern, and as it was one of the most expensive commodities in the United States, Downing warned that even moderate improvements could consume a healthy fortune: "The moment [a man] touches a spade to the ground, to plant a tree, or to level a hillock, that moment his farm is taxed three or four times as heavily as in Europe; and as he . . . 'gardens' all his life, it is evident that his out-of-door expenses must be systemized, or economised, or he will find his income greatly the loser by it." Downing was nonetheless proud of the fact that in no country was labor better paid than in the United States: the price of the cheapest labor generally averaged eighty cents to one dollar per day; in contrast, it was twenty cents in Europe. He hoped that in the future his countrymen could afford to pay even more, however, the point of his editorial was to explain how to avoid unnecessary expenditure for labor, and how to insure that the dollar a day paid for labor was "fairly and well earned." This advice was steeped in ethnic stereotyping, as Downing described what kind of work habits could be expected from Irish and German emigrants. The Irish, as a class, he warned, required "far more *watching* to get a fair day's labor from them than many of our own people." On the other hand, an Irishman would work "stoutly and faithfully" to quickly accomplish a specific piece or job of his own seeking. German families, including women and children, accustomed to laboring in the vineyard or garden, could be employed by contract for doing certain kinds of horticultural labors, at a great saving to the employer.[23]

Downing suggested using laborsaving machines, including a horse hoe to clean weeds from gravel walks (fig. 6.3). He also reminded readers about one laborsaving device provided by nature: sheep could be substituted for the English scythe to keep a lawn in order on larger country places. Although Downing would not compromise on his requirement that an estate with aspirations to be considered ornamental have a well-mown lawn (this meant once or twice a month for a velvet effect), he proposed that a flock of a half-dozen or more could do the work of two mowers. This substitution would be without expense, would possibly show a profit, and in a certain kind of picturesque or pastoral residence would heighten the interest of the scene.[24]

Downing began the new year with practical advice on transplanting large trees for those impatient owners of new sites whose predecessors had cared more for cord wood than for "the charms of sylvan landscape." He was able to offer encouraging news about the viability of transplanting large elms and maples, but his readers faced three pages of detailed instructions for selecting the specimen, digging the root ball, transporting the tree, preparing the hole, transplanting, and caring for the tree

6.3

Implement in use at Blithewood for cleaning gravel roads. In appendix 5, "Notes on Walks and Roads," in *Treatise* (1844). Kansas State University Libraries.

Economy in Gardening

afterward. In this way, he underscored the folly of destroying old trees and having to start again from "a liliputian specimen no higher than one's knee." Although there could be great delight in raising a tree from seed and watching it grow year by year, Downing recognized that some might not find it so satisfying: "To a person who has just 'settled' upon a bare field, where he has only a new house and a 'view' of his neighborhood to look at, we must not be too eloquent about the pleasure of raising oaks from the acorn. He is too much in the condition of the hungry man, who is told to be resigned, for there will be no hunger in heaven." The *Horticulturist* offered a specific case of such a hungry man. The contributing writer was a farmer living on the open prairie in Missouri, and he wrote of his impatience to set out trees around his house: "Leaving out of view the luxury of a good shade in the dog days, the idea of living a whole year with nothing to relieve the monotony of a prairie landscape, but long strings of worm fence, varied by an occasional gopher hill or haystack, I couldn't stand it."[25]

"How to Arrange Country Places" once again featured trees and lawns. The recent information on transplanting was meant to be of use to proprietors who did not already possess the indispensable trees; Downing reminded them that "a country place without trees, is like a caliph without his beard." Downing's comments and instructions concerning lawns were a far cry from those of November 1846. He still insisted that the groundwork of the residence's ornamental portion should be the lawn, but its extent could range from a "mere bit" to a number of acres, according to the owner's taste and means. Americans were also told that "no nation under the sun may have such lawns as the British," but those in the northern states could still have green and pleasant ones if they made the soil deep and kept the grass well-mown. Downing then tacitly admitted the extravagance of his former expectations: "To mow a large surface of lawn—that is to say, many acres—is a thing attempted in but a few places in America, from the high price of labor." To save money and trouble, Downing was content with the happy expedient of sheep and wire fences; with the pleasure grounds fenced in, one needed only to mow a strip around the house while animals kept the rest short.[26]

To ensure that wealthier readers understood the applicability of such economies to their own circumstances, Downing devoted an editorial to "The Management of Large Country Places." He noted that country seats, consisting of thirty to five hundred or more acres, were rapidly increasing in number around large cities. The first-class Hudson River places were commanding from fifty to seventy-five thousand dollars, and Downing attributed this trend to "a growing taste for space and beauty." Despite the impressive figures, Downing knew of ten instances of failure for one success. Considerable familiarity with the rural seats in this part of the country enabled him to state that few persons were able to keep up a fine place without being "more or less out of pocket at the end of the year"; even after considerable expense many of these places were not in good order.[27]

With this in mind, Downing sought to advise owners how to get "the greatest space and beauty at the least original expenditure, and with the largest annual profit." In many desirable locations along the Hudson River, he reported, sites could be had for sixty dollars an acre that were already prettily wooded; with "very trifling expense" they could be turned into natural parks. (In contrast, improved sites cost two or three hundred per acre.) A large part of the country seat could be turned into park meadow, "feeding it, instead of mowing and cultivating it." Downing offered the example of English parks: "very large meadows, studded with great oaks and elms—and grazed—profitably grazed, by deer, cattle and sheep." His next statement seemed to be inspired by a new understanding gained the previous summer when he had toured England: "We believe it is a common received idea in this country, with those who have not travelled abroad, that English parks are portions of highly dressed scenery—at least that they are kept short by frequent mowing, etc. It is an entire mistake." The mown lawn with its polished garden scenery, Downing affirmed, was confined to the pleasure grounds proper that immediately surrounded the house and was wholly separated from the park, which received no other attention than that of caring for its grazing animals. By managing property in the English way, Americans could maintain their parks at a profit and compress pleasure grounds and gardens into small spaces—lessening and concentrating labor in a space where it could make a difference. Downing promised that this plan would offer "a relief from a multitude of embarrassing details . . . [and] an equal relief to the debtor side of the cash account."[28]

It was still "a matter of *money*" when, in February 1852, Downing informed Americans of the dangers of unrealistic expectations upon retiring to the country and trying to create a paradise:

Is the *country*, which all poets and philosophers have celebrated as the Arcadia of this world,—is the country treacherous? Is nature a cheat, and do seed-time and harvest conspire against the peace of mind of the retired citizen? . . . Everything seems to be a matter of money now-a-days. The country life of the old world, of the poets and romancers, is cheap. The country life of our republic is *dear.*

Since 1841 Downing's name had become inextricably linked with the raised estimation of country life in America. *He* was the rural philosopher whose descriptions of sweetly flower-bedecked country homes had implanted ideas of security, contentment, and peace into his readers' imaginations. Nonetheless, after daily contact with people who were building country places, Downing felt obliged in the *Horticulturist* to remind improvers about economy and to forewarn those about to begin this supposed "voyage of pleasure" that it was not "all smooth water." With the simple expedient of offering an alternative technique for maintenance, Downing addressed American economic constraints while retaining the velvetlike lawn as a basic element of landscape gardening. He also strove with increasing insistence to teach Americans about their country's rich "permanent warp" of existing forests.[29]

The Neglected American Plants

In truth, Downing was partially to blame for the nation's indifference to its indigenous plants. Following J. C. Loudon's lead, the lesson of the 1841 *Treatise* had been that a necessary and tasteful appearance of art in a work of landscape gardening could be achieved only by introducing foreign trees and shrubs. In 1844 Downing relaxed this stance, still suggesting however that the "finest foreign sorts" of plants should be conspicuous in the more polished scenes. A further retreat was evident in the 1849 edition, as Downing incorporated ideas from Ruskin's theory of Typical Beauty; but the full extent of Downing's changed

The Neglected American Plants

opinion on this matter emerged only in the *Horticulturist*. Early in 1847 he began a campaign to convince readers that "the finest, indigenous, ornamental trees in the world were growing in America's native forests." Then, after his trip to England during the summer of 1850, Downing fully committed himself to what one editorial labeled "The Neglected American Plants." His former encouragement of the use of exotics became an embarrassment as he realized that adopting Loudon's thinking in this regard made neither practical nor aesthetic sense in America. By the time of his final editorial, Downing would condemn "the cast off nuisances of the gardens of Asia and Europe" that filled America's lawns and avenues.[30]

In March 1847, when Downing gave advice on the best trees for adorning the streets of rural towns and villages, he commented on the tendency to be captivated with exotic novelties: "There is a fashion in trees, which sometimes has a sway no less rigorous than that of a Parisian *modiste*." Americans, like the British, were fascinated with the marvels of newly available foreign plants, and Downing, with his years of experience in the family nursery business, had firsthand knowledge of the various epidemics in taste that had swept the country. He knew that it was not unusual to see fine native trees blindly overlooked for foreign species with "not half the real charms, and not a tenth part of the adaptation" to the American soil and climate. With this in mind, Downing set forth a simple rule to govern planting the streets of rural towns: "Select the finest indigenous tree or trees; such as the soil and climate of the place will bring to the highest perfection." He moved through a list of American trees (elm, Sugar Maple, oak, Tulip Tree, White Pine, *Magnolia grandiflora*) and observed: "We know how little common minds appreciate these natural treasures; how much the less because they are common in the woods about them." In cities like Philadelphia, rather than replace infested European Lindens with vigorous American maples, "that foreign tree" the Ailanthus (also known as the "tree of heaven") was becoming a great metropolitan favorite.[31]

Downing's nativism was not yet absolute, however, and he should have recognized himself as a modiste with a hand in shaping the American fashion in trees. That summer, despite his earlier lecture, he devoted an editorial to two exotic evergreens and urged planters to consider the great charms of the "world-renowned" Cedar of Lebanon and the Chili Pine of South America (fig. 6.4). He recommended the Cedar of Lebanon, "as rich in sacred and poetic association as Mount Sinai itself," and the singular Chili Pine, with its striking symmetry and edible fruit, for the country's ornamental plantations. The following spring, while pointing out the "lamentable poverty of evergreens" on the grounds of America's country places, Downing approved equally of both native and foreign trees (fig. 6.5). Silver Firs were grand and majestic features of the northern California landscape, and few trees were more strikingly picturesque, he noted, than a fine Norway Spruce. An "intelligent European horticulturist" was quoted as saying that America possessed the finest evergreens.[32]

A distinct change in the tenor of Downing's commitment to American plants occurred after his return from Europe in September 1850. Seeing American plants away from home increased Downing's awareness of his country's indigenous treasures, and the following spring the *Horticulturist* carried a fervent editorial devoted to the subject. "Yes," he admitted, "our hot-houses are full of the heaths of New-Holland and the Cape, our

A THEORY AND PRACTICE ADAPTED

6.4

A Cedar of Mount Lebanon. In *Garden and Forest* (March 1889). Kansas State University Libraries.

6.5

Plantation of Norway Spruce, Silver Firs, Larches, &c. &c. In the Grounds of Joseph Walker at Green Bank near New York—Nine Years Planted, Height from 20 to 25 Ft. In David Griscom's Evergreen Nursery's *Descriptive Catalogue of Foreign and Native Evergreen and Deciduous Trees* (1855–56). Library, Pennsylvania Horticultural Society, Philadelphia.

parterres are gay with the Verbenas and Fuchsias of South America, our pleasure-grounds are studded with the trees of Europe and Northern Asia." Sadly, it was rare on an American country place to see more than three or four native trees, rarer still to find any but foreign shrubs, and rarest of all to find any native wildflowers. As early as 1836 a contributor to Loudon's *Gardener's Magazine* had noted the American "perfect indifference" to beautiful native plants. Rhododendrons grew as plentifully in many parts of the eastern states as furze in Britain, yet vast numbers of this plant were shipped from Liverpool to Philadelphia— "although millions of the same variety could have been obtained for the trouble of lifting, at no great distance from the city." Downing confessed that an enthusiastic Belgian plant collector had made him keenly sensible of the "apathy and indifference of Americans, to the beautiful sylvan and floral products of their own country." He explained his former stance and illuminating experience abroad: "We had always, indeed, excused ourselves for the well known neglect of the riches of our native Flora, by saying that what we can see any day in the woods, is not the thing by which to make a garden distinguished. . . . One has only to go to England, where 'American plants' are the fashion, (not undeservedly, too,) to learn that he knows very little about the beauty of American plants." Downing told of the Tulip Trees on German avenues and the magnolias in the gardens in the south of France. His biggest revelation had come in seeing the masses of Mountain Laurel embellishing the English pleasure grounds: "What new shrub," Downing challenged, "surpasses the American Laurel when in perfection.... If it came from the high-lands of Chili, and were recently introduced, it would bring a guinea a plant, and no grumbling!"[33]

Of course, Downing was also reading Ruskin, whose "truth to nature" creed was grounded in "particular" nature—not in the classical vision of "general" nature. Therefore it was no surprise that when he offered "A Few Hints on Landscape Gardening" in November 1851, Downing called the attention of the planting public to "the study of nature"—to the trees found in America's beautiful woodland slopes, broad river meadows, steep hills, and deep valleys (fig. 6.6). These trees could be used as the finest elements of beauty in the embellishment of country places; forget about certain exotics, Downing urged, the "miserable rage for 'trees of heaven' [Ailanthus] and other fashionable tastes of the like nature." The Ailanthus was an easy target because of its heavy, sickening odor and abominable suckers. Downing condemned nurseries that did not stock the native Tulip Tree, Sassafras, and Pepperidge, and while praising the unrivaled beauty of these trees he also offered practical reasons for their superiority (fig. 6.7). All of them were freer from insect attacks than either larches, lindens, elms, or a dozen other favorite foreign trees; they remained unaffected by the summer sun, which burned the Asiatic Horse-chestnut brown; and "like native-born Americans," they held their foliage through the season when foreigners shriveled and died.[34]

6.6

Schuylkill Valley. In A. Kollner, *Bits of Nature and Some Art Products in Fairmount Park at Philadelphia, Pennsylvania* (1878). The Library Company of Philadelphia.

In July 1852 Downing again censured the "odorous Ailanthus and filthy poplars"; he felt that persons who planted these to the neglect of more salubrious native plants lacked any taste for rural beauty. The next month, apparently believing his audience had not yet grasped the seriousness of this mistake, Downing began what would be his last editorial with a clarion call: "'Down with the Ailanthus!' is the cry we hear on all sides, town and country,—now that this 'tree of heaven,' (as the catalogues used alluringly to call it,) has penetrated all parts of the union, and begins to show its true character. Down with the Ailanthus!" (fig. 6.8). He presented a list of complaints as if overheard from his readers: a young lady demanded that papa take her to Newport to escape the disagreeable smell; a country gentleman railed that the Ailanthus had ruined his lawn for fifty feet around each tree. Voicing the more disturbing aspects of the period's nationalism and racism, Downing himself declared:

We look upon it as an usurper in rather bad *odor* at home, which has come over to this land of liberty, under the garb of utility to make foul the air, with its pestilent breath, and devour the soil, with its intermeddling roots—a tree that has the fair outside and the treacherous heart of the Asiatics, and that has played us so many tricks, that we find we have caught a Tartar which it requires something more than a Chinese wall to confine within limits.[35]

Downing's crowning objection to this "miserable pigtail of an Indiaman" was patriotic—he felt that the Ailanthus had drawn attention from America's "own more noble native trees," and he made the most of it being a "petted foreigner." Also coming under his censure was the Abele or Silver Poplar; its fine white down unpleasantly filled the air every spring, and its suckers were even worse than those of the Ailanthus. Downing wondered who had not planted either one of these trees, and sent

6.7

The Sassafras Tree. In J. C. Loudon, *Arboretum et Fruticetum Britannicum* (1838). Library, Pennsylvania Horticultural Society, Philadelphia.

out a call for the "discreet, sagacious individual" who had escaped the national ecstasy for "foreign suckers." In urging his readers with this kind of rhetoric to plant "the freshest and comliest of American forest trees," Downing displayed the recent convert's passionate devotion to his cause. To take full advantage of native sylvan charms, Downing attempted in the *Horticulturist* to balance the opposing claims of fidelity to American nature and to the ideal.[36]

The Type of All True Art in Landscape Gardening

The *Horticulturist* adopted a much stronger nationalism than the *Treatise* in the promotion of neglected American plants while maintaining that landscape gardening was "a more refined kind of nature." Successive editions of the *Treatise* exhibited a retreat from the ideal abstractions of classicism and a growing fascination with the varied, "particular" aspects of the American landscape. In 1849 Downing added the example of an elm as the embodiment of perfected existence—"the finest form of a fine type." Significantly, however, he did not omit his earlier definition concerning the beau ideal; a footnote reiterated that the materials of the scene that constituted the *"beau ideal in Landscape Gardening as a fine art"* were different from those in wild nature because they were composed "of the floral and arboricultural riches of *all climates* . . . a scene characterized as a work of art, by the variety of the materials, as foreign trees, plants, &c." In contrast, readers of the November 1851 *Horticulturist* who wished to embellish their places "in the best and purest taste" were given this directive: "Let us take it then as the type of all true art in landscape gardening—which selects

6.8

The Glandulous-leaved Ailanthus. In J. C. Loudon, *Arboretum et Fruticetum Britannicum* (1838). Library, Pennsylvania Horticultural Society, Philadelphia.

from natural materials that abound in any country, its best sylvan features, and by giving them a better opportunity than they could otherwise obtain, brings about a higher beauty of development and a more perfect expression than nature itself offers." In other words, every country contained an abundance of indigenous material that through careful selection and subsequent care could be used to create a landscape garden.[37]

Americans would be able to avail themselves of treasures found in their own backyards once they understood how to cultivate a tree's type-form, and Downing explained this fundamental concept. "In what does the beauty of a tree consist?" he began, specifying that the question concerned the ornamental tree that stood alone in the lawn or meadow, grew in groups in the pleasure ground, arched over the roadside, or bordered a stately avenue. Downing defined the type-form stamped upon a species by nature as the highest beauty that such a tree could possess; the individual tree had to adhere perfectly to the character of its species. The oak, for example, branched out "boldly and grandly"; the chestnut had a "broad and stately" top; and the elm was "drooping and elegant." For a tree of any kind to be considered beautiful, it required a congenial soil and climate, and it had to stand quite alone to allow its boughs to stretch freely upward to the sky or downward toward the earth. Only then would it constitute "the finest picture of symmetry and proportion"—aspects of Ruskin's Divine will and plan.[38]

Any tree properly treated and situated could attain its type-form, and this interpretation allowed the native American tree to hold a place of honor in its own country. The opening statement of the May 1851 *Horticulturist* referred to this timeworn adage: "It is an old and familiar saying that a prophet is not without honor, except in his own country, and as we were making our way this spring through a dense forest in the state of New-Jersey, we were tempted to apply this saying to things as well as people." Downing offered a folksy analogy to explain how native flora could be rendered appropriate for artistic purposes, and his choice of contrasting images revealed the mid-nineteenth-century fascination with the extremes of civilization and savagery. Increasing contact with the world's primitive peoples had engendered a strange mixture of hostility and didactic paternalism—Charles Darwin's observations in his *H.M.S. Beagle Journal of Researches . . . From 1832 to 1836* (1839) may have inspired Downing's analogy. Darwin spent several months in Tierra del Fuego and found the inhabitants a "curious and interesting spectacle"; he could not believe "how wide was the difference between savage and civilized man. It is greater than between a wild and domesticated animal." Downing looked to America's far west for an example of a savage to use in comparison, not with a domesticated animal but with a cultivated plant. There was an enormous difference, he remarked, between an oak or Tulip Tree grown in a park with nothing but sky and air to interfere with its expansion and the same tree shut up in a forest (fig. 6.9). The former was comparable to "the best bred and highly cultivated man of the day," and the latter to "the best buffalo hunter of the rocky Mountains, with his sinewy body tattooed and tanned till you scarcely know what is the natural color of the skin." Those people accustomed only to the wild Indian might think they knew perfectly well what constituted a man; however Downing assured them that the "civilizee" was as different from the aboriginal man of the forest as the cultivated

A THEORY AND PRACTICE ADAPTED

6.9

Study of Trees in Park Scenery. Frontispiece in *Horticulturist* (September 1851). Author's collection.

and perfect garden tree was from the tree of the woods. Through cultivation, the plants of America's woods and swamps could be made to embellish any garden. If *Horticulturist* readers wanted something new and beautiful, Downing urged them to plant the American Laurel and the native holly.[39]

In contrast to the truly beautiful in an ornamental tree—"the most perfect standard of sylvan grace, symmetry, dignity, and finely balanced proportions"—Downing offered an image of a pruned tree: "a bare pole with a top of foliage at the end of it." Anyone with a perception of the beautiful in nature would no more wish to touch a fine elm or oak with saw or ax "than to give a nicer curve to the rainbow, or add freshness to the dew-drop." He drew a corollary to art, and for the first time

referred to Ruskin's favorite painter Joseph M. W. Turner, suggesting that "no great master of landscape, no Claude, or Poussin, or Turner" painted mutilated trees. In recognizing both the established masters and Turner, Downing differed from Ruskin, who found Claude, Poussin, and Rosa wanting when he compared their landscape paintings with actual trees, mountains, and clouds. Downing was selective in his borrowings from Ruskin and retained a loyalty to certain traditional artistic principles. His theory of landscape gardening was in fact more in line with a critic of Ruskin. Franklin B. Dexter, reviewing *Modern Painters I* for the *North American Review*, suggested that Ruskin had tried upon insufficient grounds to shake well-established opinions. Dexter asserted:

The Type of All True Art in Landscape Gardening

The true purpose of art . . . is not simply to put into gilt frames that which can be seen at any time, or even more occasionally, by looking out of doors; but to select the finest realities of nature and combine them into one consistent ideal scene, in which all things and all parts of things shall be omitted that contribute nothing to the general effect of physical beauty and moral sentiment.[40]

Similarly, when Downing declared that the American woods and fields offered ample instruction and admonished *Horticulturist* readers to "study landscape in nature more, and the gardens and their catalogues less," he hastened to qualify the statement. The finest pleasure grounds should not precisely resemble woods and fields:

We rather wish to *select* from the finest features of nature, and to recompose the materials in a choicer manner—by rejecting anything foreign to the spirit of elegance and refinement which should characterize the landscape of the most tasteful country residence—a landscape in which all that is graceful and beautiful in nature is preserved—all her most perfect forms and most harmonious lines.

His descriptive terms were markedly idealistic, but Downing had found a way to incorporate the country's richest and most diversified features into this scene: deliberate care could confer the requisite refinement on natural beauty "without impairing its innate spirit of freedom, or the truth and freshness of its intrinsic character."[41]

Again Downing chose the American Elm to reinforce his point. He painted a picture of a planted elm standing gracefully on a smooth lawn. For Downing, the elm had "all the freedom of character of its best prototypes in the wild woods, with a refinement and a perfection of symmetry which it would be next to impossible to find in a wild tree" (fig. 6.10). Downing achieved reconciliation much like the one that Asher B. Durand described five years later in his "Letters on Land-

6.10

American Elm (*Ulmus americana*). Drawing by James S. Jones.

scape Painting." The term *realism* was misapplied when used in opposition to *idealism,* Durand proposed: "The ideal is, in fact, nothing more than the perfection of the real." Downing based his idealism in the perfection of American nature rather than in a foreign beau ideal. Trees that were part of the intrinsic character of the native landscape, with the beauty of its "varied and exhaustless forests—the richest in the temperate zone," now could be accepted as landscape gardening's basic elements.[42]

7

AFTER TWENTY
YEARS TRIAL

Already in press when Downing drowned in a Hudson River steamboat accident on July 28, 1852, the August number of the *Horticulturist* indicated how far both its editor and the nation had progressed since the early 1830s when Downing joined his brother Charles in the family nursery business. With an easy familiarity of language, Downing now spoke to his "good friends" about the freshest and comliest of the country's native trees: North America was richer in oaks, maples, elms, and ashes than any country in the Old World, and its Tulip Trees and magnolias were "the exotic glories of the princely grounds of Europe." His conviction was born of experience, and the barbs were self-deprecating as well, as he asked: "Who plants an American tree—in America? And who, on the contrary, that has planted shade trees at all in the United States, for the last fifteen years, has not planted either Ailanthuses or Abele Poplars?" The statement constituted a review of his own misjudgments and former fascination with things foreign:

In this confession of our sins of commission in planting filthy suckers, and omission in not planting clean natives—we must lay part of the burden at the door of the nurserymen.... "Well! then, if the nurserymen *will* raise Ailanthus and Abeles by the thousands, (reply the planting community,) and telling us nothing about pestilential odors and suckers, tell us a great deal about "rapid growth, immediate effect—beauty of foliage—rare foreign trees," and the like, it is not surprising that we plant what turn out, after twenty years trial, to be nuisances instead of embellishments.[1]

The 1841 *Treatise* had optimistically proclaimed: "A taste for rural improvements of every description is advancing silently, but with great rapidity in this country." Yet the taste was of the old-world aristocratic variety, and in truth the young author's firsthand knowledge of his own country was limited to the eastern seaboard. He had yet to see Europe. Eleven years later Downing's inclination was markedly republican, and study, professional practice, travel, and a broadening access to information and opinions from the far reaches of the United States and its territories had given him the confidence to modify his theory and practice.[2]

As an editor Downing learned vicariously of different regions: *Horticulturist* correspondents in August 1852, for example, ranged from Louisville, Kentucky, and Northfield, Illinois, to Fayetteville, Arkansas, and the "Domestic Notices" carried a piece on "The Climate of San Francisco." Appending his editorial comment to a contributing essay on "Fruit Culture" from Macon, Georgia, Downing noted that it gave him "a new feeling of the breadth of our country, to know that before strawberries are ripe at the northern part of the Union peaches are in perfection at the other." This consciousness of the resources that could contribute to a national expression in landscape gardening—assets much beyond those in the "older portions bordering the Atlantic" that were highlighted in the *Treatise*—placed Downing in a position similar to that of the European arboriculturist whom he described in his last editorial. Traveling in America, this visitor had been "delighted and astonished at the beauty of [the country's] varied and exhaustless forests." These comments prompted Downing to remind *Horticulturist* readers (and himself) that nature in the New World could offer lessons as instructive and poetic as old-world architecture and art (fig. 7.1). The native Tulip Tree had a trunk that was as "finely proportioned, and smooth as a Grecian column"; its leaf was "cut like an arabesque in a Moorish palace"; its form as a whole was as "stately and regal as that of Zenobia," queen of ancient Palmyra.[3]

Downing's opportunity to put his mature theory of landscape gardening into practice and to realize what Calvert Vaux recalled as his partner's "great desire—Public Pleasure grounds *every where*" was cut short at his death when the Hudson River steamboat *Henry Clay* caught fire and sank. He was in the midst of supervising the improvements to the public grounds of the capital. The L-shaped area extending from the president's house along the Mall to the foot of Capitol Hill, which he designed in 1851 at the request of President Millard Fillmore, would have fulfilled many of Downing's aspirations: expressing on a grand scale what he considered the national style in landscape gardening; remedying the country's lack of a national garden such as the one he had admired at the Royal Botanic Gardens at Kew; and ultimately, of course, promoting an American taste for public pleasure grounds.[4]

In October 1848 even Downing and Henry Colman did not envision that their dream of public parks and gardens—"salubrious and wholesome breathing places" filled with beautiful trees, grass, fountains, and rare plants, shrubs and flowers—would be allowed such a scope for realization. They hoped to persuade "some country town of the first class" to build a public park; the people living there would be able to experience for themselves the moral and healthful effects of this amenity and would set an example for the rest of the country. How much better for such a place to be in the capital of the United States, for Downing believed that the true policy of republics was "to foster the taste for great public libraries, sculpture and picture galleries, parks and gardens, which *all* may enjoy."[5]

7.1
The Tulip Tree. In J. C. Loudon, *Arboretum et Fruticetum Britannicum* (1838). Library, Pennsylvania Horticultural Society, Philadelphia.

AFTER TWENTY YEARS TRIAL

The explanatory notes of March 3, 1851 that accompanied Downing's plan described the six "different and distinct scenes" in the National Park (fig. 7.2). The President's Parade was encircled by a carriage drive shaded by an avenue of elms—the tree that represented for Downing the type of all true art in landscape gardening. Surrounding the Washington Monument and bordered by the Potomac, Monument Park was planted "wholly with American trees, of large growth, disposed in open groups" to allow fine vistas of the river. Americans would no longer have to travel to Europe to view the beautiful sylvan products of their own country. In this park, with nothing to inhibit expansion, grand oaks, magnolias, Tulip Trees, and other native specimens would be grown in such a way as to encourage the type-form of the individual species.[6]

The Evergreen Garden collected all of the evergreens both foreign and native that thrived in the Washington climate. Broad-leaved evergreens in addition to the usual pines and firs with narrow leaves formed a pleasant winter garden for the capital's busiest and most populous season. The garden (shown in plan as an ellipse) was, according to Vaux, "arranged in the general form of a mound completely drained so that the Washingtonians would always have a dry, cheerfully green walk

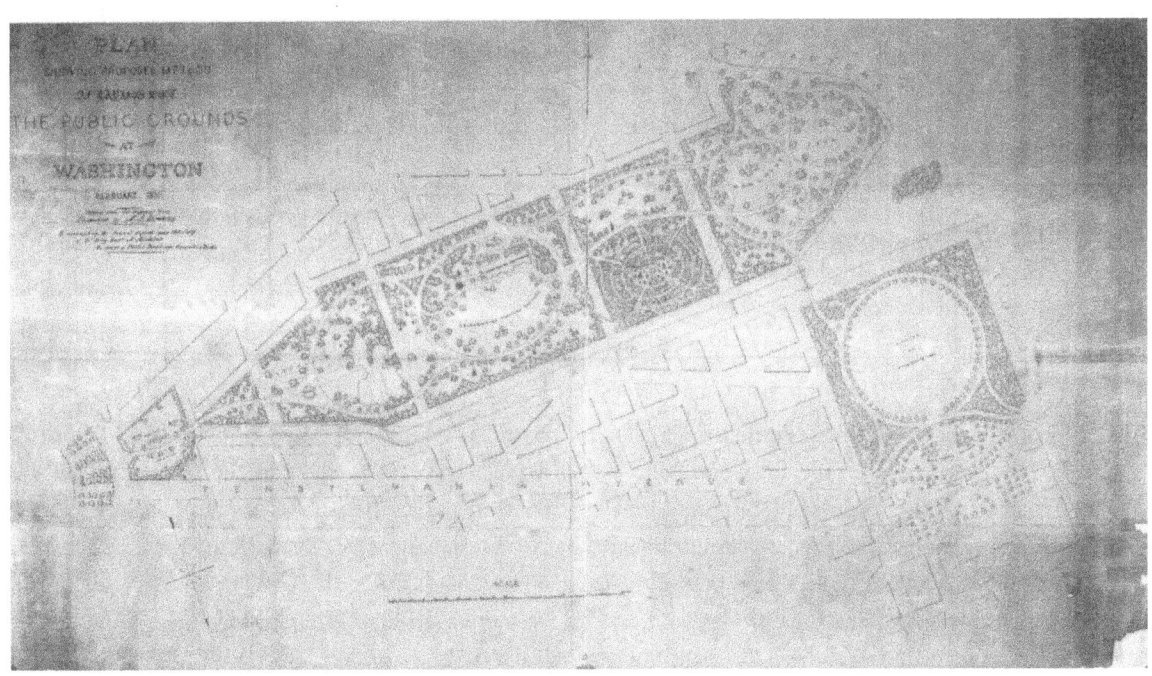

7.2

Plan Showing Proposed Method of Laying Out the Public Grounds at Washington, by A. J. Downing, February 1851. Headquarters Map File, F116–1; Records of the Office of the Chief of Engineers, Record Group 77; National Archives, College Park, Maryland.

in winter." The *Horticulturist* mirrored Downing's preoccupation with this design commission; he editorialized about "The Neglected American Plants" two months after submitting the park plans: "Our ornamental plantations, so far as they are evergreen, consist almost entirely of pines and firs—all narrow-leaved evergreens—far inferior in richness of foliage to [broad-leaved evergreens]." He specifically recommended the native holly and the American Laurel.[7]

The fourth area, called the Smithsonian Park, was "an arrangement of choice trees in the natural style," which Downing promoted as the national taste in landscape gardening. Visitors would be able to experience what he meant by "the spirit of nature, only softened and refined by art"; in these pleasure grounds, the paths were wide and smoothly curved, and every tree and shrub would be allowed free and luxuriant growth. The *Treatise* emphasized that good taste dictated that the more polished parts of the grounds be nearest the house and that the most rare and beautiful trees be displayed there. In this particular design, "the plots near the [Smithsonian] Institution would be thickly planted with the rarest trees and shrubs, to give greater seclusion and beauty to its immediate precincts."[8]

Water features distinguished the Fountain Park, which included an irregular lake and a fountain supplied from a basin on Capitol Hill. In determining "to form a National Park, which should be an ornament to the Capital of the United States," Downing surely remembered Chatsworth's impressive water spectacles—"the whole wealth of fountains and *grandes eaux*" that the Duke of Devonshire showed his American guest; moreover, Uvedale Price considered fountains among the most refined of all garden ornaments. They were appropriately placed in the public grounds of the nation's capital; Downing constantly sought "a desirable state of inter-national opinion" about the level of civilization in the United States.[9]

Downing realized when he visited England's Royal Botanic Gardens at Kew that such a public place in America "might not only be a beautiful, but a most useful and popular establishment" and designed his park to include a botanic garden with three greenhouses (fig. 7.3). Alexander von Humboldt considered the cultivation of exotic plants to have a powerful effect on the poetic imagination; in *Cosmos* he suggested that hothouses filled with groups of such plants could excite a pure love of nature. Downing, too, believed that once a certain portion of the population developed the capacity to perceive and enjoy the beauty of ornamental plants, the taste for embellishment would become contagious and rapidly diffuse itself "among all conditions of men."[10]

In sum, the Washington Public Grounds were intended to be, according to Vaux, "as nearly perfect as [Downing's] taste and experience would allow." However, after Downing's death, a new superintendent allowed the larger sense of the design to be lost; although the 1851 plan guided work on the Mall until the turn of the century, no trace of it remains. Downing's vision, described to President Fillmore in the March 1851 letter, thus was realized not in the nation's capital but rather in the city he so eloquently championed in the *Horticulturist* editorial "The New-York Park." The 1858 "Greensward Plan" for Central Park, designed by Calvert Vaux and Frederick Law Olmsted, became that "public school of instruction" for everything relating to the tasteful arrangement of parks and grounds; New York's rather than Washington's straight lines were "pleasantly relieved and con-

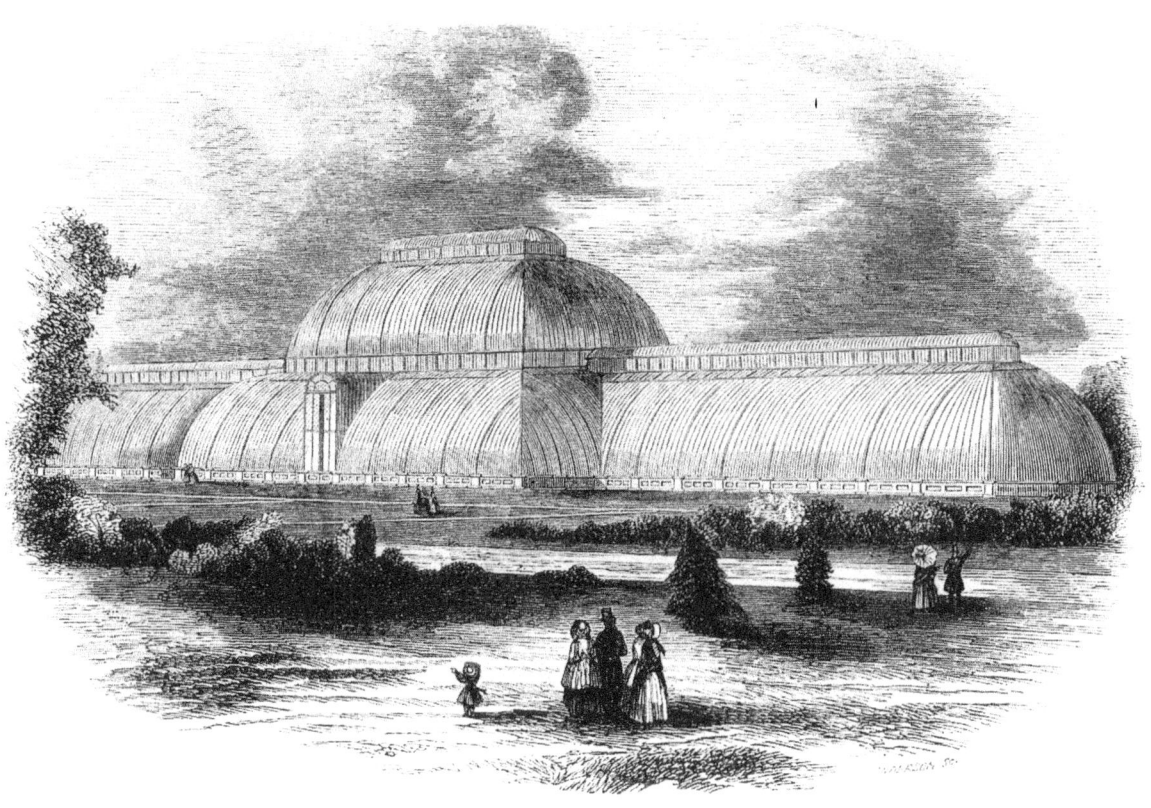

7.3

New Palm-house, Kew. In *Horticulturist* (April 1852). Author's collection.

trasted by the beauty of curved lines and natural groups of trees"; and Central Park still forms "the most perfect background or setting to the City" (fig. 7.4). Vaux and Olmsted—the English architect whom Downing brought to America and the gentleman farmer whose queries to the editor appeared in the *Horticulturist*—collaborated on landscape projects throughout the country until the late 1880s, carrying forward the experiment in public park design initiated by Downing.[11]

One of Henry Colman's remarks in "A Talk About Public Parks and Gardens" turned out to be prophetic, for it indicated Downing's most important legacy: "It is the province of the press—of writers who have the public ear—to help those to see . . . how much these outward influences have to do with bettering the condition of a people." Master of an articulate yet unaffected style of writing, Downing was also an acute social observer who understood the psychology of an emerging nation and its inhabitants. "Mr. Downing is . . . *one of us*," a reviewer in the *Home Journal* proudly claimed, "a man to whom his countrymen owe much, and to whom they feel happy to acknowledge their obligations." Comparing the effectiveness of Downing to John Ruskin in regard to an American audience, the author astutely recognized that, notwithstanding the genius of the En-

7.4

The Meadows in Central Park. In *Garden and Forest* (May 1888). Kansas State University Libraries. The accompanying article noted that "broad, open landscapes . . . offer the most pleasing of contrasts to the hard confinement of city streets."

glish critic, Downing shed as much light on issues as the newly opened eyes of his generation could bear. Americans in the 1840s found a man who spoke with their feelings, who precisely understood their difficulties, who encouraged their enthusiasm for "the works of nature, and the ideal of art," and who quietly pointed out in a plain, practical way "the very things they so much wanted to know": how to create or simply appreciate beautiful homes, gardens, schoolhouses, parks, and villages. Just as "after twenty years trial" in the nursery business Downing learned to critically assess foreign plants for their practicality, value, and appropriateness for American conditions, he came to realize that he needed to turn an equally discerning eye on the needs and wants of the people in order for the art of landscape gardening to flourish in the New World.[12]

APPENDIX

Horticulturist *Editorials*

The appendix offers a chronological list of Downing's seventy-four *Horticulturist* editorials. Confusing and often mistaken interpretations of Downing's ideas have resulted from the practice of citing the editorials as collected in *Rural Essays,* a memorial volume published in 1853. Relying on this collection is problematic not only because several editorials were omitted but, most importantly, because they were grouped by subject and not ordered chronologically. A reference to *Rural Essays* offers no indication of *when* within Downing's six-year editorship a statement was made. Conclusions drawn from such random reading are suspect, for Downing's theory and practice of landscape gardening changed during this period. The appendix also provides a list of persons quoted or referred to in each of the editorials; references made to books and journals; the use of foreign words; and a concise summary of the ideas addressed. This information provides a useful outline and overall picture of Downing's editorial work.

The last notation in the second line of each entry indicates the subject heading under which this editorial appeared in *Rural Essays,* along with its position within that sequence, using the following abbreviations:

APPENDIX

H	*Horticulture*
LG	*Landscape Gardening*
RA	*Rural Architecture*
T	*Trees*
A	*Agriculture*
F	*Fruit*
LE	*Letters from England*
n.i.	*not included*

Following this is a list of authorities, books, and journals referred to or quoted (at times Downing's own books appear on it); names with an asterisk are estate owners; fictional, mythical, and biblical characters are indicated by a cross (†). Finally, the "Subjects" listing goes beyond the editorial's title to give a better sense of its content. Whatever the month's particular topic, Downing wove in his ideas on the value of country living, taste, emulation, American progress, economy, republicanism, etc. The subject listing is meant to show the timing and frequency of these ideas (for example, how often he held up England as an exemplar). In addition to reiterating such general themes, Downing digressed on events or fads that were in the news of the day. Thus, even under such unpromising titles as "The Philosophy of Manuring Orchards," the discussion ranges from the laws of nature to quack doctors. Certain of Downing's phrases are given in full; foreign words or phrases are listed in italics to show the frequency with which Downing inserted them into his essays.

Horticulturist *Editorials*

VOLUME 1

July 1846
["Introduction"] / pp. 9–10 / (H #1)

† Flora [goddess of flowers]
† Pomona [goddess of fruit trees]
• [François Marie Voltaire]—quotation in French

Subjects:

Nature; God made the *country;* politics; beautiful & useful; sound practice & ingenious theory; patriotism; progress of horticulture & its kindred pursuits; *"Allons mes amis, il faut cultiver nos jardins!"*

August 1846
["New Vinery at Blithewood"] / pp. 57–58 / (n.i.)

★ Robert Donaldson, Esq., Blithewood
• Reference to *Landscape Gardening*

Subjects:

tasteful architecture; simplicity & functionality; climate; economy

September 1846
"On Simple Rural Cottages" / pp. 105–10 / (RA #7)

• Vitruvius [Pollio]
• [John Claudius] Loudon (quotation)
• Reference to *Cottage Residences*

Subjects:

tasteless & meager imitations; progress in rural architecture; setting an example; decoration; Greek temple mania; fitness & propriety; true character; style; class of dwelling; simplicity; proportion; expression; economy; American adaptations; color

October 1846
"On Country Houses" / pp. 153–55 / (n.i.)

• Mr. [Alexander Jackson] Davis (*A Design for a Simple Country House*)

Subjects:

Downing's correspondence; simplicity; architectural expression; American style of architecture; farmers = plain & simple; relationship of house & grounds; *atelier;* ornament; economy; climate; propriety; imitations of highly ornate styles

November 1846
"A Chapter on Lawns" / pp. 201–4 / (LG #14)

• [Matthew] Prior (quotation)
† Tom Thrifty, the farmer
• [William] Shakespeare (quotation)
• [Lodovico] Ariosto (quotation)
★ Mrs. Mary Livingston
★ [Mrs. William M.] Camac
• [Edmund] Spenser (quotation)
• Reference to *Landscape Gardening*

Subjects:

elements of landscape gardening; trees; grass; ideal of grass = lawn; water; England as exemplar; climate; adaptations in practice; expenditure in ornamental gardening; refined manner; labor

December 1846
"How to Build Ice-Houses" / pp. 249–53 / (RA #11)

• Mr. N. J. Wyeth, Cambridge, Mass. (lengthy excerpt from letter)
★ Frederic Tudor, Esq., Boston

Subjects:

architectural types; Sandwich islanders; influence of climate; *dolce far niente* (sweet do nothing); happiness = variety of sensations; Old vs. New World; Downing's correspondence; economy; character

APPENDIX

January 1847
"Impressions of Chatsworth" / pp. 297–302 / (n.i.)

- ★ Duke of Devonshire, Chatsworth
- • Prince Pückler Muskau (description cited)
- • Mr. [J. C.] Loudon
- • Mr. [Joseph] Paxton
- • Sir Jeffrey Wyattville (architect to the Duke)
- • "A—." (lengthy quotation)
- • *London Horticultural Magazine* (illustration)

Subjects:

wealthy aristocracy vs. *Hort* audience; ideal race of happiness; England as exemplar; gardening; compensations of being poor; truth; trumpery imitations; Niagara Falls; natural type; exotic plants; arboretum; first-class country place; labor; imagination; caste

February 1847
"A Chapter on Hedges" / pp. 345–55 / (T #12)

- • Homer
- † Ulysses
- † Laërtes
- • [Alexander] Pope (quotation from *Odyssey*)
- • William Cobbett (quotation)
- • [Geoffrey] Chaucer (quotation)
- ★ Mr. Godfrey, farm near Geneva, N.Y.
- ★ Hon. John Lowell, Roxbury
- ★ J[ohn]. P[erkins]. Cushing, Esq., Belmont Place, near Boston
- • Mr. Derby, Salem (extract from *Transactions of the Essex Agricultural Society*)
- • Messrs. Landreth & Fulton, Philadelphia (nursery)
- • Landreth & McMahon, near Philadelphia (nursery)
- ★ John C. Lee, Esq., Salem, Mass. (illustration of hedge on his grounds)

Subjects:

classical precedent; simplicity; art vs. nature; city vs. country; propriety; settlers; progress of labors on the soil; economy; the Prairie; American restlessness; impatience; American adaptations; native plants; practice; labor; mere imitation

March 1847
"Trees, in Towns and Villages" / pp. 393–97 / (T #4)

- † Mrs. Jeffs
- • Christopher North [John Wilson] (lengthy quotation)
- • Dr. [Thomas] Malthus

Subjects:

love of nature; destructiveness; pioneers; wise means of progress; patriotism; New England as exemplar; American character; the public good; principle of imitation [i.e. emulation]; novelty; fashion; *modiste;* native trees; adaptation for America; character; cities

April 1847
"Hints on Flower Gardens" / pp. 441–45 / (H #2)

- • Mary Howitt (poetry)
- • Mr. [J. C.] Loudon (quotation)
- ★ Baron Von Hügel, near Vienna
- • M. Peinter (quotations from *Allgemeine Garten Zeitung*)
- • Duchess of Bedford
- ★ Mrs. Edward Livingston, Montgomery Place
- • *Gardener's Magazine* (quotation)

Subjects:

Nature; geometric, natural, & gardenesque styles; selection & arrangement; novelty; breadth of effect; climate; expression; *sine qua non;* England as exemplar; practice; adaptations for America; Montgomery Place as exemplar

May 1847
"On the Colour of Country Houses" / pp. 489–93 / (RA #8)

- • Charles Dickens (quotation)
- • [Lancelot "Capability"] Brown (quotation)
- † Mr. Broadcloth

Horticulturist Editorials

† Miss Miggs
- Mr. Uvedale Price (reference to *Essays on the Beautiful and Picturesque*)
- Horace Walpole (quotation)
- [William] Wordsworth (quotations from *Scenery of the Lakes*)
- [Edmund] Spenser (quotation)
- Sir Joshua Reynolds (quotation)
- Reference to *Cottage Residences*

Subjects:

England as exemplar; protest against white paint; economy; nature as basis for practice; landscape painting for its principles; *soubriquet;* natural landscape; union of house with surroundings; expression; fashion as powerful teacher

June 1847
"Rare Evergreen Trees" / pp. 537–42 / (T #6)

† Moses
† Solomon
† Prophet Ezekiel (quotation)
- [Alphonse de] Lamartine (lengthy quotation)
- Queen Elizabeth
- Duke of Richmond
★ Duke of Wellington, Strathfieldsaye
- [J. C.] Loudon (quotation from *Arboretum Britannicum*)
★ Duke of Northumberland, Syon House
★ Sir Uvedale Price, Foxley
★ Thomas Ash, Esq., Throg's Neck, N.Y.
- Dr. Poeppig (quotation)
- Mr. [Robert] Buist, Philadelphia nurseryman
- Dr. Valk, Flushing
- *London Horticultural Magazine* (quotation)
- Reference to *Revue Horticole*

Subjects:

native trees; pride in American nature; association; Cedar of Lebanon; England as exemplar; character; republicanism; adaptations for America; challenge to taste; Chili Pine; ornamental plantations

VOLUME 2

July 1847
"Influence of Horticulture" / pp. 9–11 / (H #3)

† Tantalus [son of Zeus]
- [Alexis] de Tocqueville (lengthy quotation)
† Ishmael
† Noah

Subjects:

American character; political & moral influence; mere gratification of the senses; spirit of unrest; growth; repose; sable representative; Old World as exemplar; ideal of life; love of home & garden; property; pioneers; older portions of country as exemplar; local attachments; association; challenge to intelligence of *Hort* readers

August 1847
"Mr. Tudor's Garden at Nahant" pp. 57–59 (LG #15)

† Boreas [Greek god of the north wind]
★ Frederic Tudor, Esq., Nahant, near Boston

Subjects:

resort from city; triumph of art over nature; improvement; practice

September 1847
"A Talk with Flora and Pomona" / pp. 105–8 / (H #4)

† Flora
† Pomona
- Mr. Longworth, Cincinnati
- Mr. [Joseph] Paxton (reference to *Paxton's Magazine of Botany*)
- Mr. [Henry Ward] Beecher
- Dr. [Jean Baptiste] Van Mons [Belgian pomologist]
- Mr. [Robert] Fortune [British horticulturist & plant collector]
- Titian
- Raphael

APPENDIX

Subjects:

dolce far niente; rural nature; *en rapport;* making the wilderness blossom like a rose; American vs. foreign fruits; novelty; ladies vs. rude men; simplicity; painting vs. landscape reality

October 1847
"A Visit to Montgomery Place" / pp. 153–60 / (LG #16)

- Gen. [Richard] Montgomery
- ★ Mrs. [Janet Livingston] Montgomery
- ★ Hon. Edward Livingston
- † Rip Van Winkle
- ★ Mr. Catherwood, architect
- ★ [Samuel] Rogers (poetry)

Subjects:

speed of transportation; prosperity of America; town vs. country; dignity in repose; historical association; pride in American landscape; *coup d'oeil;* improvement; simplicity; arboretum; natural beauty elicited & heightened

November 1847
"On Planting Shade Trees" / pp. 201–3 / (T #3)

- Homer
- Virgil
- Cicero
- Manlius [sic—Manilius]
- Tully
- Mr. [James] Hillhouse, New Haven

Subjects:

Downing's correspondence; improvement of private grounds; private vs. public good; advantages of education; New England as exemplar; setting an example; challenge to intelligence of *Hort* readers; character indicated by appearance of town; patriotism; native trees; property

December 1847
"How to Choose a Site for a Country Seat" / pp. 249–52 / (LG #10)

- Ex-President [John Quincy Adams]

Subjects:

rural retirement; landscape gardening = labor, patience, taste, time, & money; superiority of trees & lawns to all other features; availability of good sites in America; finishing touch of rural artist; good patrimony from nature; beautiful & useful; economy; the West; cultivation of eye & taste; mental culture; metaphysicians; spirit of destruction; *gens d'armes;* agricultural schools; associations in old trees

January 1848
"The Philosophy of Manuring Orchards" / pp. 297–303 / (F #3)

- [Baron Justus von] Liebig (reference to *Agricultural Chemistry*)
- Dr. [Ebenezer] Emmons (lengthy excerpt from *Agriculture of New-York*)
- † Noah
- Reference to *Fruits and Fruit-Trees of America*

Subjects:

culture of the soil = natural & noble employment; transformation of unproductive nature; laws of Nature; challenge to intelligence of *Hort* readers; value of science; knowledge into practice; chemistry; progress in scientific cultivation; future progress; patient experimentation; new & improved system of agriculture; quack doctors

February 1848
"On the Moral Influence of Good Houses" / pp. 345–47 / (RA #2)

- Dr. [Timothy] Dwight (lengthy excerpt from *Travels in America*)

Subjects:

shelter vs. domestic architecture; primitive vs. civilized; grosser wants of life vs. fitting, appropriate, & beautiful forms; fine architecture & tasteful grounds; new era in U.S.; expression; public virtue & general good; Old vs. New World; improvement to all classes; property; primogeniture; feeble imitation; want of fitness & propriety; architectural progress; classes of dwelling

March 1848
"A Chapter on School-Houses" / pp. 393–96 / (RA #10)

- Rembrandt

Subjects:

free government depends on education; older portions of country as exemplar; fertile invention of our age; clearer terms & captivating style rob learning of half its terrors; adaptations for American character; narrow sectarianism; expression; phrenology; cultivation of children; foretaste of the millennium; ideal picture of common schoolhouses; millennium of schoolboys; importance of external objects on the mind, heart, manners, & life; rural cemeteries; insane asylums; influence of nature; trees, flowers, gardens, country, & home vs. politics, commerce, & professions

April 1848
"A Few Words on the Kitchen Garden" / pp. 441–44 / (A #6)

- [J. C.] Loudon (quotation from *Suburban Horticulturist*)
- Mr. Stafford, gardener at Willersly Castle, near Mattock
- Reference to *Journal of the Agricultural Society of England*

Subjects:

the useful; unsuitable soil; pride in American climate; labor; practice; economy

May 1848
"A Word in Favor of Evergreens" / pp. 489–93 / (T #7)

- [J. C.] Loudon (illustration and lengthy quotation from *Arboretum Britannicum*)
- ★ Col. [Thomas Handasyd] Perkins, near Boston
- ★ Mr. Winter, Flushing, Long Island
- ★ Capt. Forbes, Milton Hill, near Boston
- Mr. [Robert] Nelson, correspondent from Newburyport, Mass.
- Elwanger & Barry, nursery, Rochester, N.Y.
- Douglass [sic—David Douglas] (quotation)
- Landreth nursery, Philadelphia

Subjects:

fine indigenous trees of our country; ornamental plantations; useful as well as picturesque; England as exemplar; character & practical aspects of four evergreens; tree grown alone in a smooth lawn

June 1848
"Cultivators—The Great Industrial Class of America" / pp. 537–40 / (A #1)

- Mr. Burke, commissioner of patents (excerpt from report)

Subjects:

republic vs. Old World monarchical institutions; class equality; practical & busy American spirit; agriculture over manufactures; transportation; labor; aid & direct nature; landholding vs. leasing; farming class = nursery of all professions; city vs. country; agricultural education

VOLUME 3

July 1848
"Hints to Rural Improvers" / pp. 9–14 / (LG #3)

- [Johann Wolfgang von] Goethe (poetry)
- ★ [Daniel] Webster, Marshfield
- ★ [Zachary] Taylor
- ★ Washington Irving, Sunnyside
- ★ [Thomas] Cole

APPENDIX

- ★ Col. [Thomas Handasyd] Perkins, Brookline
- ★ Thos. Lee, Esq., Brookline, near Boston
- ★ Mr. [John Perkins] Cushing, Watertown
- ★ Mrs. [William M.] Camac, near Philadelphia
- ★ Mrs. Edward Livingston, Montgomery Place
- ★ R[obert]. Donaldson, Esq., Blithewood
- ★ W. Langdon, Esq., Hyde Park
- • [Victor] Cousin

Subjects:

progress of refinement = increase in ornamental gardening & rural embellishment; older portions of northern & middle states; city vs. country; old-world class distinctions; landscape gardening = a more refined kind of nature; beautiful & useful in transportation; ideal of retired life; property; England as exemplar; bad taste; aesthetic capacities of improver; cultivated taste vs. sensibility (natural taste); amateur vs. professional; American residences as models; moderate fortunes; republican vs. aristocratic modes of life; taste vs. genius; Anglo-Saxon traits

August 1848
"A Chapter on Roses" / pp. 57–63 / (H #5)

- • Dr. [Charles] Darwin
- • Duke of Guise
- • Leigh Hunt (poetry)
- • Martial (excerpt from Latin *Ode to Caesar*)
- • [Francis] Beaumont and [John] Fletcher (poetry)
- • Barry Cornwall (poetry)
- † Imogen
- † Ophelia
- • Mr. Paul, English nurseryman
- • [Jean-Jacques] Rousseau (reference to *Nouvelle Héloïse*)
- • Mr. [Robert] Buist, nurseryman, Philadelphia
- • Dr. [William W.] Valk
- • Mr. [Thomas] Rivers [nurseryman, Sawbridgeworth, Herts., England]

Subjects:

rose = type of everything fair & lovely on earth; rose = type of infinity; associations; expression; western readers looking for practical advice; *ultima thule;* improved roses; symbol of female loveliness; culture = rose & feminine beauty; *embarras de richesses;* republicans; leveller; a smile once a year vs. a golden temper, always sweetness & sunshine = all other vs. everblooming roses

September 1848
"Pomological Reform" / pp. 105–9 / (n.i.)

- • Mr. [J. J.] Thomas, Macedon, N.Y.
- • Dr. [J. P.] Kirtland, Cleveland
- • Mr. [Samuel] Walker, Boston
- • Mr. [Henry Ward] Beecher, Indiana (lengthy quotation)
- • Reference to *Fruits and Fruit-Trees*

Subjects:

nursery business; public good; cost & labor

October 1848
"A Talk About Public Parks and Gardens" / pp. 153–58 / (LG #7)

- • Count Rumford, Munich
- • [Queen] Victoria

Subjects:

American nationalism; revolutions in Europe; *ouvriers;* millennium; growth of country; Old vs. New World; *avoirdupois;* patriotism; France & Germany as exemplars of social life; cultivation of social & intellectual nature; republican simplicity; *gens d'armes;* democracy worth imitating; German public grounds = drawing rooms of whole population; Anglo-Saxon race; class distinctions; *gêne;* women's health; American feverish unrest; *modus operandi;* public good; influence of beauty on daily lives; beautiful/true/good; influence of the press; elevation of national character; setting an example; temperance

Horticulturist *Editorials*

November 1848
"The Art of Transplanting Trees" / pp. 209–12 / (T #10)

- Sir Henry Stewart [sic—Stuart]
- † Capt. Bragg

Subjects:

multitude of complaints & inquiries received by Downing; practical knowledge; theory vs. practice in different climate of America

December 1848
"A Chapter on Green-Houses" / pp. 257–62 / (H #6)

Subjects:

variety; triumph of art over nature; address not to wealthy readers but to readers interested in economy

January 1849
"On the Mistakes of Citizens in Country Life" / pp. 305–9 / (LG #5)

- [William] Cowper (poetry)
- [Abraham] Cowley (poetry)
- Sir Walter Scott

Subjects:

Book of Nature; Anglo-Saxon inheritance; manifest destiny; *otium cum dignitate;* city vs. country; beau ideal = retirement to the country; practical ability; expecting & undertaking too much; prose in country life; with us labor is always costly; *patés de foie gras;* economy; continual distribution of fortunes; servants; true philosophy of living in America = moderation; amateurs vs. professionals; perfect model of beauty & convenience; *en grand seigneur;* house & surroundings; simplicity; suburban country life; most expressive vs. most expensive kind of rural beauty

February 1849
"On the Drapery of Cottages and Gardens" / pp. 353–59 / (H #14)

- Mr. [Samuel] Morse
- † Theseus [Greek hero]
- † Ariadne [daughter of Minos who gave Theseus the thread to escape the labyrinth]
- † Tim Steady
- † Widow Winning
- † Daphne [nymph transformed into a laurel tree to escape Apollo]
- Ovid
- † Hector [husband of Andromache & bravest Trojan in Homer's *Iliad*]
- † Andromache
- ★ Washington Irving, Sunnyside
- ★ Mr. Alfred Smith, Newport
- Monsieur Van Houtte, Ghent

Subjects:

ladies = natural mistresses of the art of embellishment; romantic vs. common place; utility vs. beauty; grace; Home; appearance of taste; expression; practice

March 1849
"Fruit Trees and the Best Manures for Them" / pp. 401–4 / (n.i.)

- Messrs. Reybold, Delaware peach-growers

Subjects:

inquiries, propositions, & suggestions in Downing's correspondence; secret of good cultivation; passion for novelty & variety

April 1849
"On Feminine Taste in Rural Affairs" / pp. 449–55 / (H #7)

- † John Bull [character typifying the English nation in *The History of John Bull* (1712) by John Arbuthnot]
- Mr. [Henry] Colman (lengthy excerpt from *European Agriculture*)
- Duchess of Portland
- Madame de Sevigne (excerpt from letter)
- M. [Michael] Chevalier (excerpt from *Society, Manners and Politics*)

APPENDIX

Subjects:

national characters of French, English, & American; *ennuyant;* city vs. country; no profound philosophical dissertation; address to ladies; love of nature; English as exemplar for out-of-door pursuits; social manners of French; *morale; la Belle France;* beau ideal of principal apartments; *en suite;* progress of buildings; *Française;* chivalry; exercise/fresh air/health

May 1849
"Economy in Gardening" / pp. 497–500 / (H #8)

- Mr. [Henry] Colman (reference to *European Agriculture*)
- Reference to *Landscape Gardening*

Subjects:

American character = careless spenders; labor = one of the dearest commodities; improvements; ease of accumulating wealth; *cottage ornée;* economy; Irish emigrants as a class; laborsaving machines; practical advice; practice for imitation = substitution of sheep for the scythe; lawn & trees vs. mere flowers; England as exemplar

June 1849
"On the Improvement of Country Villages" / pp. 545–49 / (RA #5)

- Sir Walter [Scott]
- Professor [Louis] Agassiz
- Mr. [James] Hillhouse, New Haven
- *Rockingham Farmer's Club* (lengthy excerpt)

Subjects:

quotation from correspondent; apostle of taste; enjoyment from orderly, tasteful, agreeable dwellings & streets; domestic virtues; reflection of character; graceless villages; visionary = ideas rise above the level of own accustomed vision; national character = imitation [i.e., emulation] & progress; improvement; language of the trees; California gold; heathen piratical Malay; utility vs. beauty; tasteful models; competent architect; American space; England as exemplar for public parks; common enjoyment; New England as exemplar for street trees; principle of progress; ornamental tree associations; Home; Book of Nature; challenge to intelligence of *Hort* readers

VOLUME 4

July 1849
"Public Cemeteries and Public Gardens" / pp. 9–12 / (LG #9)

Subjects:

rise & progress of our rural cemeteries; Greenwood, Laurel Hill, Mount Auburn; imagination; nature embellished by art; associations; character: progress of horticulture; predominant passion for rural pleasures; didactic use of public gardens; better class; city; practical economics; setting an example; public amenities; primogeniture

August 1849
"The Philosophy of Rural Taste" / pp. 57–60 / (LG #1)

- [Alexander von] Humboldt (quotations from *Cosmos*)
- Lieu-Tscheu (Chinese writer quoted on rural taste)
- Livy
- Tacitus
- Cicero
- Pliny
- Ovid
- Virgil
- Julius Caesar

Subjects:

England as exemplar for taste in landscape gardening; national character; spirit of nature softened & refined by art; a higher ideal of nature; races of mankind; national sensibility; poetic or northern taste vs. artistic or symmetric taste; Anglo-Saxon love of nature

September 1849
"Cockneyism in the Country" / pp. 105–9 / (RA #4)

- [William] Hogarth
- Cruikshanks [sic—George Cruikshank]

Subjects:

country vs. city; insults to nature & truth; countryman vs. "cit"; association; improvement; following nature's hint; adaptation to country life; facsimile of town house; display vs. use; propriety; tawdry & tinsel imitation; simplicity & modesty of expression; true taste = union of beautiful & significant; imitations of city splendor; progress in all things; progress of taste; models

October 1849
"A Chat in the Kitchen Garden" / pp. 153–56 / (A #7)

- Christopher North [John Wilson]

Subjects:

how much better the sun shines for us [Americans]; improved varieties; *ménage;* recipes; *modus operandi*

November 1849
"How to Enrich the Soil" / pp. 201–4 / (A #4)

- M. Soyer (reference to his cookbook)

Subjects:

good cultivation; practical hints; economy; labor is too dear; experience worth more than theory drawn from observation in other climates; American adaptations

December 1849
"A Chapter on Agricultural Schools" / pp. 249–52 / (A #5)

- "A great continental statesman" (lengthy quotation)
- † Leander [legendary Greek youth noted for swimming Hellespont nightly to visit Hero]
- [George] Washington
- Hamilton Fish
- Reference to *Working Farmer*

Subjects:

property in land; Home; agricultural life = presence of God; agriculture's influence on character; monarchical vs. republican; education; cultivation of the powers of the mind; age of technology; agricultural schools = great topic of day; mere theory vs. mere practice; learned by imitation; wisdom = knowledge put in action; model & type

January 1850
"On Transplanting Large Trees" / pp. 297–301 / (T #11)

- Sir Henry Stuart (information from book on transplanting)
- Sir Walter Scott
- ★ Thos. [Handasyd] Perkins, Brookline

Subjects:

impatience; destruction of trees; use vs. beauty; theory & practice; adaptations for America; climate; experiment; native elms & maples

February 1850
"The Fruits in Convention" / pp. 345–51 / (F #2)

- [Henri Louis] Duhamel [du Monceau] [French botanist]
- [Dr. Jean Baptiste] Van Mons [Belgian pomologist]

Subjects:

national characters; pride in America; republican vs. aristocratic tastes; translate foreign names into plain English; assertion of nationality; native American; associations; plain English essence; progress in horticulture

March 1850
"How to Arrange Country Places" / pp. 393–96 / (LG #11)

- Jeffreys (correspondent)
- Pericles
- Mr. [Henry Winthrop] Sargent
- [Sir] Walter Scott

APPENDIX

Subjects:

convenience, comfort, & beauty; beauty = harmony between real & ideal; privacy & seclusion; Greek architecture; necessary & truthful part of the dwelling; taste & means of owner; climate; Britain as exemplar for lawns; high price of labor; sheep & wire fences; economy; character of the place; improvement; imagination

April 1850
"A Look About Us" / pp. 441–43 / (H #9)

- Dr. Lee, editor of *Genesee Farmer*
- [Dr. Jean Baptiste] Van Mons
- M. Van Houtte, horticulturist from Ghent
- Mr. President [Samuel] Walker, [Massachusett's Horticultural Society]

Subjects:

old-fashioned vs. modern travel; field of progress; undeviating straight forward line; agricultural press; farming class; republic; improvement; progress in culture of gardens in West; America as exemplar in fruit culture; landholders among all classes; native varieties; practical school for gardeners

May 1850
"A Spring Gossip" / pp. 489–93 / (H #10)

- [James Russell] Lowell (poetry)
- † Mynheer
- [William] Shakespeare (poetry)
- [Carolus] Linnaeus
- † Richard III
- † Lord Ely
- † Falstaff
- Leigh Hunt (lengthy excerpt)
- [Alexander] Pope (poetry)

Subjects:

love of Nature; sober & practical men; lady readers; types; associations; beauty in common & familiar objects; English hold key to the poetry of rural life; *a fortiori*

June 1850
"Our Country Villages" / pp. 537–41 / (RA #6)

- [Alexander] Pope [sic—a line from William Cowper]

Subjects:

pride in America's natural features; *la belle France;* miserable towns deform the fair landscape; land of peace & plenty; beauty = taste, symmetry, order, space, & proportion; "God made the country, but man made the town"; utility & beauty; true rural faith; millennium of country towns; Massachusetts as exemplar for country villages; education; patriotism; Home; property; improvement; appearance = outward mark of character; force of example; association; manifest destiny; beau ideal of newly planned villages; city; summer boarding in farm house; rural character; public amenities; communist; power & virtue of individual home; we are republican; all classes

VOLUME 5

July 1850
"A Few Words on Rural Architecture" / pp. 9–11 / (RA #1)

- Reference to *Architecture of Country Houses*

Subjects:

a national American architecture & music; practical wants of life; all landlords; moderate sums to spend; national spirit of progress; modern improvements; popular taste requires right direction; character; pseudo-classical architecture; miniature imitations in wood; naturalization of type; absolute & relative beauty; *cottage ornée;* meaning in beauty

August 1850
"The Vineyards of the West" / pp. 57–60 / (F #4)

- Major Adlum, Washington, D.C.
- Nicholas Longworth, Esq., Ohio
- Dr. Flagg, Cincinnati
- † Noah

Horticulturist *Editorials*

- R. Buchanan, Esq., Cincinnati (reference to pamphlet on *Grape Culture*)
- Mr. Rentz

Subjects:

our own vine & fig tree = sacred idea of a life of security, contentment & peace; foreign vs. native grapes; inquiries from readers; temperance; men not content with merely living and breathing; cities

September 1850
"The Horticultural Shows" / pp. 105–7 / (n.i.)

Subjects:

spirit of emulation; practical information; free-masonry; severe abstract address to the eye & imagination; progress of horticulture; progress of the art; progress depends on experimental knowledge

October 1850
"Mr. Downing's Letters from England" / [August 1850, Cambridgeshire] pp. 153–60 / (LE #1)

- Sir William Hooker
- George III
- Queen Charlotte
- Sir Joseph Banks
- Capt. [James] Cook
- [Allan] Cunningham
- Mr. [Charles] Barry
- Earl and Countess of H[ardwicke], Wimpole
- Van Dyck
- Rubens

Subjects:

London parks as exemplars; *en passant;* healthful breathing zone; *coup d'oeil;* indirect & direct benefits in educating, refining, & elevating the people; address to ladies; health; land ownership; temperance; republicanism; domestics; primogeniture

November 1850
"The Favorite Poison of America" / pp. 201–6 / (RA #12)

† Hebe [Greek goddess of youth]
- [Dr.] Arnott, London
- [Frederick] Emerson, Boston
- Reference to *Architecture of Country Houses*

Subjects:

temperance; national health & constitution; national poison is not: slavery, socialism, abolition, mormonism, tobacco, patent medicines, or coffee; poison = vitiated air of close stoves in unventilated apartments; national invention; national pride & sensitiveness = warp & woof of national improvement; Europe as exemplar for healthy physical conditioning; daily exercise in open air; *tête montée;* economy; labor

December 1850
"Country Places in Autumn" / pp. 249–51 / (LG #13)

† Hercules

Subjects:

improvement; tongues in trees; poets or lovers of nature; earnest, practical working owners

VOLUME 6

January 1851
"A Short Chapter on Country Churches" / pp. 9–12 / (RA #9)

Subjects:

expression in building = human face; type; Beauty = harmony, grace, proportion, symmetry, & expression; shabby imitation of Greek temples; *chef d'oeuvres;* associations; simplicity

APPENDIX

February 1851
"The Beautiful in a Tree" / pp. 57–59 / (T #1)

- Claude [Gelée Lorrain]
- [Nicolas] Poussin
- [Joseph M. W.] Turner

Subjects:

ornamental tree; symmetry & proportion; left to nature; type-form; species; beau ideal; tree in a state of nature; pruning; amelioration by art; local truthfulness to landscapes by Dutch & French artists

March 1851
"The Management of Large Country Places" / pp. 105–8 / (LG #12)

Subjects:

two classes of country residences; definition of pleasure grounds in suburban residence; Boston as exemplar for little places; country seats of thirty to five hundred acres; distinct character in treatment; adaptations for America; sylvan & pastoral beauty; facility of management; high price of labor; England as exemplar for park pasture; simple feeling of nature; poetic idea of Arcadia; ideal nature = softened, refined, & ennobled; primogeniture; republicans

April 1851
"The Great Discovery in Vegetation" / pp. 153–56 / (H #11)

† John Bull
† Solomon

Subjects:

editor = oracle; correspondents; *sub rosa;* canine millennium; progress of dogs; hard words thrown in to puzzle terriers without a scientific education

May 1851
"The Neglected American Plants" / pp. 201–3 / (T #9)

- [Mr.] Summer, Belgian horticultural collector

Subjects:

native vs. foreign plants; wild plants; *Voilà le goût République;* novelty; cultivated man vs. buffalo hunter is to tree in pleasure ground vs. tree in the woods; perfection of form & foliage

June 1851
"A Few Words on Our Progress in Building" / pp. 249–54 / (RA #3)

- Thomas Jefferson (quotation)
- Mr. [John] Ruskin
- [Sir William] Blackstone
- Vitruvius [Pollio]
- [A. W. N.] Pugin
- [James Russell] Lowell ("The Rural Cot of Mr. Knott" reprinted)
- Reference to *Architecture of Country Houses*

Subjects:

aristocratic vs. republican; improvement; *ornée;* novelty; progress of building taste; foreign vs. new order of styles; invention; local modifications; American style of architecture; national type in character, manners & art; froth of foreign affectations; amateur vs. professional; ambitiously imitate; *cognoscenti; cottage ornée;* superior charm of simplicity; beauty of expression; lack of propriety [re: Fonthill built 1848–52 for Edwin Forrest]

July 1851
"A Few Words on Fruit Culture" / pp. 297–301 / (F #1)

- Mr. [R. G.] Pardee [correspondent from Palmyra, N.Y.]

Subjects:

U.S. as exemplar in fruit cultivation; rapid communication by railroads & steamboats; want of knowledge; high price of labor; destruction of forests & birds; improved varieties; adaptations to American soil & climate; hints drawn from the facts immediately around us

August 1851
"The New-York Park" / pp. 345–49 / (LG #8)

- Mayor [Ambrose C.] Kingsland
- Sir Philip Sidney

Subjects:

health; exercise; country vs. city; cities of Old World as exemplar for public parks; didactic uses of park; social influence; elevating influence of the beautiful in nature & art; all classes; exclusiveness; popular refinement = republican in its very idea & tendency; knowledge; manifest destiny

September 1851
"The National Ignorance of the Agricultural Interest" / pp. 393–96 / (A #2)

Subjects:

prosperity of U.S.; manifest destiny; migratory habits of Americans; concern about maintenance of natural resources; ruinous system of husbandry; decrease in rural population; increase in towns; the West = Arcadia of American farmer; slow progress of farming as an honest art; high cost of labor; agricultural education

October 1851
"A Reform Needed" / pp. 441–43 / (n.i.)

Subjects:

low point of civilization = allowing animals to run at large; progress of good government; Massachusetts as exemplar for order, cleanliness, & good government; external marks of civilization; improvement; challenge to intelligence of *Hort* readers; personal cleanliness; health of cities; liberty; property; setting an example

November 1851
"A Few Hints on Landscape Gardening" / pp. 489–91 / (LG #4)

Subjects:

improvement; embellishment; country vs. city; familiar vs. rare; finer native vs. poorer sorts of foreign plants; nurserymen; Book of Nature; the study of nature = real lessons in the beautiful & picturesque; climate; gardens vs. nature; selection & recomposition of nature; innate spirit of freedom; truth & freshness of a landscape's intrinsic character; type of all true art in landscape gardening = planted American Elm; more perfect expression than nature itself offers

December 1851
"The State and Prospects of Horticulture" / pp. 537–41 / (H #12)

Subjects:

progress in horticulture; separate & independent homes; useful & necessary vs. ornamental; England as exemplar for ornamental gardening; U.S. as exemplar in fruits & vegetables; improvement in fruit culture; progress in the art of raising good fruits; progress in the art of gardening; practical gardening school for native or naturalized ability; changes in practice for climate; formal vs. natural style; rural cemeteries; public parks & gardens; reference to Washington Mall design project; North American trees; practical art & art of taste; manifest destiny

VOLUME 7

January 1852
"The Home Education of the Rural Districts" / pp. 9–14 / (A #3)

- Major [Marsena Rudolph] Patrick (lengthy excerpt from address)
- Reference to *Landscape Gardening & Hort*

Subjects:

agricultural schools; Home; education of whole man; refined & innocent social pleasures; how to throw the sunshine of a cultivated understanding & heart upon everyday life; classes; knowledge is power, influence & position; farming; influence of women; challenge to intelligence & sensibility of *Hort* readers; honesty & dignity of rural life; beauty of propriety; pictures as faithful as Dutch master vs. pictures of Art Union; influence of surroundings; property; murderous ax

February 1852
"Citizens Retiring to the Country" / pp. 57–61 / (LG #6)

- Mr. [John Jacob] Astor

Subjects:

increase of cottage & villa residences; Anglo-Saxon nature; freehold property; fortune made in California; *otium cum dignitate;* ignorance vs. professional knowledge; the country which all poets & philosophers have celebrated as the Arcadia of this world; nature as cheat; money; republic; high cost of labor; practical knowledge of farming; choose a site where nature has done as much as possible; I will create a paradise for myself; the cost of luxury; modesty; simplicity; it is art not nature which costs money; most Americans vs. millionaires

March 1852
"The Beautiful in Ground" / pp. 105–7 / (LG #2)

- Claude [Gelée Lorrain]
- [David] Teniers

Subjects:

interest in mere surface of the ground; forms of acknowledged beauty = curved lines; "earth's smiles" = grassy slopes & swells; flat or level surface evinces art; straight line expressive of power; aim of man's existence = subjugate or level; Italian vs. Dutch painters; terracing; ground rarely ugly in nature; existing character; follow hints given by nature; variety; improvement

April 1852
"On the Improvement of Vegetable Races" / pp. 153–56 / (F #5)

- Reference to *Fruits and Fruit-Trees*

Subjects:

no progress in U.S. beyond common orchard culture; need for adaptation to climate & soil; reducing natural laws to system; naturalizing; how much may be done by a new race or generation in plants & men; subduing Western wilderness; manifest destiny; best race = individuals adapted by birth, constitution, & education to America; rights of a superior organization in certain men & races of men; public good

May 1852
"Brown Houses and Lightning Conductors" / pp. 201–4 / (n.i.)

† John Bull
† Don Quixotes [sic—Quixote]
- [Edmund] Spenser (poetry)
- Napoleon [Bonaparte]

Subjects:

fashion; imitation [i.e., emulation] as a means of improvement; progress in mental, moral, & social culture; invention; merely imitative & dull are content to follow; novelty; color of natural stone = real; imitation = false instead of real; *à la mode;* "Victoria brown" = imitation of freestone; pleasing variety of expression achieved with shades of neutral tints; country vs. city; poor innocent republicans; Weeping Elm = loveliest of all American trees; labor strikes; *chevaux de frieze;* New England as bad example for hideous display of lightning conductors on every house; *savans*

Horticulturist *Editorials*

June 1852
"American versus British Horticulture" / pp. 249–52 / (H #13)

Subjects:

real character of a country = language, manners, & customs; U.S. spirit of liberty & progress; Old & New World; progress in horticulture; lack of American professional gardeners; need for adaptations to American climate & soil; different gardening tongues of England & America; for theorists, who know little of human nature; reason vs. habit; mulching; banish ignorance by setting an example

July 1852
"How to Popularize the Taste for Planting" / pp. 297–301 / (T #2)

- Mrs. [Felicia Dorothea] Hemans
- Lord [Francis] Bacon (quotation)

Subjects:

England as exemplar of rural beauty; taste for things above the merely useful; newness of American civilization; taste, time, & means = beautiful human habitations; want of knowledge; primogeniture; taste is contagious; Boston as exemplar in pretty rural homes; how to enjoy a little well; sentiment; influence of private individuals, nurserymen, & horticultural societies; amateur; a taste for improving; the effects of opium or tobacco on confirmed *habitués;* millennium; Saxony as exemplar for individuals planting for public good; *matériel*

August 1852
"Shade Trees in Cities" / pp. 345–49 / (T #5)

- Herod
- ★ Fisher family, Wakefield, near Philadelphia
- Zenobia [queen of Palmyra]

Subjects:

down with the Ailanthus; Mason & Dixon's line; fair outside & treacherous heart of the Asiatics; patriotic objection; more noble native American trees vs. miserable pigtail of an Indiaman; down with the Abeles Poplar; beauty of native shade trees; business of the nurseryman vs. duty of the planter; take refuge in the American maples; Tulip Tree; transplanting; true sportsman needs skill & preparation

NOTES

A. J. Downing, *A Treatise on the Theory and Practice of Landscape Gardening, Adapted to North America*, is indicated by *LG*, with the various editions distinguished by date of publication.

Unless otherwise noted, pieces in the *Horticulturist* are by A. J. Downing. The letters from A. J. Downing to John Jay Smith in the Smith Manuscript Collection at the Library Company of Philadelphia on deposit at the Historical Society of Pennsylvania, Philadelphia, are indicated by "Downing to Smith, LCP in HSP"; quoted by permission of the Library Company of Philadelphia. Joseph Sill, Diary in 10 vols., Manuscript Collection, Historical Society of Pennsylvania, Philadelphia, is indicated by "Sill in HSP"; quoted by permission of the Historical Society of Pennsylvania. A. J. and Caroline Downing letters in the Houghton Library Manuscript Collection are quoted by permission of the Houghton Library, Harvard University. The letters from A. J. Downing to Luther Tucker (7 AlsS from Andrew Jackson Downing to Luther Tucker, 1849–1850, General Manuscripts [Misc.], Box: DO, Folder: Downing, Andrew Jackson, Manuscripts Division, Department of Rare Books and Special Collections, Princeton University Libraries) are indicated by "Downing to Tucker, Princeton University"; quoted by permission of Princeton University Libraries.

ABBREVIATIONS

AM	*Architectural Magazine*
CLGM	*Columbian Lady's and Gentleman's Magazine*
EG	J. C. Loudon, *An Encyclopedia of Gardening*
GC	*Gardeners' Chronicle*
GLGM	*Graham's Lady's and Gentleman's Magazine*
GM	*Gardener's Magazine, and Register of Rural and Domestic Improvement*
Godey's	*Godey's Lady's Book, and Ladies' American Magazine* (1840–43); *Godey's Magazine and Lady's Book* (1844–50); *Godey's Lady's Book* (1851–52)
Gs'M	*Gardeners' Magazine of Botany, Horticulture, Floriculture, and Natural Science*
Hort	*Horticulturist and Journal of Rural Art and Rural Taste*
JGH	*Journal of Garden History*
LG	*A Treatise on the Theory and Practice of Landscape Gardening, Adapted to North America*
NAR	*North American Review*
NYM	*New-York Mirror*
SG	J. C. Loudon, *The Suburban Gardener*
USMDR	*United States Magazine and Democratic Review*

INTRODUCTION

1

"American versus British Horticulture," *Hort* 7 (June 1852): 249; *LG* (1844, 493–95) contained a new Appendix 4, "Note on professional quackery," condemning "a mode . . . like that of Germany" employed by "a foreign *soi-disant* landscape gardener." Downing claimed that the simple grand beauty of a fine river residence had been completely spoiled. George B. Tatum suggests that the complaint was directed at Hans Jacob Ehlers, who worked at Montgomery Place. See Tatum, "Nature's Gardener," in *Prophet with Honor: The Career of Andrew Jackson Downing 1815–1852,* ed. George B. Tatum and Elisabeth Blair MacDougall (Washington, D.C.: Dumbarton Oaks, 1989), 67–68fn.

2

"Introduction," *Hort* 1 (July 1846): 9. On Whigs versus Jacksonian Democrats in the 1840s, see Christine Stansell and Sean Wilentz, "Cole's America: An Introduction," in *Thomas Cole: Landscape into History,* ed. William Truettner and Alan Wallach (New Haven: Yale University Press, 1994), 14–17.

3

The opening quotation is from the first line of the preface to A. J. Downing, *The Fruits and Fruit-Trees of America* (New York & London: Wiley & Putnam, 1845). After Downing's death his friend and colleague Marshall P. Wilder, president of the Massachusetts Horticultural Society, solicited information for a eulogy, and the responses are in the Smith Manuscript Collection. See Charles Downing to Marshall P. Wilder, 24 August 1852, LCP in HSP, vol. 14, p. 129. With this letter are notes that Caroline Downing gave to Charles; Notes by Calvert Vaux to Marshall P. Wilder, [1852], LCP in HSP, vol. 14, p. 124. Detailed biographical information can be found in David Schuyler, *Apostle of Taste: Andrew Jackson Downing 1815–1852* (Baltimore: Johns Hopkins University Press, 1996), 9–27; also see Tatum, "Introduction: The Downing Decade," in Tatum and MacDougall, eds., *Prophet with Honor,* 1–42.

4

J. C. Loudon, in *GM* 7 (April 1831): 177, as quoted in Melanie Louise Simo, *Loudon and the Landscape: From Country Seat to Metropolis: 1783–1843* (New Haven: Yale University Press, 1988), 133; N. P. Willis, "Sale of Mr. Downing's Residence," *Hort* 7 (November 1852): 528. Journalist, poet, and editor Nathaniel Parker Willis (1806–1867) also befriended Edgar Allan Poe, whom he employed at his daily newspaper the *New York Evening Mirror.* See Cortland P. Auser, *Nathaniel P. Willis* (New York: Twayne Publishers, 1969).

5

Review of *A Discourse, delivered at the Plymouth Church, Brooklyn, N.Y.,* by Henry Ward Beecher, *Hort* 2 (February 1848): 376; review of *A Manual of the Botany of the Northern States,* by Asa Gray, *Hort* 2 (April 1848): 474.

PART I

1

[Parke Godwin], "Landscape Gardening and Rural Architecture," *USMDR* 9 (December 1841): 554; "Landscape Gardening and Rural Architecture in America," *USMDR* 16 (April 1845): 348. Downing (*LG,* 1841, 20) pointed out the only other American work treating "directly of landscape gardening" published before his: Bernard M'Mahon, *American Gardener's Calendar* (Philadelphia: Printed by B. Graves, 1806), 55–72. On M'Mahon, see Brenda Bullion, "Early American farming and gardening literature," *JGH* 12 (January–March 1992): 29–51. Downing (*LG,* 1841, 21) also mentioned André Parmentier, whose article appeared in Thomas G. Fessenden, *The New American Gardener* (Boston: J. B. Russell, 1828), 184–87. The article was also included in Parmentier's own nursery catalogue. Ann Leighton reprints this essay in *American Gardens of the Nineteenth Century* (Amherst: University of Massachusetts Press, 1987), 129–32. On Parmentier, see Therese O'Malley, "Art and Science in the Design of Botanic Gardens, 1730–1830," in *Garden History,* ed. John Dixon Hunt (Washington, D.C.: Dumbarton Oaks, 1992), 297–98.

2

Tatum suggests that Downing is the author of an article signed XYZ, "Rural Embellishments," *New-York Farmer* 5 (1832): 329–30. See introduction, in Tatum and MacDougall, eds., *Prophet with Honor,* 21. Articles by Downing in the journal edited by C. M. Hovey and P. B. Hovey, Jr. included "On the employment of Ornamental Trees and Shrubs in North America," *American Gardener's Magazine* 1 (December 1835): 444–52. This article had been published the previous year in the *New England Farmer* and reprinted in translation in the *Annales de Fromont*. Also see "On the Cultivation of Hedges in the United States," *Magazine of Horticulture* 4 (February 1838): 41–44 [now edited by C. M. Hovey]. The Hoveys published seventeen pieces in all from 1835 to 1841. Downing contributed four notices to J. C. Loudon's *Gardener's Magazine* from 1838 to 1841. [Charles Francis Adams], "Downing on Landscape Gardening," *NAR* 53 (July 1841): 262.

3

Downing's 1836 letter (no detailed date is given) to the Hoveys is quoted in C. M. Hovey, "Arboricultural Notices," *MH* 25 (March 1859): 134, on the occasion of H. W. Sargent's 1859 edition of the *Treatise;* A. J. Downing, "Notices on the State and Progress of Horticulture in the United States," *MH* 3 (January 1837): 8. In the novel *Home as Found* (1838), James Fenimore Cooper similarly pointed out that although the climate and forests of America offered so many inducements to encourage landscape gardening, it was the branch of ornamental art "perhaps the least known in this country." As quoted in Blake Nevius, *Cooper's Landscapes* (Berkeley: University of California Press, 1976), 68.

4

Downing's October 1838 letter to the Hoveys is quoted in C. M. Hovey, "Arboricultural Notices," *MH* 25 (March 1859): 134. A. J. Downing to A. J. Davis, 12 December 1838, and A. J. Downing to Judge Buel, 2 August 1838, are both quoted in George Bishop Tatum, "A. J. Downing: Arbiter of American Taste, 1815–1852" (Ph.D. diss., Princeton University, 1950), 53–54, 255. Downing wrote to Judge Jesse Buel (1778–1839), editor of the *Cultivator,* requesting a loan of Loudon's *Suburban Gardener:* "I believe it has . . . scarcely found its way into this country—at least I cannot learn of any subscribers in N.Y. (all his other publications we have)."

5

[Luther Tucker], "Mr. Downing and the Horticulturist," *Hort* 7 (September 1852): 394; A. J. Downing, "Notices on the State and Progress of Horticulture in the United States," *MH* 3 (January 1837): 9; Alexis de Tocqueville, *Democracy in America,* the Henry Reeve text as revised by Francis Bowen, 2 vols. (New York: Alfred A. Knopf, 1945), 2: 55. Volume 1 of the American edition was originally published in 1838, and volume 2 appeared in 1840. Henry Reeve translated the first American edition. Harriet Martineau, *Society in America,* 3 vols. (London: Saunders and Otley, 1837), 3: 217; William E. Channing, "Remarks on National Literature" (1830), in *The Works,* vol. 1 (Boston: James Munroe & Co., 1841), 260. Channing (1780–1842) felt that the nation gained immensely from having men of distinguished intellect "among its own sons."

6

Ralph Waldo Emerson, "The American Scholar" (1837), in *Complete Works,* vol. 1 (Boston: Houghton Mifflin Co., 1903), 81; "The Great Nation of Futurity," *USMDR* 6 (November 1839): 428; on the writers who contributed to the *Democratic Review,* see Russel Blaine Nye, *Society and Culture in America: 1830–1860* (New York: Harper & Row, 1974), 79. For a study of "the attempt of American authors, critics, and patriots to design and foster a national literature during the three centuries after the first settlements," see Benjamin T. Spencer, *The Quest for Nationality* (Syracuse, N.Y.: Syracuse University Press, 1957); "Landscape Gardening and Rural Architecture," *USMDR* 9 (December 1841): 554.

7

For example, see A. Davezac, "A Chapter on Gardening," *USMDR* 12 (February 1843): 122–28; J. C. Loudon, "Summary View of the Progress of Gardening," *GM* 17 (December 1841): 592; "Review of New Books," *GLGM* 32 (March 1848): 191; J. J. King, "Downing's Fruits and

Fruit-Trees of America," *Cultivator* 3 (May 1846): 149; "Downing on Landscape Gardening," *NAR* 53 (July 1841): 258.

8

LG (1841), i–ii; "Landscape Gardening and Rural Architecture in America," *USMDR* 16 (April 1845): 361, 358.

CHAPTER 1

1

For a discussion of "Victorian interest in the arts of persuasion," see Daniel Walker Howe, ed., *Victorian America* (Philadelphia: University of Pennsylvania Press, 1976), 25. Review of *A Treatise on the Theory and Practice of Landscape Gardening,* by A. J. Downing, *NYM* 19 (22 May 1841): 161–62; "Landscape Gardening and Rural Architecture," *USMDR* 9 (December 1841): 555–56. In a review of the second edition of Downing's *Treatise* and *Cottage Residences,* the *Democratic Review* proclaimed: "Gardening and architecture are arts that promote a genuine patriotism." See "Landscape Gardening and Rural Architecture in America," *USMDR* 16 (April 1845): 356; *LG* (1841), i, iii, 10.

2

LG (1841), iii–iv. Downing ultimately settled on an acreage of fifty to five hundred in *LG* (1844), 11. In the first edition, the number varied from five to five hundred acres (1841, 10) to fifty to three hundred acres (1841, 55).

3

"Landscape Gardening and Rural Architecture," *USMDR* 9 (December 1841): 556. Horatio Greenough, "Remarks on American Art," *USMDR* 13 (July 1843): 45.

4

Downing to Smith, 21 May 1842, LCP in HSP. For the 1840 Log Cabin campaign, see Donald Barr Chidsey, *And Tyler Too* (Nashville: Thomas Nelson, 1978), 30; and Richard L. Bushman, *The Refinement of America* (New York: Vintage Books, 1993), 425–31. Francis Bacon, "Of Gardens" (1625), in *Essays* (New York: Hurst & Co., 1883),

194. Downing quotes Bacon in "How to Popularize the Taste for Planting," *Hort* 7 (July 1852): 297.

5

LG (1841), i, 298.

6

"Country seats," *NYM* 12 (11 April 1835): 327. An article signed by Downing appeared later: "The Dans-Kamer," *NYM* 13 (10 October 1835): 117–18.

7

[Susan Fenimore Cooper], *Rural Hours* (New York: George P. Putnam, 1851), 215; "Landscape Gardening and Rural Architecture," *USMDR* 9 (December 1841): 555. Tocqueville (1945, 1: 249) noted during his 1831 tour of the U.S. that "amelioration and progress [were] the topics of inquiry."

8

LG (1841), i–ii; Johnaphene Faulkner, as quoted in Sandra L. Myres, *Westering Women and the Frontier Experience, 1800–1915* (Albuquerque: University of New Mexico Press, 1982), 142. See also Solon Robinson, "To Western Emigrants," *Cultivator* 7 (October 1840), reprinted in *Solon Robinson: Pioneer and Agriculturist,* ed. Herbert Anthony Kellar, vol. 1: 1825–1845 (Indianapolis: Indiana Historical Bureau, 1936), 140. For other contemporary descriptions of American conditions see J. S. Buckingham, *The Eastern and Western States of America,* 3 vols. (London & Paris: Fisher, Son, & Co., 1842); Francis J. Grund, *The Americans in Their Moral, Social, and Political Relations,* 2 vols. (London: Longman, Rees, Orme, Brown, Green, & Longman, 1837); Charles Lyell, *Travels in North America,* 2 vols. (London: John Murray, 1845); and Captain Marryat, *A Diary in America,* 2 vols. (Philadelphia: Carey & Hart, 1839).

9

"Landscape Gardening and Rural Architecture," *USMDR* 9 (December 1841): 555; Horatio Greenough, "Remarks on American Art," *USMDR* 13 (July 1843): 45.

10

Tocqueville, 1945, 2: 36; Francis Lieber, *The Stranger in*

America, 2 vols. (London: Richard Bentley, 1835), 1: 282; Michael Chevalier, *Society, Manners, and Politics in the United States* (Boston: Weeks, Jordan & Co., 1839), 277, 280; "Landscape Gardening and Rural Architecture in America," *USMDR* 16 (April 1845): 349.

11
See for example *NYM* 19 (22 May 1841): 161–62, and the review of Downing's second edition of the *Treatise* in "Landscape Gardening," *Cultivator* 2 (March 1845): 80–84; Washington Irving to Sarah Storrow, 23 Aug. 1847, in Washington Irving, *Complete Works,* ed. Richard Dilworth Rust, letters, vol. 4, 1846–1859 (Boston: Twayne Publishers, 1982), 144; Joseph Sill, 16 May 1845, 6: 222, and 29 Aug. 1848, 8: 280, in Sill in HSP; Nicholas B. Wainwright, ed., *A Philadelphia Perspective: The Diary of Sidney George Fisher* (Philadelphia: Historical Society of Pennsylvania, 1967), 200–1. On Sweetbrier (built in 1797), see the November 1962 issue of *Antiques,* which is dedicated to the houses of Fairmount Park; Adolph B. Benson, ed., "Fredrika Bremer's Unpublished Letters to the Downings," *Scandinavian Studies and Notes* 11 (February 1931): 150.

12
LG (1841), iii, 296–97; "The Vineyards of the West," *Hort* 5 (August 1850): 57; Martineau, 2: 31. On property as "the most critical variable in locating white Americans," see Robert H. Wiebe, *The Opening of American Society* (New York: Alfred A. Knopf, 1984), 324; and Howard Mumford Jones, *O Strange New World* (New York: Viking Press, 1964), 155–61, 189–90, 352–53.

13
LG (1841), 19; *LG* (1844), 28, with minor word changes; *LG* (1849), 39; "Mr. Downing's Letters from England," *Hort* 5 (October 1850): 158. For a discussion of American ideas of property and political thought that supports Downing's observations, see A. Whitney Griswold, *Farming and Democracy* (New York: Harcourt, Brace & Co., 1948), 36.

14
Sill, 18 Sept. 1845, 6: 328, Sill in HSP; John Quincy Adams, *Memoirs,* ed. Charles Francis Adams, vol. 10 (Philadelphia: J. B. Lippincott & Co., 1876), 346; Mrs. H. Marion Ward, "Home," *GLGM* 32 (February 1848): 129.

15
James K. Paulding, "The Quiet Home," *CLGM* 5 (January 1846): 35; "Landscape Gardening and Rural Architecture in America," *USMDR* 16 (April 1845): 356; Mrs. M. St. Leon Loud, "The Voices of Home," *USMDR* 8 (August 1840): 135. Concerning the "home feeling," see also S. B. Parsons, *Address* (New Haven: n.p., 1849), 5–6.

16
Henry P. Tappan, *A Step from the New World to the Old, and Back Again,* 2 vols. (New York: D. Appleton & Co., 1852), 1: 202; Lieber, 1: 68; Mrs. Lydia H. Sigourney, "Horticulture," *Godey's* 21 (October 1840): 179.

17
LG (1841), ii; Tocqueville, 1945, 2: 4, as quoted in *LG* (1841), iii. A belief in a continental destiny became a principal ingredient in American nationalism after the War for Independence. See Henry Nash Smith, *Virgin Land* (Cambridge: Harvard University Press, 1950), 9.

18
Lewis F. Allen, *Address* (Albany: Weed, Parsons & Co., 1849), 32; Marryat, 1: 14; Charles Augustus Murray, *Travels in North America,* 2 vols. (London: Richard Bentley, 1839), 1: 148; Henry Meigs, *Address* (New York: James Van Norden & Co., 1845), 6; Allen, 32; *LG* (1841), 25fn; *LG* (1844), 40fn–41fn; and *LG* (1849), 55fn.

19
"Influence of Horticulture," *Hort* 2 (July 1847): 9; Tocqueville, 1945, 2: 137, as quoted in "Influence of Horticulture," 10.

20
N. Parker Willis, *The Rag-Bag* (New York: Charles Scribner, 1855), 36. This book collects articles written in the late 1840s for the *Home Journal.*

21
LG (1841), ii, 10; "Hints to Rural Improvers," *Hort* 3 (July 1848): 9.

22

G. R. Nicholl, "Town and Country Contrasted," *Godey's* 43 (September 1851): 176; review of *Rural Letters*, by N. P. Willis, *Literary World* 4 (21 April 1849): 353; Linda S. Ferber, "Themes in American Genre Painting: 1840–80," *Apollo* 115 (April 1982): 250. For a description of Horace's life on his Sabine Farm, see Edward Townsend Booth, *God Made the Country* (New York: Alfred A. Knopf, 1946), 21–28. For a discussion of agricultural literature inspired by the classical back-to-nature tradition, see Paul H. Johnstone, "The Rural Socrates," *Journal of the History of Ideas* 5 (April 1944): 152.

23

LG (1841), 334–35. The notice was reworded and moved into the "Historical Sketches" section in *LG* (1844), 38, and *LG* (1849), 51. George P. Morris, "New York in the Dog Days: Rime of the Auncient Editour," *Godey's* 41 (September 1850): 180; Washington Irving to Sabina O'Shea, 8 Nov. 1846, in Irving, *Works,* 4: 105; Irving to Henry Lee, Jr., 18 Dec. 1850, in Irving, *Works,* 4: 237. On Sunnyside, see Robert M. Toole, "An American Cottage Ornée: Washington Irving's Sunnyside, 1835–1859," *JGH* 12 (January–March 1992): 52–72. Sunnyside, Tarrytown, New York, is now a property of Historic Hudson Valley, a nonprofit educational organization.

24

William Cowper (1731–1800) illustrated the pleasures of country life in *The Task*. The line appears near the end of book 1. See William Cowper, *The Task* (London: Printed for J. Johnson, 1785; reprint, London: Scolar Press Facsimile, 1973). Downing used this phrase in the opening paragraphs of "Introduction," *Hort* 1 (July 1846): 9. Miss C. M. Sedgwick, "Country Life," *Godey's* 36 (April 1848): 221; "Rural retirement, gardens, etc.," *NYM* 12 (6 June 1835): 391.

25

Historians including Neil Harris, Paul H. Johnstone, Perry Miller, and Roderick Nash note this exaggerated comparison of country and city life. H. W. Rockwell, "City Life," *Godey's* 37 (July 1848): 36; Morris, "New York in the Dog Days," 180; Emerson, *Nature* (1836), in *Works,* 1: 16.

26

Unlike the Greek attachment to the *polis*, "enthusiasm for the American city has not been typical or predominant in our intellectual history." See Morton White and Lucia White, *The Intellectual Versus the City* (Cambridge: Harvard University Press, 1962), 1. For the Wall Street versus West Point quotation, see "Town and Country," *NYM* 13 (10 October 1835): 119. For Downing's comments on the city versus the country, see "The New-York Park," *Hort* 6 (August 1851): 346; "Hints to Rural Improvers," *Hort* 3 (July 1848): 9; and *LG* (1841), iii. For the reference to a "moss-covered bucket," see A Mississippi Reader, "Public Parks and Gardens," *Hort* 3 (January 1849): 347.

27

Gunther Barth, *City People* (New York: Oxford University Press, 1980), 21–22; Tocqueville, 1945, 1: 289.

28

Review of *European Agriculture and Rural Economy,* Parts 1 to 7, by Henry Colman, *Hort* 1 (March 1847): 424–26; Henry Colman, *European Agriculture and Rural Economy,* 2nd ed. (Boston: Charles C. Little & James Brown, 1849), 251; "Landscape Gardening and Rural Architecture in America," *USMDR* 16 (April 1845): 350. This reviewer also cited Henry Colman's European agricultural survey. See also "Corner Loungers," *USMDR* 13 (August 1843): facing 154, and "The Card Players," *USMDR* 13 (November 1843): facing 451; Nicholl, "Town and Country Contrasted," *Godey's* 43 (September 1851): 176; Mrs. C. H. Butler, "Retribution," *CLGM* 7 (November 1847): 208.

29

Parsons, 4; "Landscape Gardening and Rural Architecture in America," *USMDR* 16 (April 1845): 363; Lydia H. Sigourney, "Taste," *Godey's* 20 (February 1840): 88. For an explanation of the Book's lessons, see John Mason Good, *The Book of Nature* (New York: J. & J. Harper, 1831); Warren Burton, *The District School as It Was* (Boston: T. R. Marvin, 1852), 313; Miss C. M. Sedgwick, "Country Life," *Godey's* 36 (April 1848): 221. On Downing's friendship with Sedgwick, see Downing to Smith, 21 Oct. 1842, LCP in HSP; "Landscape Gardening and Rural Architecture in America," *USMDR* 16 (April 1845): 348.

30

LG (1841), iii–iv; "Landscape Gardening and Rural Architecture in America," *USMDR* 16 (April 1845): 349.

31

"Landscape Gardening," *Cultivator* 2 (March 1845): 80; "Landscape Gardening and Rural Architecture in America," *USMDR* 16 (April 1845): 357; *LG* (1841), iii–iv.

32

"On the Moral Influence of Good Houses," *Hort* 2 (February 1848): 347. Fredrika Bremer related the story about the workingman's house in *Homes of the New World,* trans. Mary Howitt, 2 vols. (New York: Harper & Bros., 1854), 1: 48; Washington Irving, "Rural Life in England," *Godey's* 38 (January 1849): 23.

33

For Downing's "first-class" remark, see "The New-York Park," *Hort* 6 (August 1851): 349. On class and status in America, see Bushman, 402–47; and Henry Nash Smith, 215. The story of the Taylors is told in Mary Win Walter Norris, "A Present from the Past," *Fine Gardening,* January/February 1990, 46–50.

34

Many observers stated that all Americans started out on equal footing and that every honest exertion resulted in its adequate reward. See Bremer, 1: 48; Chevalier, 287; Grund, 1: 279, and 2: 161; Marryat, 1: 12; and Martineau, 2: 353. Tocqueville most lucidly formulated the egalitarian thesis, according to Edward Pessen, "The Egalitarian Myth and the American Social Reality," in *The Many-Faceted Jacksonian Era: New Interpretations,* ed. Edward Pessen (Westport, Conn.: Greenwood Press, 1977), 7–46. Pessen draws evidence from a variety of sources and discloses a society, at least in the great cities of the Northeast, markedly unlike the egalitarian one depicted by Tocqueville and others. "On the Moral Influence of Good Houses," *Hort* 2 (February 1848): 346; *LG* (1841), 26; *LG* (1844), 12, 45, 60; and *LG* (1849), 20, 60, 78–79.

35

LG (1844), 10–11; and *LG* (1849), 18–19.

36

Johann Wolfgang von Goethe, as quoted in A. J. Downing, *Cottage Residences* (New York & London: Wiley & Putnam, 1842), ii. The source of this quotation may have been "Architectural Maxims," *AM* 1 (November 1834): 351, although the translation from the German varies slightly. Downing dropped the end of the last sentence: "the generality of people take delight in silly and insipid things, provided they be new." Perhaps he did not want to insult the people of obviously good taste who had purchased his new book.

37

LG (1844), 37, 39–40; and *LG* (1849), 50, 52, 54.

38

LG (1844), 12; and *LG* (1849), 20; "A Few Words on Rural Architecture," *Hort* 5 (July 1850): 11. This editorial referred to the recently published *Architecture of Country Houses.* Prince von Pückler Muskau, "Observations on Landscape Gardening," *GM* 12 (February 1836): 92.

39

LG (1841), ii, 20; *LG* (1844), 29; and *LG* (1849), 40.

40

N. P. Willis, *Out-Doors at Idlewild* (New York: Charles Scribner, 1855), 213.

41

[N. P. Willis,] "How to Make a Paradise in the Country," *Hort* 1 (June 1847): 552; *LG* (1841), i, 262; review of *Landscape Gardening* and *Cottage Residences,* by A. J. Downing, *NAR* 56 (January 1843): 13.

42

J. C. Loudon, *The Suburban Gardener, and Villa Companion* (London: Longman, Orme, Brown, Green & Longmans, 1838), 136; *LG* (1841), 42, 28–29. Downing strengthened this statement by making a slight change in *LG* (1844), 47–48: "To attempt the *smallest* work in any art, without knowing either the capacities of that art, or the schools, or modes, by which it has previously been characterized" [my emphasis].

43

Edmund Burke, *A Philosophical Inquiry into the Origin of Our Ideas of the Sublime and Beautiful,* ed., introd., and notes by James T. Boulton (Oxford: Basil Blackwell, 1987), 13. See also David Hume, "Of the Standard of Taste," in *Four Dissertations* (London: Printed for A. Millar, 1757; reprint, New York: Garland Publishing, 1970); "Hints to Rural Improvers," *Hort* 3 (July 1848): 11.

44

Downing to Smith, 15 Nov. 1841 and 21 Oct. 1842, LCP in HSP.

45

Wainwright, 223–24, 227–28. An 1852 Landreth Nursery catalogue lists the prices of various agricultural, horticultural, botanical, and rural publications: Downing's *Cottage Residences,* $2; Downing's *Fruits and Fruit-Trees,* $1.50; Loudon's *Encyclopedia of Agriculture,* $10; and Dana's *Muck Manual,* $1. For a description of Springside, see Harvey K. Flad, "Matthew Vassar's Springside: '. . . the hand of Art, when guided by Taste,'" in Tatum and MacDougall, eds., *Prophet with Honor,* 219–57.

46

For the "elegant and graceful style" comment, see *NYM* 19 (22 May 1841): 161; for the comparison of Downing to Reynolds, see "Landscape Gardening and Rural Architecture in America," *USMDR* 16 (April 1845): 348; "Trees, in Towns and Villages," *Hort* 1 (March 1847): 424. See section 4, "Deciduous Ornamental Trees," and section 5, "Evergreen Ornamental Trees," in all editions of *LG,* referred to in "Landscape Gardening and Rural Architecture in America," 361.

47

"Landscape Gardening," *Cultivator* 2 (March 1845): 84; *LG* (1841), 45; and *LG* (1844), 67; review of *Landscape Gardening* and *Cottage Residences,* by A. J. Downing, *NAR* 56 (January 1843): 1. For the "accustomed vision" remark, see "On the Improvement of Country Villages," *Hort* 3 (June 1849): 546.

CHAPTER 2

1

LG (1841), ii; Bremer (1: 17) reported that during her trip to the New World in 1849 she relied on Downing for assistance in understanding "the conditions and the questions" of the United States.

2

Howe (3–4) states that in the Victorian period, "reflective Americans worried lest their culture be insufficiently distinctive to sustain a proper national identity." For a discussion of nationalism and the arts in America, see Jones (313, 328); and F. O. Matthiessen, *American Renaissance* (New York: Oxford University Press, 1941; reprint, New York: Oxford University Press, 1980); "Traits of American Authorship," *Literary World* 1 (17 April 1847): 245.

3

James Marston Fitch, *Historic Preservation* (New York: McGraw Hill, 1982), 268. Washington Irving experienced and wrote about rural life in England and did not hesitate to defer to its superiority in this regard: "The rudest habitation, the most unpromising and scanty portion of land, in the hands of an Englishman of taste, becomes a little paradise." As quoted in *LG* (1841), 332. Prince Pückler-Muskau also found England far superior "in respect to desirable and . . . gentlemanly enjoyments, particularly in reference to a country life." Loudon published these remarks, translated from the German, in "Observations on Landscape Gardening," *GM* 12 (February 1836): 85; *LG* (1841), ii.

4

The description of Cheshunt Cottage reprinted in appendix 2 in *LG* (1841), 413–51, originally appeared in *GM* 15 (December 1839): 633–74.

5

Thomas Whately's *Observations on Modern Gardening* appeared in 1770, but late seventeenth-century France had already witnessed "the quarrel of the ancients and moderns" in architecture. "The history of garden design is bedeviled by problems of nomenclature even more than that of other arts," Kenneth Woodbridge notes in "The Nomenclature of Style in Garden History," in *British and American Gardens in the Eighteenth Century,* ed. Robert P. Maccubbin and Peter Martin (Williamsburg, Va.: Colonial Williamsburg Foundation, 1984), 19.

6

LG (1841), iv. Downing quoted extensively from J. C. Loudon's *Encyclopedia of Gardening* (1835), *Suburban Gardener* (1838), *Arboretum et Fruticetum Britannicum* (1838), and two London-based journals, *The Gardener's Magazine* (1826–43) and *The Architectural Magazine* (1834–38).

7

Mrs. Hofland, *White-Knights* (London: Printed for His Grace the Duke of Marlborough, [1819]), 1; as quoted with slight word changes in *LG* (1841), 9–10. Loudon used the same Hofland quotation in the introduction to *EG,* 2. A contemporary reported that Downing owned a copy of *White-Knights,* "a work very rare in this country." See "Residence of A. J. Downing, Botanical gardens and Nurseries, Newburgh, New York," *MH* 7 (November 1841): 407; Jacques Delille, *Les Jardins* (Paris: Michaud Frères, 1813), 53, as quoted in *LG* (1841), 9. The name is variously spelled De Lille or De Lisle. Downing or his wife Caroline evidently had a knowledge of French, for his library contained volumes of the *Annales Horticole de Fromont,* the publication of the Chevalier Soulange Bodin's institution for young horticulturists, and a copy of M. Loiseleur-Deslongchamps, *L'Herbier général de l'amateur* (Paris: H. Cousin, 1839–44). This series contained colored illustrations of new, rare, and interesting plants from European gardens.

8

Delille's *Les Jardins* was much admired by English devotees of gardening. Delille in turn was an admirer of Thomas Whately. See Elizabeth Wheeler Manwaring, *Italian Landscape in Eighteenth Century England* (New York: Oxford University Press, 1925), 164. On Versailles, see *LG* (1841), 12. Downing's description of Versailles was culled from Loudon, *EG,* 83.

9

LG (1841), 29, 50, 52; Delille (3) similarly disparages "la partie mécanique de l'art des jardins." M'Mahon, 66; Hofland, 1.

10

Loudon, *SG,* 168–69; review of *An Essay on the Nature, the End, and the Means of Imitation in the Fine Arts,* by Quatremère de Quincy, *GM* 13 (December 1837): 600; review of *Cottage Residences,* by A. J. Downing, *GM* 18 (November 1842): 570; *LG* (1841), 54.

11

LG (1841), 14, 16, 16fn. Downing's main text and footnote on Addison and Pope followed the lead of Loudon (*EG,* 319). Joseph Addison, no. 411, *Spectator,* 21 June 1712, and no. 414, 25 June 1712, in *The Spectator,* ed. G. Gregory Smith, 4 vols. (New York: E. P. Dutton, 1909), 3: 56, 65–66, 68. For a concise view of the development of the English landscape garden, see the introduction to John Dixon Hunt and Peter Willis, eds., *The Genius of the Place* (Cambridge: MIT Press, 1988). Also see Walter John Hipple, Jr., *The Beautiful, the Sublime, and the Picturesque in Eighteenth-Century British Aesthetic Theory* (Carbondale: Southern Illinois University Press, 1957); and Heinz-Joachim Müllenbrock, "The 'Englishness' of the English landscape garden and the genetic role of literature: a reassessment," *JGH* 8 (October–December 1988): 97–103.

12

LG (1841), 16, 50; Alexander Pope, no. 173, *Guardian* (29 September 1713) in *Works,* 10 vols. (London: John Murray, 1886), 10: 530–33. This is one instance in which Downing's use of the term *ancient* for the despised artificial mode can cause confusion. Pope actually held up as a standard the taste of the ancients in their gardens. Furthermore, John Dixon Hunt argues that Pope's garden at Twickenham is an expression of traditional ideas, with a debt to Rome. See John Dixon Hunt, "Pope's Twickenham Revisited," in Maccubbin and Martin, eds., 26; Alexander Pope, "Epistle IV to Richard Boyle, Earl of Burlington," in *Epistles to Several Persons,* ed. F. W. Bateson (New Haven: Yale University Press, 1951), 144, as quoted in *LG* (1841), 51.

13

LG (1841), 14–17. These men were typically cited; see Loudon, *EG,* 318: "Mason the poet states, in a note to the English Garden, that 'Bacon was the prophet, Milton the herald, of modern gardening; and Addison, Pope, and Kent, the champions of true taste.'" Lines 223 through 268, book 4, of Milton's *Paradise Lost* were quoted in *LG* (1841), 15–16. Richard E. Quaintance remarks: "For over half a century the Eden of Book IV of *Paradise Lost* had been cited as England's discovery of its proper model." See his "Walpole's Whig Interpretation of Landscaping History," *Studies in Eighteenth-Century Culture* 9 (1979): 292. For the *jardin anglo-chinois,* see Christopher Hussey, *The Picturesque* (London: Frank Cass & Co., 1967), 151–60; Arthur O. Lovejoy, "The Chinese Origin of a Romanticism," in *Essays in the History of Ideas* (Baltimore: Johns Hopkins University Press, 1948; reprint, New York: Capricorn Books, 1960), 113; Manwaring, 121; and Dora Wiebenson, *The Picturesque Garden in France* (Princeton: Princeton University Press, 1978), 39–63. The "Asiatics" comment is in "Shade Trees in Cities," *Hort* 7 (August 1852), 345.

14

LG (1841), 17.

15

Thomas Whately, *Observations on Modern Gardening* (London: Printed for T. Payne, 1770; reprint, New York: Garland Publishing, 1982), 52, 96–97, 136–37, 256. Downing (*LG,* 1841, 90, 264fn) cited Whately on variety and contrast in trees and praised his treatment of improving ground. For a discussion of the problem of "how to intensify Nature without distorting it; how to attain the universal without abandoning the particular," see Basil Willey, *The Eighteenth Century Background* (New York: Columbia University Press, 1962), 21. See also Norman Crowe, *Nature and the Idea of a Man-Made World* (Cambridge: MIT Press, 1995), 15, 18; Delille, 51. This particular passage was not quoted by Downing. See Delille in *LG* (1841), 28, 272, 292, 392, and 402.

16

LG (1841), 18–19. Humphry Repton started work in 1813 at Ashridge Park, Hertfordshire. J. C. Loudon's *The Landscape Gardening and Architecture of the Late Humphry Repton* (London: Longman & Co., 1840) contained descriptions of both Ashridge (525–36) and Woburn Abbey (536–57). It is unlikely that Downing saw this book until after the 1841 *Treatise* was in press.

17

LG (1841), 21–22, 19. On primogeniture, see Alexis de Tocqueville, *Democracy in America,* ed. J. P. Mayer and trans. George Lawrence (New York: Harper & Row Perennial Library, 1988), 721; and Griswold, 42–45.

18

Tocqueville, 1945, 1: 48–50; Martineau, 3: 37.

19

Buckingham (2: 152) recorded the exception that he encountered: "Mr. Charles Carroll was himself the only son of an only son, and . . . he left an only son, who now possesses an only son, to whom the property of Carrollton Manor still belongs." William Wynne, "Some Account of the Nursery Gardens and the State of Horticulture in the Neighbourhood of Philadelphia," *GM* 8 (June 1832): 275.

20

LG (1841), 19–20, 22–26. Hyde Park, Waltham House, Monte Video, Joseph Bonaparte's former seat at Bordentown, New Jersey, and the residence of General Van Rensselaer were all described in Loudon, *EG,* 401–2. Downing praised the Mount Vernon of Washington's lifetime as "one of the largest and loveliest estates in America." See review of *Letters on Agriculture, from His Excellency George Washington, to Arthur Young and Sir John Sinclair, Hort* 2 (November 1847): 236–38. See also "Purchase of Mt. Vernon," *Hort* 2 (April 1848): 481: "It is . . . most strongly to be desired that this estate should become public property; that it should be restored to, and kept in the best condition."

21
LG (1841), 22. On Hyde Park, see J. E. Spingarn, "Henry Winthrop Sargent and the Landscape Tradition at Wodenethe," *Landscape Architecture* 29 (October 1938): 25. Hyde Park was cited by Alexander Gordon, "Notices of some of the principal Nurseries and private Gardens in the United States of America," *GM* 8 (June 1831): 282. The embellishments at Hyde Park disappointed the visitor in review of *A Tour through North America,* by Patrick Shirreff, *GM* 11 (April 1835): 197.

22
LG (1841), 23; Spingarn (28) attributes the design of Blithewood to Downing. Haley (13fn) reports that Donaldson employed Downing and A. J. Davis to design the landscape and structures on his estate, but Tatum is convinced that Downing did not design the landscape. See Tatum, "Nature's Gardener," in Tatum and MacDougall, eds., *Prophet with Honor,* 67. On the Livingstons, see Clare Brandt, *An American Aristocracy: The Livingstons* (Garden City, N.Y.: Doubleday & Co., 1986), 145–46, 165–66; "A Visit to Montgomery Place," *Hort* 2 (October 1847): 153–60; "Messina—A Country Seat on the Hudson," *Hort* 7 (May 1852): 230–31.

23
LG (1841), 24–26, 25fn. On Lemon Hill, see John T. Faris, *Old Gardens in and about Philadelphia* (Indianapolis: Bobbs-Merrill Co., 1932), 283–85; and Virginia Norton Naude, "Lemon Hill," *Antiques,* November 1962, 531–33. On the Boston country seats and their owners, see Tamara Plakins Thornton, *Cultivating Gentlemen: The Meaning of Country Life among the Boston Elite 1785–1860* (New Haven: Yale University Press, 1989). For Perkins's Brookline estate, see Carl Seaburg and Stanley Paterson, *Merchant Prince of Boston: Colonel T. H. Perkins, 1764–1854* (Cambridge: Harvard University Press, 1971), 389–93, 424; and Tanya Boyett, "Thomas Handasyd Perkins: An Essay on Material Culture," *Old-Time New England* 70 (1980): 45–62. The information on Monte Video was corrected in *LG* (1844, 39); Loudon, *EG,* 402; "Bordentown," *Graham's* 31 (March 1845): 131, and "View of the Delaware near Bordentown," before 97.

24
LG (1841), 27.

25
LG (1841), 29, 31–32, 34. Downing was not consistent, and a confusing variety of terms confronted the reader. Downing also referred to the "picturesque or simply beautiful" and "the elegant or picturesque."

26
Uvedale Price, *Essay on the Picturesque, as Compared with the Sublime and the Beautiful,* 3 vols. (London: Printed for J. Mawman, 1810), 1: 39; William Gilpin, *Three Essays* (London: Printed for R. Blamire, 1794; reprint, Westmead, Farnborough, Hants, England: Gregg International Publishers, 1972). In 1841 Downing did not mention Gilpin's *Essay* but included numerous citations of his *Remarks on Forest Scenery* (London: Printed for R. Blamire, Strand, 1791; reprint, New intro. by Sutherland Lyall, Richmond, Surrey: Richmond Publishing Co., 1973). See *LG* (1841), 86, 86fn, 89fn, 96, 98fn, 114, 166, 241.

27
Burke, 32–33, 39–40, 57–78. On Burke, see Samuel H. Monk, *The Sublime, a Study of Critical Theories in XVIII-Century England* (New York, 1935; reprint, Ann Arbor: University of Michigan Press, 1960), 86, 92, 98. Hipple (88) states that "before [Alexander] Gerard and Burke, no aesthetician had found the fearful, considered in itself, a source of aesthetic satisfaction."

28
Burke, 92, 113–17.

29
Ibid., 115–16; William Hogarth, *The Analysis of Beauty,* ed. and introd. Joseph Burke (Oxford: Clarendon Press, 1955), xiv, 21, 65 and illustration facing 164, 68 and illustration facing 165; also see Hipple, 56–57; *LG* (1841), 262.

30
Price, 1: 38–42, 92–93; Gilpin, *Three Essays,* 5–6.

31
Price, 1: x, 14, 22–23, 103–12; R. P. Knight, *The Landscape* (London: Printed by W. Bulmer & Co., 1794), book 1, lines 261–66, p. 16. For a defense of Capability Brown's style and techniques, see Roger Turner, *Capability Brown and the Eighteenth-Century English Landscape* (New York: Rizzoli, 1985), 68–91.

32
Price, 1: 2–3, 15–20, 44, 49–69, 83–86, 102.

33
H. Repton, *An Enquiry into the Changes of Taste in Landscape Gardening* (London: Printed for J. Taylor, 1806), 154–55; idem, *Sketches and Hints on Landscape Gardening* (London: Printed by W. Bulmer & Co., [1794]), 59–60, 64; idem, *Observations on the Theory and Practice of Landscape Gardening* (London: Printed for T. Bensley, 1803), 11.

34
LG (1841), 60, 60fn, 279fn, 284, 260.

35
Ibid., 17, 18, 32, 268. The eight rules were from Repton, *An Enquiry,* 109. For the criticism of Repton, see J. Loudon, *Observations on the Formation and Management of Useful and Ornamental Plantations* (Edinburgh: Printed for Archibald Constable & Co., 1804), 224–28, 294. On the relationship of Loudon and Repton, see Simo, 34. Frank A. Waugh mistakenly states that "Downing was influenced chiefly by Repton." See *The Landscape Beautiful* (New York: Orange Judd Co., 1912), 160. Haley (9) also links Downing to Repton: "[Downing] acquired his theoretical background in the English or 'natural' style of landscape gardening through the works of Humphrey Repton."

36
LG (1841), 29–31.

37
Ibid., 32.

38
Ibid., 31.

39
Ibid., 33, 10. For a discussion of classicism and idealistic aesthetics, see Erwin Panofsky, *Idea: A Concept in Art Theory,* trans. Joseph J. S. Peake (Columbia: University of South Carolina Press, 1968), 103–11.

40
Aristotle's "Poetics," trans., introd., and notes by James Hutton (New York: W. W. Norton & Co., 1982); Horace, *The Art of Poetry,* intro. Burton Raffel (Albany: State University of New York Press, 1974). For a discussion of the assumption that good painting, like good poetry, is the ideal imitation of human action, see Rensselaer W. Lee, *Ut Pictura Poesis* (New York: W. W. Norton & Co., 1967); and John Dixon Hunt, "Ut Pictura Poesis, Ut Pictura Hortus, and the Picturesque," in *Gardens and the Picturesque* (Cambridge: MIT Press, 1992), 105–36; Paul Oskar Kristeller, "The Modern System of the Arts: A Study in the History of Aesthetics (I)," *Journal of the History of Ideas* 12 (October 1951): 496–527; and idem, "The Modern System of the Arts (II)," *JHI* 13 (January 1952): 17–46. For "The Three Sister Arts and the Picturesque," see Isabel Wakelin Urban Chase, *Horace Walpole: Gardenist* (Princeton: Princeton University Press, 1943), 105ff. On imitation, see Irving Babbitt, *The New Laokoon* (Cambridge: Riverside Press, 1910), 3–19; John W. Draper, "Aristotelian 'Mimesis' in Eighteenth Century England," *PMLA* 36 (1921): 372–400; Wladyslaw Tatarkiewicz, *A History of Six Ideas: An Essay in Aesthetics* (Warsaw: Polish Scientific Publishers, 1980), 266–309; Anthony Vidler, "The 'Art' of History: Monumental Aesthetics from Winckelmann to Quatremère de Quincy," *Oppositions* 25 (Fall 1982): 52–67; and Rudolf Wittkower, "Imitation, Eclecticism, and Genius," in *Aspects of the Eighteenth Century,* ed. Earl R. Wasserman (Baltimore: Johns Hopkins University Press, 1965), 143–61; *Lotus International,* no. 32 (1981) is devoted to mimesis/imitation.

41
LG (1841), 34. "Nature," in the sense of objects to be reproduced or represented in art, can have numerous and conflicting meanings. See Lovejoy, "'Nature' as Aesthetic Norm," in *Essays,* 69–77. On general nature, see *LG* (1841), 10. This interpretation of imitation goes back to

Aristotle, who wrote that the arts imitate not individual events but general states of things. See Tatarkiewicz, 104. Three writers cited by Downing used the term *general nature* or *general beauty:* Joshua Reynolds, Archibald Alison, and J. C. Loudon.

42
Giovanni Pietro Bellori, "The Idea of the Painter, Sculptor and Architect, Superior to Nature by Selection from Natural Beauties," trans. and repr. as an appendix in Panofsky. On Bellori, see Babbitt, 9–11; Lee, 10–16; Panofsky, 105–9; and Tatarkiewicz, 277–78.

43
Charles Batteux, *Les Beaux Arts réduits à un même principe* (n.p., 1773; reprint, Geneva: Slatkine Reprints, 1969), 6–7, 33, 45. On Batteux, see Frank P. Chambers, *The History of Taste* (New York: Columbia University Press, 1932), 111–12; and Tatarkiewicz, 22, 60–62.

44
Sir Joshua Reynolds, *Discourses on Art,* ed. Robert R. Wark (New Haven: Yale University Press, 1975), xviii–xx, xxx–xxxi, 42–43, 233, 244, 240. Reynolds's writings are described as "the last major assertion in English of the classical principle of 'general nature.'" See Walter Jackson Bate, *From Classic to Romantic* (Cambridge: Harvard University Press, 1949), 79–92; and Hipple, 133–48.

45
Simo (1, 170) reports that Reynolds nurtured Loudon's eye. For Quatremère's influence on Loudon, see Simo, 12–13, 132, 138, 172–73. Downing was praised as "this Sir Joshua Reynolds of our rural decorations," in "Landscape Gardening and Rural Architecture in America," *USMDR* 16 (April 1845): 348, and he quoted Reynolds in *Cottage Residences* (1842, 26fn). The Quatremère articles started with "On the Principles of Taste, with reference to Architecture, and the Fine Arts generally," in *AM* 2 (January 1835): 7–11, and ran for two years. In *AM* 4 (January 1837): 43–44, Loudon reviewed Quatremère's *Essay on Imitation,* which had just been translated by J. C. Kent at his request. On Quatremère, see Sylvia Lavin, *Quatremère de Quincy and the Invention of a Modern Language of Architecture* (Cambridge: MIT Press, 1992); Nikolaus Pevsner, *Some Architectural Writers of the Nineteenth Century* (Oxford: Clarendon Press, 1972), 197–98; René Schneider, *Quatremère de Quincy et son intervention dans les arts: 1788–1830* (Paris: Librairie Hachette, 1910); Anthony Vidler, "The Idea of Type: The Transformation of the Academic Ideal, 1750–1830," and his introduction to "Type: Quatremère de Quincy," *Oppositions* 8 (Spring 1977): 95–115, 147–50.

46
A. C. Quatremère de Quincy, *An Essay on the Nature, the End, and the Means of Imitation in the Fine Arts,* trans. J. C. Kent (London: Smith, Elder & Co., 1837), 10. The original French edition appeared in 1823.

47
Ibid., 139, 150, as quoted in *LG* (1841), 33.

48
Ibid., 165–68, 170–71.

49
Loudon, "Miscellaneous Intelligence," *GM* 10 (November 1834): 558–61. Earlier, Loudon introduced ideas on imitation based on Quatremère, although he did not mention him by name. See review of *Practical Hints on Landscape-Gardening,* by S. Gilpin, *GM* 8 (December 1832): 701.

50
Loudon, "Miscellaneous Intelligence," *GM* 10 (November 1834): 558. The work was published as *Arboretum et Fruticetum Britannicum* in 1838.

51
Ibid., 558–59; Knight, Book 1, lines 1–7, p. 1.

52
J. C. Kent, "Introduction," in Quatremère, ix–x; *LG* (1841), 34.

53
Loudon, *SG,* 136–37.

54
Downing reported: "The Royal Garden at Kew, near London, has lately received . . . some specimens of the Cactus family, which are of enormous proportions." See "Giant Mexican Cactus," *Hort* 1 (November 1846): 223–25. Nicolette Scourse, *The Victorians and Their Flowers* (Portland, Oregon: Timber Press, 1983), 1, 18; Anonymous, as quoted in Scourse, 20.

55
Loudon, *SG,* 164, 166. The term *gardenesque* did not appear in print until 1832, when Loudon first defined it in *GM* (December 1832): 701. He presented his most fully developed concept of the gardenesque in the 1838 works *The Suburban Gardener* and *Arboretum et Fruticetum Britannicum.*

56
"'On the Philosophy of Architecture,' from the German of Weinbrenner, trans. by M.L.," *AM* 5 (September 1838): 393, 396–97, 399. This translation was the source of the lengthy quotation in *LG* (1841), 35fn; *LG* (1844), 52fn; and *LG* (1849), 66–67fn. On Weinbrenner, see David B. Brownlee, ed., *Friedrich Weinbrenner: Architect of Karlsruhe* (Philadelphia: University of Pennsylvania Press, 1986).

57
LG (1841), 33–35. The example of a "counterfeit of the human figure in wax" appeared only in the first edition.

58
Downing to Smith, 15 Nov. 1841, LCP in HSP.

59
LG (1841), 34–35, 100, 105, 114, 121, 130, 192–97.

60
Ibid., 35, 37–38. The description of the "gardenesque" was first published by Loudon in "Remarks on laying out Public Gardens and Promenades," *GM* 11 (December 1835): 664–65. It was repeated under "Gardenesque Imitation" in *SG,* 164–66. Downing printed it only in *LG* (1841), 36–37.

61
LG (1841), 38–39.

62
Ibid., 13, 11. Downing was undoubtedly influenced by Archibald Alison, *Essays on the Nature and Principles of Taste* (Dublin: Printed for Messrs. P. Byrne, J. Moore, Grueber & M'Allister, W. Jones, & R. White, 1790), 286: "In the infancy of Society, when Art was first cultivated . . . such Forms would be employed in those Arts which were intended to please, as were most strongly expressive of design or Skill."

63
See "Taste" in Raymond Williams, *Keywords* (New York: Oxford University Press, 1976), 264–66; Alison, 296, as quoted in *LG* (1841), 13fn.

64
Alison, 204. For Alison and British associationism and "character," see G. L. Hersey, "Associationism and Sensibility in Eighteenth-Century Architecture," *Eighteenth-Century Studies* 4 (Fall 1970): 71–89. Rudolf Wittkower gives a concise summary of the overthrow of "the whole structure of classical aesthetics" in *Architectural Principles in the Age of Humanism,* 4th ed. (New York: St. Martin's Press, 1988), 134–37.

65
Alison, 74. Twenty years earlier, Whately had distinguished between emblematic and expressive gardening in his *Observations on Modern Gardening,* and Alison (250) referred his readers to "Mr. Whately's excellent [book]." For a discussion of emblematic versus expressive, see Hunt and Willis, eds., 37–38; and Ronald Paulson, *Emblem and Expression* (London: Thames & Hudson, 1975).

66
LG (1841), 305, 33–34.

67
Ibid., 13–14.

68
Ibid., 43.

69

Perhaps the philosopher Victor Cousin inspired Downing to link the recognition of art to "the immutability of the true as well as the beautiful." Cousin centered his philosophical system on the concepts of the good, the true, and the beautiful. See Kristeller, 1952, 24. Downing referred to Cousin's *Philosophy of the Beautiful* in "Hints to Rural Improvers," *Hort* 3 (July 1848): 13. Downing (*LG*, 1841, 40–41) illustrated the principle of "the production of a whole" with examples from both architecture and landscape gardening. According to Simo (37–38), Loudon derived his two leading principles from Girardin's *Essay on Landscape,* which emphasized "l'unité et la liaison des rapports." On variety, see *LG* (1841), 16, 42; and Addison, 3: 66.

70

On Loudon and scientific order, see Simo, 56, 172–73. On the rejection of French system, see Michel Baridon, "Ruins as a Mental Construct," *JGH* 5 (January–March 1985): 84–96.

71

For the French interpretation of *la belle nature,* see Donald Drew Egbert, *The Beaux-Arts Tradition in French Architecture* (Princeton: Princeton University Press, 1980), 99–120; and R. G. Saisselin, "The French Garden in the Eighteenth Century: From Belle Nature to the Landscape of Time," *JGH* 5 (July–September 1985): 284–97.

72

Frank Chambers, *The History of Taste* (148) compares ideal versus real and classicism versus romanticism; Loudon, *GM* 13 (December 1837): 598.

CHAPTER 3

1

Toward the end of a long life, John Jay Smith (1798–1881) recorded in his autobiography: "Though considerably younger than myself, I may be said to have been [Downing's] pupil, and so far profited by his teaching as to become his unworthy but enthusiastic successor" as editor to the *Horticulturist* in 1855. See John Jay Smith, *Autobiography of John Jay Smith: A Legacy for My Descendants* (Germantown, Pa., 1872), 359–60. Stored at HSP for LCP. Five Downing to Smith letters are transcribed in Judith K. Major, "The Downing Letters," *Landscape Architecture* 76 (January/February 1986): 50–57.

2

Downing to Smith, 15 Nov. 1841; and 3 Dec. 1841, LCP in HSP.

3

Downing to Smith, 3 Dec. 1841, LCP in HSP; *LG* (1844), 11–12.

4

Downing to Smith, 21 Oct. 1842; 27 Jan. 1843; 14 April 1843; and 11 Aug. 1843, LCP in HSP.

5

Downing to Smith, 26 Feb. 1844, LCP in HSP. Loudon's book was entitled *On the Laying Out, Planting and Managing of Cemeteries, and on the Improvement of Churchyards* (London: Longman, Brown, Green, & Longmans, 1843). In the last year of Loudon's life, his chief occupation was the planning and layout of cemeteries, according to John Gloag, *Mr. Loudon's England* (Newcastle upon Tyne: Oriel Press, 1970), 66.

6

Downing to Smith, 21 Feb. 1844, LCP in HSP; *LG* (1841), 21–22.

7

Thomas Dick Lauder, *Sir Uvedale Price on the Picturesque* (Edinburgh: Caldwell, Lloyd, & Co.; London: Wm. S. Orr & Co., 1842). Hipple (159) states that Lauder edited Price "partly with the idea of supplying the proper associational underpinnings for Price's theories, his introductory 'Essay on the Origin of Taste' being a version of [Francis] Jeffrey's version of Alison."

8

LG (1844), v, 12–13.

9

Ibid., 13–20; Pope, *Works,* 10: 532–33, as quoted in *LG* (1844), 19–20.

10

Pope, *Epistles,* 137–39; *LG* (1844), 22–23.

11

LG (1844), 24–25.

12

Ibid., 25–26, 48–49; Addison, 3: 68; review of *A Treatise on the Theory and Practice of Landscape Gardening* . . . by A. J. Downing, *Gardeners' Magazine* 2 (July–December 1850): 167.

13

Loudon, *SG,* 168–69; *LG* (1844), 26. Downing used the American spelling "Humphrey" for Repton's first name.

14

LG (1844), 26; Loudon, *Repton;* "Literary Notice," *GM* 14 (October 1838): 491.

15

LG (1844), 26fn, 26.

16

John Lindley (1799–1865) was one of the founders and principal editor of the *Gardeners' Chronicle* from 1841 until his death. See John Lindley, *Gardeners' Chronicle* 7 (October 9, 1847): 667, as quoted in "English and American Landscape Gardening," *Hort* 2 (December 1847): 261, 263. See Loudon, *EG,* 11 passim. In time Downing's publishers heeded the poor reviews. Beginning with the 1859 edition, sixteen pages from this portion of the work were omitted. The historical notices were still included in *LG,* 5th ed. (New York: G. P. Putnam & Co., 1853), 20–37. In *LG,* 6th ed. (New York: A. O. Moore & Co., 1859), pages 21 through 36 from the fifth edition were cut out.

17

Lindley, *GC* 7 (October 9, 1847): 667. The statement about estate size was added to *LG* (1844), 11: "Most of its beauty, and all its charms, may, however, be enjoyed in *ten to twenty acres,* fortunately situated, and well treated" [my emphasis]. In *LG* (1841), 10, it read: "The principles of the art may be applied, and its beauties realized to a certain degree, in the space of *half an acre* of ground–wherever grass will grow, and trees thrive luxuriantly" [my emphasis].

18

Downing to Smith, 15 Nov. 1841, LCP in HSP; *LG* (1844), 35.

19

Downing to Smith, 3 Dec. 1841, LCP in HSP; *LG* (1844), 37.

20

LG (1844), 43. On Sheaff and Camac, see Downing to Smith, 21 Feb. 1844, LCP in HSP. In Downing to Smith, 27 Jan. 1843, LCP in HSP, Smith was asked to request a sketch. Sheaff's former seat is now a state-owned property, The Highlands, located in Fort Washington, Pennsylvania. The three-hundred-year-old oak tree was felled by hurricane winds in August 1991. See "At the Highlands Estate near Philadelphia," *Historic Preservation News,* November 1991, 11.

21

LG (1844), 44; Wainwright, 132–33, 137, 141; "A Chapter on Lawns," *Hort* 1 (November 1846): 204. The now demolished Camac house (formerly at Eleventh Street and Montgomery Avenue, Philadelphia) was the work of John Notman. See Constance M. Greiff, *John Notman, Architect 1810–1865* (Philadelphia: Athenaeum, 1979), 235.

22

LG (1844), 31–32, 202–03. William Hamilton (1745–1813) corresponded with Thomas Jefferson and supplied plants for the grounds at Monticello. In 1839 what remained of the estate became a cemetery. The Woodlands Cemetery and house can be visited at 40th and Woodland streets near the University of Pennsylvania. For a contemporary report on Hamilton and the Woodlands, see A Massachusetts Subscriber, "The Rare Trees and Pleasure Grounds of Pennsylvania," *Hort* 6 (March 1851): 127–30.

23
LG (1844), 39–43. On the Boston trips, see Downing to Smith, 15 Nov. 1841, and 21 Oct. 1842, LCP in HSP. For Perkins, see Thornton, 148–51. Seaburg and Paterson (424) report that the Brookline house was demolished after Perkins's death in 1854, but a large part of the estate remained intact and was passed down in one line of descent. "How to Popularize the Taste For Planting," *Hort* 7 (July 1852): 298–99. On Belmont, see Horticola, "Notes on Gardens and Country Seats Near Boston," *Hort* 7 (March 1852): 127. Downing editorialized that his correspondent hardly did justice to the place. For Joseph Lee and his sons Thomas, George, and Henry, see Thornton, 152–53. For Gardiner's Oaklands, see Robert Hallowell Gardiner, *Early Recollections of Robert Hallowell Gardiner, 1782–1864* (Hallowell, Maine: White & Horne Co., 1936), 214–15; and Deborah Thompson, ed., *Maine Forms of American Architecture* (Camden, Maine: Downeast Magazine, n.d.), 160. Oaklands is listed on the National Register of Historic Places. For this information, I am indebted to Ophelia Lepore, Community Room volunteer in the Gardiner Public Library. For comments on Trinity Church and Richard Upjohn's work on a Van Rensselaer manor in Albany, see Downing to Smith, 21 Oct. 1842, LCP in HSP.

24
LG (1844), 45.

25
Ibid., 11, 29.

26
Ibid., 54, 52. Alison as quoted in Lauder, 34, 43 [my emphasis].

27
The footnote citing Weinbrenner on the beauty of nature and the beauty of art was retained in *LG* (1844), 52–53, 52fn. The lengthy quotation was appended to the sentence concerning "*an expressive, harmonious, and refined imitation.*" In the 1841 edition it had been linked to the explanation of "fac-simile" versus "artistical" imitation.

28
LG (1844), 53.

29
Ibid., 56–57, 64. Downing gathered the 1841 principles of "Production of a Whole," which referred to the necessity of a unity of sensation, and the "Production of Variety," which included intricacy and harmony, into the principle of the "Production of Unity, Harmony, and Variety." The discussion in the text remained essentially the same, with a new paragraph devoted to "Harmony."

30
Downing omitted the 1841 footnote that quoted Alison. Lauder, 2; *LG* (1844), 58–59.

31
LG (1844), 49–51, 53, 54, 55–60. As in the earlier edition, there was a confusing mixture of terms: Downing referred to "general" (dropping "or natural") and "picturesque beauty" as "striking examples of expression in natural scenery" and explained these characters using the 1841 descriptions with only minor word changes.

32
Ibid., 55fn. This footnote appeared only in the 1844 edition.

33
Ibid., 59, 57.

34
Ibid., 53, 56, 490–93.

35
Loudon, *Repton*, vii, 203, 234, 180; *LG* (1844), 55–56.

36
Loudon, *Repton,* 57–58, 84; *LG* (1844), 55–57, 58.

37
LG (1844), 58, 54, 59. Loudon (*Repton,* viii) actually described the gardenesque as combining a display of the natural form and habit of plants with a unity of expression and character.

38
LG (1844), 55fn.

CHAPTER 4

1
A. J. Downing, *A Treatise on the Theory and Practice of Landscape Gardening adapted to North America,* 4th ed., enlarged, revised, and newly illustrated (New York: George P. Putnam; London: Longman, Brown, Green & Longmans, 1849), v. Charles B. Wood III states:

We cannot provide conclusive proof that the third edition was never published, but the backs of the original printed wrappers of *The Horticulturist* provide some interesting evidence to support this theory. In January 1848, the second edition was advertised; in November 1848, a *new* edition was advertised; and in May 1850, the fourth edition was advertised. There is no contemporary reference to a third edition as such.

See "The New 'Pattern Books' and the Role of the Agricultural Press," in Tatum and MacDougall, eds., *Prophet with Honor,* 187–88; "Notices of New Publications," *Cultivator* 2 (July 1845): 226; Downing to Smith, 11 Aug. 1843, LCP in HSP. See also Downing to Joel Rathbone, 17 June 1845, Gratz Case 6, Box 2, HSP: "I feel quite a leisurely man once more as the 'Fruits & Fruit-trees of America' is published today. This volume of 600 pages has cost me four times the labour of any former work." Downing to Smith, 29 Dec. 1847, LCP in HSP; Wood (*Prophet With Honor,* 166) cites 1853 sales figures for *Fruits* at 15,000 copies, compared to 9,000 copies of the *Treatise.* A printed notice dated 15 Feb. 1847, one of which is in the Smith Manuscript Collection, LCP in HSP, announced Downing's retirement. Downing to Smith, 19 Feb. 1847, LCP in HSP: "I have sold out all my nursery interest, stock of trees &c, & am rejoiced at the freedom from ten thousand details & a very heavy business correspondence of which I am relieved." Downing to Smith, 29 Dec. 1847, LCP in HSP. In 1853, the prominent editor George William Curtis (1824–92) wrote that in the winter of 1846–47 Downing had been in serious financial difficulty and under pressure to give "unremitting" attention to the *Horticulturist.* He also noted that Downing's interest in the management of the nursery had decreased. See George William Curtis, "Memoir of the Author," in *Rural Essays* (New York: George P. Putnam & Co., 1853), xlii. David Schuyler suggests that Downing's "period of acute financial distress" lasted until 1849, when a lawsuit between Downing and his father-in-law John Peter DeWint was settled. See Schuyler, *Apostle of Taste: Andrew Jackson Downing 1815–1852* (Baltimore: Johns Hopkins University Press, 1996), 89–90. Downing wrote to the owner of the *Horticulturist,* Luther Tucker, on April 19, 1849, to inform him "that the great lawsuit . . . yesterday was satisfactorily & amicably settled." See Downing to Tucker, 19 April 1849, Princeton University.

2
LG (1849), 79. He actually added a few elements: to the basic requirements of the 1844 "soft verdant lawn, and a few forest or ornamental trees, well grouped," the 1849 edition added "walks, and a few flowers." Downing made these changes in response to John Lindley's comments in *GC* 7 (December 4, 1847): 795: "We conclude that Downing does not prohibit paths—that he does not command us to walk on wet Grass. That is an omission on his part—by mere accident. The curious thing, however, is that he leaves out flowers altogether."

3
LG (1849), v; John Ruskin, *Modern Painters,* vol. 2, in John Ruskin, *The Works,* vol. 4, ed. E. T. Cook & Alexander Wedderburn (London: George Allen, 1903). The volume was published in England in 1846.

4
LG (1849), 27–30. Downing footnoted only one quotation in the entire section (1849, 29fn). For the source of this material, see Loudon, *EG,* 307–15. Other minor

changes included a moderation of his 1844 insult of Capability Brown (*LG,* 1849, 35) and an inexplicable switch from Warwick Castle to Arundel Castle in his list of celebrated English residences (*LG,* 1849, 38).

5

Haley, 11–27; "A Visit to Montgomery Place," *Hort* 2 (October 1847): 153.

6

LG (1849), 47–49; Downing to Thomas P. Barton, 31 Dec. 1846, Sleepy Hollow Restorations, Tarrytown, New York; reprinted in Haley, 33. Barton was Mrs. Livingston's son-in-law. Montgomery Place, Annandale-On-Hudson, New York, is now a National Historic Landmark and a property of Historic Hudson Valley.

7

LG (1849), 52–53; Downing to Smith, 24 Aug. 1846, LCP in HSP; "The Meadow Park at Geneseo," *Hort* 3 (October 1848): 164–65. Asher Brown Durand (1796–1886) was an American engraver and painter.

8

See Roger B. Stein, *John Ruskin and Aesthetic Thought in America, 1840–1900* (Cambridge: Harvard University Press, 1967), 14–18; Asher B. Durand, "Letters on Landscape Painting, Letter II," *Crayon* 1 (17 January 1855): 34–35, as quoted in Stein, 14. Durand stressed the depiction of the real as opposed to the painting of ideal subjects. "Hints to Rural Improvers," *Hort* 3 (July 1848): 9. For Bryant, see *LG* (1849), 160, 186, 280.

9

LG (1849), v. A Professor of Taste in Landscape Gardening, "Landscape Gardening," *GC* 8 (January 8, 1848): 22; John Lindley, *GC* 8 (March 18, 1848): 187.

10

Ibid., 63, 73–75 (there were a few minor word changes); Lindley had also used the word *vague* in an article examining the terms employed in landscape gardening: "Vague application of terms already existing, and equally unmeaning terms newly invented, are but so much dust thrown into the eyes." See Lindley, *GC* 7 (October 23, 1847): 699; *LG* (1849), 67; Loudon, *Repton,* 105. Lindley devoted four of his articles to Sir Thomas Dick Lauder's edition of *Price on the Picturesque,* which Downing had recommended to his readers in 1844. One excerpt from the fourth—*GC* 8 (May 13, 1848): 315–16—suffices to give a sense of Lindley's opinion:

> It would be an endless task to expose the mere platitudes—the small talk—and often (so far as any attempt to lay down principles is concerned) the nonsense which disfigure his interpolations. . . . We have only a glaring example of a classical author spoiled, and, by the very process of disfigurement, rendered less accessible to the mass of those who would desire to read him.

The others appeared in *GC* 8 (February 12, 1848): 99–100; *GC* 8 (April 8, 1848): 235–36; and *GC* 8 (April 22, 1848): 267. Downing made no mention of Lauder in the 1849 *Treatise.*

11

LG (1849), 67. See Price, 1: 39: "These definitions seem to me . . . at once too vague, and too confused." Downing (*LG,* 1849, 65) made these changes: "In the inimitable pictures of this great master [Claude]" became "In the best pictures of this master"; that Claude's compositions had been "nowhere surpassed" became "seldom surpassed." Ruskin, *Modern Painters I* (1843), as quoted in Franklin B. Dexter, "Modern Painters," *NAR* 66 (January 1848): 116. For a discussion of Ruskin, Turner, and Claude, see Stein, 37–38.

12

LG (1849), 71–72. Lindley, *GC* 8 (April 1, 1848): 219.

13

LG (1849), 72–73.

14

Ibid., 68. Carlo Dolci (1616–1686)—spelled Dolce by Downing—was a Florentine painter known for delicately colored religious canvases. Gerrit Dou, or Gerard Douw (1613–1675), was a Dutch painter who studied under Rembrandt.

15

Ibid., 66, 68 [my emphasis]; Ruskin, *Modern Painters II,* in *Works,* 4: 76fn (this note was added in 1883), 76–145, 210. For an outline of the major principles of *Modern Painters II* and their potential for an American audience, see Stein, 39–41.

16

LG (1849), 68–69, 69fn. Downing apparently was unaware that Hogarth, too, in the preface to *The Analysis of Beauty,* had emphasized this expressive quality of infinity while referring to an even earlier artist: "Shakespear, who had the deepest penetration into nature, has sum'd up all the charms of beauty in two words, Infinite Variety." Ruskin, *Works,* 4: 88, 81.

17

Ruskin, *Works,* 4: 88–89. In *Modern Painters II,* "Of Symmetry" (4: 127), Ruskin had in fact noted: "In landscape the same sense of symmetry is preserved . . . even to artificialness, by the greatest men; and it is one of the principal faults in the landscape of the present day, that the symmetry of nature is sacrificed to irregular picturesqueness." For a discussion of Ruskin and his "two modes of the picturesque," see George P. Landow, *The Aesthetic and Critical Theories of John Ruskin* (Princeton: Princeton University Press, 1971), 221–40; *LG* (1849), 69–71. These contrasting expressions were similar to those described by Ruskin (4: 113–24) in his chapter "Of Repose, or the Type of Divine Permanence": "Repose demands for its expression the implied capability of its opposite, Energy. . . . In architecture, in music, in acting, in dancing, in whatsoever art, great or mean, there are yet degrees of greatness or meanness entirely dependent on this single quality of repose." Referring to "the convulsions of the Laocoon," Ruskin criticized its absence of repose: "No group has exercised so pernicious an influence on art as this." The Italian painter Raphael lived from 1483 to 1520. The Spaniard Bartolomé Esteban Murillo (1618–1682) painted religious works, scenes of gypsy life, and beggar children.

18

LG (1849), 76.

19

Ibid., 76–77.

20

Ibid., viii, 18; Frank J. Scott, *The Art of Beautifying Suburban Home Grounds of Small Extent* (New York: D. Appleton & Co., 1870; reprint, American Life Foundation, n.d.), 12–13.

21

"Landscape Gardening and Rural Architecture in America," *USMDR* 16 (April 1845): 357.

PART II

1

"Introduction," *Hort* 1 (July 1846): 9; "New Magazine," *Cultivator* 3 (June 1846): 195. The *Cultivator* duly reported on each of Downing's new works. See for example, *Cultivator* 2 (July 1845): 226: "[*Fruits and Fruit-Trees*] shows thorough devotion of the author to his subject, as well as his indefatigable research and untiring industry." For information on the professional relationship of Tucker and Downing, see Tatum, "Introduction," and Wood, in Tatum and MacDougall, eds., *Prophet with Honor,* 29, 169, 178, 186–87; "Landscape Gardening," *Cultivator* 2 (March 1845): 80; "Notices of 'The Horticulturist,'" *Cultivator* 3 (December 1846): 362.

2

Luther Tucker recalled Downing's "plain sayings and wholesome counsel" under the guise of "An Old Digger" in Luther Tucker, "Mr. Downing and the Horticulturist," *Hort* 7 (September 1, 1852): 394. See An Old Digger, "Raising Peas—Kitchen-Garden Talk," *Hort* 6 (March 1851): 142–44; idem, "Seasonable Hints," *Hort* 6 (May 1851): 235–37. Downing wrote eleven of these pieces. Within two years of its founding, the *Horticulturist* had the largest circulation of any magazine of its class in America (see Wood in Tatum and MacDougall, eds., *Prophet with Honor,* 186); statements in Downing's editorials indicate his extensive correspondence and his attempts to respond to readers' comments. See for example, "The Art of Transplanting Trees," *Hort* 3 (November 1848): 209: "the multitude of complaints and inquiries which beset us." Visitors and colleagues noted Downing's considerable correspondence: "His business was varied and his correspondence really enormous. He has often and truly said he could fully employ a secretary merely to answer his letters." Calvert Vaux to Marshall P. Wilder, 18 August [1852], LCP in HSP.

3

See A. J. Downing to S. G. Ward, 1 July 1850, bMS Am 1465 Houghton Library Harvard *42M–2088 (267): "My work on 'Country Houses' will be published on Thursday." Samuel G. Ward (1814–1884) was an American financier and author. See Downing to Tucker, 28 [June] 1850, Princeton University: "I intend to sail on the Pacific on the 6th of July—and will of course write you again with copy (several times) for next no. before then." Downing returned in September. See Caroline Downing to J. R. Lowell, 15 September 1850, bMS Am 765 Houghton Library Harvard (293). Caroline wrote to Lowell in "Mr. Downing's absence" saying that she was going to meet her husband in New York the next day; Calvert Vaux described the circumstances of their meeting in Vaux to Wilder, 18 Aug. [1852], LCP in HSP. In 1857 Vaux wrote *Villas and Cottages,* dedicating it to "Caroline E. Downing, and to the Memory of her Husband, Andrew J. Downing."

4

"Mr. Downing's Letters From England," *Hort* 5 (September 1850): 121; *Hort* 5 (November 1850): 222. Downing gave the Latin names as *Abies Douglassi* (now *Pseudotsuga menziesii*) and *Abies nobilis* (now *Abies procera*). Downing noted that the trees had been brought to England "about 18 years ago"; however, the tree list for the garden at Stourhead, Wiltshire, England (where there are magnificent specimens of both), indicates that the Douglas Fir was introduced into England in 1827, the Noble Fir in 1830. See National Trust Wiltshire, *Stourhead Tree List,* compiled and written by Michael Lear (London: National Trust Enterprises Ltd., 1995); "Mr. Downing's Letters From England," *Hort* 6 (March 1851): 137; *Hort* 6 (February 1851):

85. The essential core planting in the typical "American garden" consisted of rhododendrons, azaleas, and kalmias according to Mark Laird, "Approaches to Planting in the Late Eighteenth Century: Some Imperfect Ideas on the Origins of the American Garden," *JGH* 11 (July–September 1991): 167; "Mr. Downing's Letters From England," *Hort* 6 (June 1851): 281.

5

"Mr. Downing's Letters From England," *Hort* 5 (November 1850): 220. On Niagara Falls, see John F. Sears, *Sacred Places: American Tourist Attractions in the Nineteenth Century* (New York: Oxford University Press, 1989), 12–30; "Mr. Downing's Letters From England," *Hort* 6 (June 1851): 281–86; *Hort* 5 (October 1850): 153. Downing apparently visited Kew on the morning of July 23, 1850, sending ahead several plants of *Torreya taxifolia* (a cedar native of Florida) that he had brought from America for the garden. He also carried volumes of the *Horticulturist* for the director, botanist Sir William Jackson Hooker (1785–1865). See A. J. Downing to Sir William Hooker, 20 July 1850, vol. 63: 168. A few days after the tour Downing assured Hooker: "I have passed few pleasanter days than that at Kew—which I owe to your kindness." He also reminded the director of the promised letter "which will enable me to see Chatsworth to the best advantage." See Downing to Hooker, 26 July 1850, vol. 63: 169. Both letters are in the Director's Correspondence, Library and Archives, Royal Botanic Gardens, Kew, Richmond, Surrey, England; quoted by permission of the Library and Archives, Kew. Two eighteenth-century estates originally in the royal family formed the basis of the botanic gardens, and it was not until 1840 that Kew was taken over by the state. Downing's host had been director since 1841. "Mr. Downing's Letters From England," *Hort* 6 (March 1851): 139.

6

"Mr. Downing's Letters From England," *Hort* 5 (October 1850): 157–58. Downing's readers did not learn the full name of his host and hostess; he simply referred to "the property of the Earl of H—." However, Downing speaks of his visit in his final letter to Hooker, which warrants a full transcription:

My dear Sir William

I promised myself the pleasure of passing an hour or two at Kew again before leaving England—but as I return earlier than I at first intended I fear I shall not be able to do so.

I have had a most agreeable visit & shall carry away the most satisfactory impression of England. I passed a couple of days at Lord Hardwicke's fine place in Cambridgeshire (where there is an avenue of elms three miles long!) The Duke of Devonshire (to whom I went with your letter & one from Lord Hardwicke) showed me Chatsworth in great perfection—setting the Emperor fountain & all the water works in play. Chatsworth more than realized all my expectations & unites magnificence & *taste* more completely than anything I have seen in England. At the home of Mrs. Marsh—the authoress—I got a most charming impression of the domestic life of the educated middle class of England.

And now, my dear Sir William, you must allow me to thank you for your very kind attentions—& finally for the excellent letters you had the goodness to send me. Let me add how much gratification it would give me to receive & welcome you in my American home in the beautiful scenery of the Hudson. If any of your family or friends ever come to America pray remember that you have a friend there to whom to commend them.

I will only add that if you can send me the print of yourself which you were so good as to promise I will be greatly obliged. I intend running over to Paris to day but shall be here again on the 6th & shall take the steamer from Liverpool on the 7th of September.

With great respect & regard yours

A J Downing

See Downing to Hooker, 30 August 1850, vol. 63: 170, Kew. Anne Marsh-Caldwell (1791–1874) was a domestic novelist whose popularity, according to one conservative journal, was evidence of England's moral integrity. She published anonymously, and although some reviewers knew her name, others referred to her as "the authoress." See Paul and Jane Schlueter, eds., *An Encyclopedia of British Women Writers* (New York: Garland Publishing, 1988), 318–20.

7

"Mr. Downing's Letters From England," *Hort* 5 (October 1850): 159; *Hort* 6 (January 1851): 41.

CHAPTER 5

1

"Introduction," *Hort* 1 (July 1846): 9, 10.

2

"Impressions of Chatsworth," *Hort* 1 (January 1847): 298. These impressions were not Downing's own, although he added comments at the beginning of the editorial. Notes concerning this visit to Chatsworth were given to him by a person identified simply by "A____." The *Horticulturist*'s articles on Chatsworth were cited in "Chatsworth," *Garden and Forest* 2 (October 23, 1889): 506–7, illustration on 511.

3

"A Visit to Montgomery Place," *Hort* 2 (October 1847): 154, 160; "Hints to Rural Improvers," *Hort* 3 (July 1848): 12. For details about the owners of Montgomery Place and the improvements made after 1802, see Haley, 11–17.

4

"Hints to Rural Improvers," *Hort* 3 (July 1848): 13.

5

"On the Mistakes of Citizens in Country Life," *Hort* 3 (January 1849): 307.

6

Ibid., 307, 309; *LG* (1844), 11–12; and *LG* (1849), 19–20.

7

LG (1849), 18; "On the Mistakes of Citizens in Country Life," *Hort* 3 (January 1849): 305.

8

"Our Country Villages," *Hort* 4 (June 1850): 541. Although the "We are *republicans*" statement was made in 1850, the sentiment permeated earlier editorials. See the appendix for specific instances. "The Fruits in Convention," *Hort* 4 (February 1850): 346. The clearest and most complete explanation of the republican moral vision is David E. Shi, *The Simple Life* (New York: Oxford University Press, 1986). On simplicity, also see Harris, 28–53; and

Jones, 327. Jones (228) also devotes a chapter to the influence of the Roman classical past on the United States: "Constitutionally we are not a democracy but a republic; that is, a 'res publica,' a phrase referring to the commonweal, which in the sense of a government by elected representatives came into English in the seventeenth century."

9
"Cultivators—The Great Industrial Class of America," *Hort* 2 (June 1848): 537.

10
"A Talk About Public Parks and Gardens," *Hort* 3 (October 1848): 154. This editorial is in the form of a dialogue between the editor and an unnamed traveller—Henry Colman, who sojourned in England and the continent from 1843 to 1848. The dialogue relied on his observations and sentiments published in *The Agriculture and Rural Economy of France, Belgium, Holland, and Switzerland* (London: John Petheram, 1848), 56–64. Cooper, 215; "Republican Simplicity," *NYM* 18 (22 August 1840): 71. This unsigned piece may have been written by Downing's friend N. P. Willis, an editor for this weekly.

11
"On Simple Rural Cottages," *Hort* 1 (September 1846): 107; *LG* (1844), 12.

12
"On Country Houses," *Hort* 1 (October 1846): 153, 154; "On the Moral Influence of Good Houses," *Hort* 2 (February 1848): 347; "Design for a Small Cottage," *Hort* 2 (April 1848): 471–72.

13
"On the Mistakes of Citizens in Country Life," *Hort* 3 (January 1849): 309; "Cockneyism in the Country," *Hort* 4 (September 1849): 105–6, 108. The American tendency to judge harshly any unrepublican display of wealth was noted by Jesse Buel, "On the Horticulture of the United States of America," *GM* 4 (August 1828): 193.

14
"A Few Words on Rural Architecture," *Hort* 5 (July 1850): 11; "A Few Words on Our Progress in Building," *Hort* 6 (June 1851): 253; "Citizens Retiring to the Country," *Hort* 7 (February 1852): 60–61.

15
Vaux to Wilder, 18 Aug. [1852], LCP in HSP.

16
Benson, "Bremer's Unpublished Letters," 195.

17
"Influence of Horticulture," *Hort* 2 (July 1847): 9; Harris (39) notes that "Reynolds' glorification of history-painting was based on the moral ends it served, refining, purifying, restraining. Concern with such ends raised the painter's status from the craft level."

18
Theodore Dwight, 78; "On the Moral Influence of Good Houses," *Hort* 2 (February 1848): 346, 347. Lydia Sigourney was confident that "he who beautifies a garden for the eye of the community, is surely a public benefactor." See "Horticulture," *Godey's* 21 (October 1840): 179.

19
Timothy Dwight, *Travels in New England and New York* (1821), ed. Barbara Miller Solomon, 4 vols. (Cambridge: Belknap Press of Harvard University Press, 1969), 2: 348, 346–47, as quoted in *Hort* 2 (February 1848): 346 [Downing's emphasis]; Theodore Dwight, 77; Horace Bushnell, *Christian Nurture* (Edinburgh: Alexander Strahan & Co., 1861), 68. The series of articles that culminated in this book began in 1838.

20
"A Chapter on School-Houses," *Hort* 2 (March 1848): 395; L. H. Sigourney, "The Perception of the Beautiful," *Godey's* 20 (January 1840): 9, 10.

21
Henry Barnard, *Practical Illustrations of the Principles of School Architecture* [Hartford: n.p., 1851], 69, 38, 40–42.

22

Colman, *European Agriculture,* 28; Colman as the "Traveller" in "A Talk About Public Parks and Gardens," *Hort* 3 (October 1848): 154, 157, 158. On parks, see also "Public Cemeteries and Public Gardens," *Hort* 4 (July 1849): 9–12; and "The New-York Park," *Hort* 6 (August 1851): 345–49; and Senex ["Letter to the Editor,"] *NYM* 14 (3 June 1837): 391: "The pleasures of air and exercise . . . are not less conducive to moral than to physical health."

23

A Mississippi Reader, "Public Parks and Gardens," *Hort* 3 (January 1849): 348; "On the Improvement of Country Villages," *Hort* 3 (June 1849): 545, 546.

24

"Our Country Villages," *Hort* 4 (June 1850): 537, 538; Christopher Mulvey, *Anglo-American Landscapes* (Cambridge: Cambridge University Press, 1983), 175–78.

25

"On the Improvement of Country Villages," *Hort* 3 (June 1849): 546; "A Chapter on School-Houses," *Hort* 2 (March 1848): 395.

26

"On the Improvement of Country Villages," *Hort* 3 (June 1849): 546; John Adams, as quoted in Brooke Hindle, *Emulation and Invention* (New York: New York University Press, 1981), 16; "The Favorite Poison of America," *Hort* 5 (November 1850): 202; See Howe (18) on emulation: "The Victorian's educational practices frequently relied on 'emulation,' a word they always used to mean desire to excel in rivalry, never in its twentieth-century sense of imitation."

27

Review of *The Builder's Guide,* 3rd ed., by Asher Benjamin, *NAR* 52 (April 1841): 307; "The Horticultural Shows," *Hort* 5 (September 1850): 105; "A Reform Needed," *Hort* 6 (October 1851): 442. See the appendix for editorials in which Downing provided exemplars.

28

"A Talk About Public Parks and Gardens," *Hort* 3 (October 1848): 155; "The New-York Park," *Hort* 6 (August 1851): 348; "Public Cemeteries and Public Gardens," *Hort* 4 (July 1849): 12. The parks of Brussels were praised in Colman, *Agriculture and Rural Economy,* 59. Downing's contribution to "The Ideology of the Public Park" is discussed in David Schuyler, *The New Urban Landscape* (Baltimore: Johns Hopkins University Press, 1988), 59–76; "Trees, in Towns and Villages," *Hort* 1 (March 1847): 395.

29

"On Planting Shade Trees," *Hort* 2 (November 1847): 201–3. See the appendix for other instances of New England cited as an exemplar. "On the Colour of Country Houses," *Hort* 1 (May 1847): 493; "Brown Houses and Lightning Conductors," *Hort* 7 (May 1852): 201; N. P. Willis, *American Scenery,* vol. 2, illustrated in a series of views by W. H. Bartlett (London: George Virtue, 1840), 10.

30

Timothy Dwight, 2: 347, as quoted in "On the Moral Influence of Good Houses," *Hort* 2 (February 1848): 345–46; Reverend Choules, as quoted in "Thoughts on Trees and Flowers," *Farmer's Library* 1 (September 1845): 153, 151.

31

"Landscape Gardening and Rural Architecture in America," *USMDR* 16 (April 1845): 348, 350; "How to Popularize the Taste for Planting," *Hort* 7 (July 1852): 298.

32

"Citizens Retiring to the Country," *Hort* 7 (February 1852): 57, 60. Earlier Downing stated that "With us, as a people, retirement to country life, must come to be the universal pleasure of the nation." These retirees included the statesman to the mechanic. "On the Mistakes of Citizens in Country Life," *Hort* 3 (January 1849): 305.

33

"Country Places in Autumn," *Hort* 5 (December 1850): 250–51; "On the Mistakes of Citizens in Country Life,"

Hort 3 (January 1849): 309; "On Country Houses," *Hort* 1 (October 1846): 154; "Introduction," *Hort* 1 (July 1846): 10; Bremer, 1: 46. The following information aids in understanding how many people "consulted" Downing's work: 9,000 copies of the *Treatise* were sold as of 1853. The 1850 census recorded 6,893,249 people in New York, Pennsylvania, Massachusetts, and New Jersey—the states likely to provide the main audience. In 1848, the *Horticulturist* had the largest circulation of any magazine of its class in America. See Wood, in Tatum and MacDougall, eds., *Prophet with Honor,* 166, 186; and J. D. B. DeBow, *Seventh Census of the United States: 1850* (Washington, D.C.: Robert Armstrong, 1853).

34

Charles Downing to Marshall P. Wilder, 24 August 1852, LCP in HSP; Fredrika Bremer, "A Letter to his Friends," in *Rural Essays,* xix; Cooper, 161. For the Victorian woman's role in the home, see Howe, 26; Nancy Woloch, *Women and the American Experience* (New York: Alfred A. Knopf, 1984), 116, 132; and Barbara Welter, "The Cult of True Womanhood: 1820–1860," in Pessen, 47–69.

35

"A Chapter on Lawns," *Hort* 1 (November 1846): 204; "A Talk With Flora and Pomona," *Hort* 2 (September 1847): 108. For male opinions on ladies and flowers, see Meigs, 8; and Robinson, "Advice to Western Emigrants," in *Solon Robinson,* 520. "On the Drapery of Cottages and Gardens," *Hort* 3 (February 1849): 353, 354.

36

"On Feminine Taste in Rural Affairs," *Hort* 3 (April 1849): 455; "A Spring Gossip," *Hort* 4 (May 1850): 489–90; "The Home Education of the Rural Districts," *Hort* 7 (January 1852): 10; "Introduction," *Hort* 1 (July 1846); 10 [my emphasis].

37

"Introduction," *Hort* 1 (July 1846): 10; "How to Arrange Country Places," *Hort* 4 (March 1850): 393.

38

"Mr. Tudor's Garden at Nahant," *Hort* 2 (August 1847): 57, 59. On Frederic Tudor, see Thornton, 154–55; "A Visit to Montgomery Place," *Hort* 2 (October 1847): 160.

39

"How to Choose a Site for a Country Seat," *Hort* 2 (December 1847): 249, 251.

40

"On the Moral Influence of Good Houses," *Hort* 2 (February 1848): 347, 345; "Hints to Rural Improvers," *Hort* 3 (July 1848): 10, 11, 14.

41

"On the Mistakes of Citizens in Country Life," *Hort* 3 (January 1849): 307–8. The Provincial Law Association was founded in 1847. See David Brownlee, *The Law Courts: The Architecture of George Edmund Street* (New York: Architectural History Foundation; Cambridge: MIT Press, 1984), 44–45.

42

"A Few Words on Rural Architecture," *Hort* 5 (July 1850): 9, 10; "A Few Words on Our Progress in Building," *Hort* 6 (June 1851): 251–52. Sir William Blackstone (1723–1780) was a prominent English jurist.

43

"Hints on Landscape Gardening," *Hort* 6 (November 1851): 490–91.

44

"Citizens Retiring to the Country," *Hort* 7 (February 1852): 58.

45

Review of *European Agriculture and Rural Economy. From Personal Observation,* by Henry Colman, *Hort* 1 (March 1847): 425, 426.

46

Leo Marx uses the terms *vernacular* versus *genteel* styles in *The Pilot and the Passenger* (New York: Oxford University

46

Press, 1988), 3–17. "A Few Words on Our Progress in Building," *Hort* 6 (June 1851): 250; Channing, 262; "Influence of Horticulture," *Hort* 2 (July 1847): 9, 10, 11; "How to Choose a Site for a Country Seat," *Hort* 2 (December 1847): 251.

47

"A Chapter on School-Houses," *Hort* 2 (March 1848): 393; "The Art of Transplanting Trees," *Hort* 3 (November 1848): 209; "On the Mistakes of Citizens in Country Life," *Hort* 3 (January 1849): 307.

48

"The Fruits in Convention," *Hort* 4 (February 1850): 345, 346; Denison Olmsted and George Olmsted, "Notes on the *Belle et Bonne* Apple," *Hort* 3 (January 1849): 322–25.

49

"The Fruits in Convention," *Hort* 4 (February 1850): 347.

50

Ibid., 348, 349. See the appendix for foreign words and phrases used in the editorials.

51

"How to Arrange Country Places," *Hort* 4 (March 1850): 393, 395, 396. Henry Winthrop Sargent (1810–1882) retired to Wodenethe, his 22-acre estate at Fishkill Landing, New York, in 1841. A contributor to the *Horticulturist*, Sargent supervised the sixth edition (1859) of the *Treatise*, supplementing it extensively. He also wrote a supplement on terrace gardens for the 1873 edition of *Cottage Residences*, and with Downing's brother Charles revised its list of flowers, fruits, shrubs, and trees. For Sargent, see Spingarn, 24–39.

52

"A Spring Gossip," *Hort* 4 (May 1850): 489; On Downing's regard for the poetry of Britain, see "The Philosophy of Rural Taste," *Hort* 4 (August 1849): 58. Lowell is the only American poet whom Downing mentions in the editorials. See the appendix for foreign poets cited in the editorials. Bremer, 1: 27.

53

Downing to J. R. Lowell, [November 1849], bMS Am 765 Houghton Library, Harvard University (292); "A Spring Gossip," *Hort* 4 (May 1850): 489; Bremer (1: 28) noted that Caroline Downing preferred Lowell's short epic poem "The Vision of Sir Launfal." Lowell's humorous poem followed "A Few Words on Our Progress in Building," *Hort* 6 (June 1851): 254.

54

"The Horticultural Shows," *Hort* 5 (September 1850): 106, 107.

55

"A Few Words on Our Progress in Building," *Hort* 6 (June 1851): 250, 251.

56

"American versus British Horticulture," *Hort* 7 (June 1852): 249–50.

57

"Shade Trees in Cities," *Hort* 7 (August 1852): 349.

58

Major Patrick, as quoted in "The Home Education of the Rural Districts," *Hort* 7 (January 1852): 13. See the appendix for the references made or authorities quoted in each editorial.

59

[Luther Tucker], "Mr. Downing and the Horticulturist," *Hort* 7 (September 1852): 397; "How to Arrange Country Places," *Hort* 4 (March 1850): 393. American painters at this time were also demanding "a blend of the real and the ideal," see Novak, 68.

CHAPTER 6

1

"On the Mistakes of Citizens in Country Life," *Hort* 3 (January 1849): 305, 309; *LG* (1849), 68, 66.

2

LG (1849), 18; "How to Arrange Country Places," *Hort* 4 (March 1850): 393; Henry T. Tuckerman statement in 1847, as quoted in Carl Carmer, *The Hudson,* Fiftieth Anniversary ed. (New York: Fordham University Press, 1989), 156.

3

[Luther Tucker,] "Mr. Downing and the Horticulturist," *Hort* 7 (September 1852): 394–95.

4

"Hints to Rural Improvers," *Hort* 3 (July 1848): 10, 14; "On Feminine Taste in Rural Affairs," *Hort* 3 (April 1849): 450, 451. For other references to the Anglo-Saxon inheritance, see the appendix.

5

"The Philosophy of Rural Taste," *Hort* 4 (August 1849): 57; Ruskin, *Modern Painters II,* in *Works,* 4: 81.

6

"The Philosophy of Rural Taste," *Hort* 4 (August 1849): 57, 59; J. J. Baker, "Influence of External Nature on Man," *Godey's* 45 (October 1852): 375, 376; "How to Build Ice-Houses," *Hort* 1 (December 1846): 249. On climatic causality, see Glacken, 551–654; William H. Goetzmann, *New Lands, New Men* (New York: Viking, 1986), 331; Alfred W. Crosby, *Ecological Imperialism* (Cambridge: Cambridge University Press, 1986); and Edmunds V. Bunkse, "Humboldt and An Aesthetic Tradition in Geography," *Geographical Review* 71 (April 1981): 127–46.

7

"The Philosophy of Rural Taste," *Hort* 4 (August 1849): 57; Alexander von Humboldt, *Cosmos,* trans. E. C. Otte, 2 vols. (New York: Harper & Bros., 1849). The previous year, Lindley had devoted four *Gardeners' Chronicle* articles to Humboldt's *Cosmos* (second ed., London, 1847), concentrating on two sections of interest to landscape gardeners—"Incitements to the Study of Nature" and "Descriptions of Natural Scenery." Lindley posed a question: "Why should inhabitants of the northern climate be warm and eloquent admirers and describers of the beauties of natural scenery—while those who lived among the far more enchanting beauties of southern climes were cold and indifferent?" Leaving this unanswered, Lindley quoted Humboldt on Grecian art (see note 9 for Downing's use of the passage in 1849) and then stated, "How far in extent, or whether in principle, it is correct, is a matter for future application of thoughts and feelings." Perhaps Downing was prompted to respond a year later. See John Lindley, *GC* 8 (April 15, 1848): 252. See also *GC* 8 (May 6, 1848): 300; *GC* 8 (May 20, 1848): 331–32; *GC* 8 (June 3, 1848): 363.

8

Humboldt, 1: 25; 2: 26.

9

Ibid., 2: 19, 20, 22, 25, 29, as quoted in "The Philosophy of Rural Taste," *Hort* 4 (August 1849): 58. The quotations do not correspond word for word with the Otte translation; I have used Downing's version.

10

"The Philosophy of Rural Taste," *Hort* 4 (August 1849): 58, 59.

11

"The Beautiful in a Tree," *Hort* 6 (February 1851): 58, 59.

12

"The Beautiful in Ground," *Hort* 7 (March 1852): 106.

13

Ibid., 107.

14

"How to Choose a Site for a Country Seat," *Hort* 2 (December 1847): 249–50.

15

"A Chapter on Lawns," *Hort* 1 (November 1846): 201–4.

16

Ibid., 204; Downing to Smith, 15 Nov. 1841, LCP in HSP.

17
"How to Choose a Site for a Country Seat," *Hort* 2 (December 1847): 249–50.

18
Review of *A Treatise on the Theory and Practice of Landscape Gardening* and *Cottage Residences*, by A. J. Downing, *NAR* 56 (January 1843): 6; R. C. Taylor, "Foreign Notice," *GM* 8 (February 1832): 74. For the American aversion to trees, see Buckingham, 2: 294; Cooper, 213; Grund, 1: 266; and Robinson, "Odds and Ends–No. 3," *Cultivator* 8 (September 1841); reprinted in Robinson, 238; Lyell, 1: 26; "How to Choose a Site for a Country Seat," *Hort* 2 (December 1847): 251–52.

19
"Trees, in Towns and Villages," *Hort* 1 (March 1847): 393; "How to Choose a Site for a Country Seat," *Hort* 2 (December 1847): 252; John Lindley, *GC* 7 (October 9, 1847): 667, as quoted in "English and American Landscape Gardening," *Hort* 2 (December 1847): 262. On the ax as a symbol of progress, see Novak, 157; and Perry Miller, *Nature's Nation* (Cambridge: Belknap Press of Harvard University Press, 1967), 198.

20
"How to Choose a Site for a Country Seat," *Hort* 2 (December 1847): 249–52.

21
"Hints to Rural Improvers," *Hort* 3 (July 1848): 10, 13.

22
"On the Mistakes of Citizens in Country Life," *Hort* 3 (January 1849): 306–9; W. H. Scott, "Notes on the Architecture and Gardening of the Eastern States," *Hort* 3 (January 1849): 328. The interpretation that ascribes the introduction of manufacturing technologies in the U.S. to a shortage of labor created in a nation that contained a modest population and abundant land is contested by Carville Earle and Ronald Hoffman, "The Foundation of the Modern Economy: Agriculture and the Costs of Labor in the United States and England, 1800–60," *American Historical Review* 85 (December 1980): 1055–94.

23
S. B. Gookins, "Hints on the Formation of Rural Taste," *Hort* 3 (April 1849): 470; "Economy in Gardening," *Hort* 3 (May 1849): 497–99. On the constant fretting and toiling to supply labor in America, see Martineau, 2: 93–94; and Fessenden: "In Europe land is *dear,* and labour *cheap;* but in the United States the reverse is the case," as quoted in review of *The Complete Farmer and Rural Economist,* by Thomas G. Fessenden, *GM* 11 (January 1835): 88. Downing also generalized about the characters of Irish and German emigrants in "American versus British Horticulture," *Hort* 7 (June 1852): 250.

24
"Economy in Gardening," *Hort* 3 (May 1849): 499–500. Hindle (140) reports that in contrast to British workers Americans generally welcomed laborsaving machines.

25
"On Transplanting Large Trees," *Hort* 4 (January 1850): 297, 298–301; J. R. Hammond, "Transplanting on the Unbroken Prairie Sod, &c.," *Hort* 4 (November 1849): 205.

26
"How to Arrange Country Places," *Hort* 4 (March 1850): 396, 395.

27
"The Management of Large Country Places," *Hort* 6 (March 1851): 105–7.

28
Ibid., 106–8.

29
"Citizens Retiring to the Country," *Hort* 7 (February 1852): 57–58.

30
"Trees, in Towns and Villages," *Hort* 1 (March 1847): 394; "The Neglected American Plants," *Hort* 6 (May 1851): 201–3; "Shade Trees in Cities," *Hort* 7 (August 1852): 346.

31

"Trees, in Towns and Villages," *Hort* 1 (March 1847): 396, 397.

32

"Rare Evergreen Trees," *Hort* 1 (June 1847): 537–42. What Downing called the Chili Pine (*Araucaria araucana*) is now known as the Monkey-puzzle Tree. The Cedar of Lebanon is *Cedrus libani stenocoma*; "The Cedar of Lebanon," *Garden and Forest* 2 (March 27, 1889): 147–49. This illustrated article included Downing's reference (*LG*, 1849, 298) to the specimen in the grounds of Mr. Thomas Ash of Westchester Co., N.Y. "A Word in Favor of Evergreens," *Hort* 2 (May 1848): 489–93. Downing's Norway Spruce (*Abies excelsa*) is *Picea abies*. "The great California Silver Fir, (*Picea grandis*)" is likely Giant Fir (*Abies grandis*) and the "noble Silver Fir, (*P. nobilis*)" the Noble Fir (*Abies procera*).

33

"The Neglected American Plants," *Hort* 6 (May 1851): 201–2, 203; Patrick Shirreff, "A Tour through North America," *GM* 12 (April 1836): 189–92. C. M. Hovey's *Magazine of Horticulture,* in its twenty-fifth anniversary volume (1859), happily recorded "a more general appreciation of our splendid native plants, the Rhododendron, Kalmia, Azalea, Magnolia, &c., which are now being more freely introduced into our gardens." Nevertheless, Hovey noted that "there are thousands, if not tens of thousands, of these plants grown in England to one in our own gardens." See C. M. Hovey, "The Progress of Horticulture," *MH* 25 (January 1859): 10.

34

"A Few Hints on Landscape Gardening," *Hort* 6 (November 1851): 490–91.

35

"How to Popularize the Taste for Planting," *Hort* 7 (July 1852): 298; "Shade Trees in Cities," *Hort* 7 (August 1852): 345–46.

36

"Shade Trees in Cities," *Hort* 7 (August 1852): 346–47, 349. Downing's "Abele" is likely *Populus alba nivea*.

37

LG (1849), 68, 76fn; "A Few Hints on Landscape Gardening," *Hort* 6 (November 1851): 491; "Hints to Rural Improvers," *Hort* 3 (July 1848): 9.

38

"The Beautiful in a Tree," *Hort* 6 (February 1851): 57.

39

"The Neglected American Plants," *Hort* 6 (May 1851): 201–3; Charles Darwin, *Journal of Researches into . . . the Various Countries Visited by H.M.S. Beagle* (London: Henry Colburn, 1839), 228. Downing refers to Darwin in "A Chapter on Roses," *Hort* 3 (August 1848): 57. For a discussion of Darwin and Victorian ideas of civilization, see Donald Worster, *Nature's Economy* (New York: Cambridge University Press, 1977); Goetzmann (365–98) discusses the discovery of strange new people and cultures that occurred during the explorations of the eighteenth and nineteenth centuries. Howe (24) notes that the prevalence of racial and ethnic stereotypes among even enlightened Victorians is often startling.

40

"The Beautiful in a Tree," *Hort* 6 (February 1851): 58, 59. According to Stein (1), John Ruskin's *Modern Painters I* was "the most extended defense of the painter [J. M. W. Turner] yet to be written and the most sweeping in its denunciation of the accepted old masters of painting." He also states (37–38) that Ruskin "claimed that Turner was true to nature and Claude merely to tradition." [Franklin B. Dexter,] review of *Modern Painters I,* by John Ruskin, *NAR* 66 (January 1848): 113.

41

"A Few Hints on Landscape Gardening," *Hort* 6 (November 1851): 491.

42

Ibid. Durand, as quoted in Stein, 115; "Shade Trees in Cities," *Hort* 7 (August 1852): 346.

Notes to Pages 159–163

CHAPTER 7

1
"Shade Trees in Cities," *Hort* 7 (August 1852): 347.

2
LG (1841), i.

3
In *Hort* 7 (August 1852), a subscriber from Louisville, Kentucky, wrote "On Summer Pruning Hardy Grapes," 370–71. From Northfield, Illinois, John A. Kennicott sent in "Illinois Horticulture–Insects–Prof. Turner, Etc.," 372–75. From Fayetteville, Arkansas, J. M. J. Smith commented upon "The Cold Winter in Arkansas," 383–84. "The Climate of San Francisco" was an extract from a scientific account by Dr. Gibbons, 382. Editorial comment to Testis, "Fruit Culture in Upper Georgia," *Hort* 7 (August 1852): 366; "Shade Trees in Cities," *Hort* 7 (August 1852): 346, 348.

4
Vaux recalled that on the day of his death Downing had been on his way to Newport, Rhode Island, to supervise construction of Daniel Parish's villa. See Calvert Vaux, *Villas and Cottages; A Series of Designs Prepared for Execution in the United States* (New York: Harper & Brothers, 1857), xi; Vaux described the design of the "Park at Washington" in Vaux to Wilder, 18 August [1852], LCP in HSP.

5
"A Talk About Public Parks and Gardens," *Hort* 3 (October 1848): 154, 158; "Public Cemeteries and Public Gardens," *Hort* 4 (July 1849): 12.

6
A. J. Downing, "Explanatory Notes to Accompany the Plan for Improving the Public Grounds at Washington, D.C.," 3 March 1851, Records of the Commissioners of Public Buildings, Letters Received, RG 42, LR, vol. 32, National Archives, Washington, D.C. A transcription of these notes is in John W. Reps, "Romantic Planning in a Baroque City: Downing and the Washington Mall," *Landscape* 16 (Spring 1967): 6–11; and in Wilcomb E. Washburn, "Vision of Life for the Mall," *AIA Journal* 47 (March 1967): 52–59. On Downing's design, also see David Schuyler, "The Washington Park and Downing's Legacy to Public Landscape Design," in Tatum and MacDougall, eds., *Prophet with Honor*, 291–311; and Therese O'Malley, "'A Public Museum of Trees': Mid-Nineteenth Century Plans for the Mall," *Studies in the History of Art* 30 (1991): 60–76.

7
Downing, "Explanatory Notes" in Reps, 11; "The Neglected American Plants," *Hort* 6 (May 1851): 203.

8
Downing in Reps, 11; and Downing in Washburn, 55; There is a difference in Reps's and Washburn's transcriptions of a key word in the section "Smithsonian Park or Pleasure Grounds." The document in the National Archives is a handwritten copy of Downing's original text. In Reps, the sentence reads "An arrangement of choice trees in the *national* style." Washburn correctly reports it as "in the *natural* style." I am obliged to Joseph Disponzio for verifying the word as written in the archives document. For the "spirit of nature" comment, see "The Philosophy of Rural Taste," *Hort* 4 (August 1849): 57; *LG* (1849), 111.

9
Downing, in Reps, 10; "Mr. Downing's Letters From England," *Hort* 5 (November 1850): 219. On Price and fountains, see H. Noel Humphreys, "Notes on Decorative Gardening—Fountains," *Hort* 5 (November 1850): 208. For the "inter-national opinion" comment, see "Trees, in Towns and Villages," *Hort* 1 (March 1847): 424.

10
"Mr. Downing's Letters From England," *Hort* 5 (October 1850): 156; Downing in Reps, 11. See "The Great Palm House at Kew," *Hort* 7 (April 1852): 191: "The rich collection of plants . . . are worthy of the great national garden in which it stands, and which the British nation keeps up at a large annual cost." Humboldt, 2: 99–100; "How to Popularize the Taste for Planting," *Hort* 7 (July 1852): 297–98.

11
Vaux to Wilder, 18 August [1852], LCP in HSP; Downing in Reps, 11. On subsequent changes to the Mall, see Washburn; and Richard Longstreth, ed., *The Mall in Washington, 1791–1991* (Hanover, N.H.: University Press of New England, 1991). On Vaux and Olmsted's collaboration on the design for Central Park, see Charles E. Beveridge and David Schuyler, eds., *The Papers of Frederick Law Olmsted,* vol. 3, *Creating Central Park: 1857–1861* (Baltimore: Johns Hopkins University Press, 1983). Downing labeled Olmsted "one of our original young Yankee farmers" in review of *Walks and Talks of an American Farmer in England,* by Fred. Law Olmsted, *Hort* 7 (March 1852): 135; F. L. Olmsted, "Queries on Sea-Coast Culture," *Hort* 2 (August 1847): 100. For Vaux and Olmsted's later work, see David Schuyler and Jane Turner Censer, eds., *The Papers of Frederick Law Olmsted,* vol. 6, *The Years of Olmsted, Vaux & Company: 1865–1874* (Baltimore: Johns Hopkins University Press, 1992).

12
Henry Colman as the "Traveller," in "A Talk About Public Parks and Gardens," *Hort* 3 (October 1848): 158; N.H., "Review," *Home Journal,* as quoted in "Architecture of Country Houses," *Hort* 5 (September 1850): 140–41.

BIBLIOGRAPHY

Primary Sources

Adams, John Quincy. *Memoirs of John Quincy Adams, comprising portions of his diary from 1795 to 1848.* Vol. 10. Ed. Charles Francis Adams. Philadelphia: J. B. Lippincott & Co., 1876.

Addison, Joseph. *The Spectator.* Ed. G. Gregory Smith. 4 vols. New York: E. P. Dutton, 1909.

Alison, Archibald. *Essays on the Nature and Principles of Taste.* Dublin: Printed for Messrs. P. Byrne, J. Moore, Grueber and M'Allister, W. Jones, and R. White, 1790.

Allen, Lewis F. *Address delivered before the New-York State Agricultural Society, 18th January, 1849.* Albany: Weed, Parsons & Co., 1849.

Bacon, Francis. "Of Gardens" [1625]. In *Essays.* New York: Hurst & Co., [1883].

Barclay, Captain [R. Barclay-Allardice]. *Agricultural Tour in the United States and Upper Canada, with Miscellaneous Notices.* Edinburgh: William Blackwood & Sons, 1842.

Barnard, Henry. *Practical Illustrations of the Principles of School Architecture.* [Hartford: n.p., 1851].

Batteux, Charles. *Les Beaux Arts réduits à un même principe.* N.p., 1773; reprint, Geneva: Slatkine Reprints, 1969.

Benson, Adolph B., ed. "Fredrika Bremer's Unpublished Letters to the Downings." *Scandinavian Studies and Notes* 11 (February 1930): 1–10; 11 (May 1930): 39–53; 11 (August 1930): 71–78; 11 (November 1930): 109–24; 11 (February 1931): 149–72; 11 (May 1931): 187–205; 11 (August 1931): 215–28; 11 (November 1931): 264–74.

Bremer, Fredrika. *The Homes of the New World: Impressions of America.* Trans. Mary Howitt. 2 vols. New York: Harper & Bros., 1854.

Bryant, William Cullen. *Letters of a Traveller; or, Notes of things seen in Europe and America.* New York: George P. Putnam, 1850.

BIBLIOGRAPHY

The Letters of William Cullen Bryant. Ed. William Cullen Bryant II and Thomas G. Voss. Vol. 2, *1836–1849*. New York: Fordham University Press, 1977.

The Letters of William Cullen Bryant. Ed. William Cullen Bryant II and Thomas G. Voss. Vol. 3, *1849–1857*. New York: Fordham University Press, 1981.

Buckingham, J. S. *The Eastern and Western States of America.* 3 vols. London & Paris: Fisher, Son, & Co., 1842.

Burke, Edmund. *A Philosophical Inquiry into the Origin of Our Ideas of the Sublime and Beautiful.* Ed. with an introduction and notes by James. T. Boulton. Oxford: Basil Blackwell, 1987.

Burton, Warren. *The District School As It Was, Scenery-Showing, and Other Writings.* Boston: T. R. Marvin, 1852.

Bushnell, Horace. *Christian Nurture.* Edinburgh: Alexander Strahan & Co., 1861.

Chambers, William. *A Dissertation on Oriental Gardening.* 1772; reprint, Westmead, Farnborough, Hants, England: Gregg International Publishers, 1972.

Channing, William E. "Remarks on National Literature." In *The Works of William E. Channing.* Vol. 1. Boston: James Munroe & Co., 1841.

Chevalier, Michael. *Society, Manners and Politics in the United States: Being a Series of Letters on North America.* Translated from the third Paris edition. Boston: Weeks, Jordan & Co., 1839.

Colman, Henry. *The Agriculture and Rural Economy of France, Belgium, Holland, and Switzerland.* London: John Petheram, 1848.

European Agriculture and Rural Economy. 2d ed. Boston: Charles C. Little & James Brown, 1849.

[Cook, Clarence]. "The Late A. J. Downing." *The New-York Quarterly* 1 (October 1852): 367–82.

[Cooper, Susan Fenimore]. *Rural Hours by a Lady.* New York: George P. Putnam, 1851.

Cowper, William. *The Task.* London: Printed for J. Johnson, 1785; reprint, London: Scolar Press Facsimile, 1973.

Darwin, Charles. *Journal of Researches into the Geology and Natural History of the Various Countries Visited by H.M.S. Beagle, Under the Command of Captain Fitzroy, R.N. From 1832 to 1836.* London: Henry Colburn, Great Marlborough Street, 1839.

DeBow, J. D. B. *Seventh Census of the United States: 1850.* Washington, D.C.: Robert Armstrong, 1853.

DeLille, Abbé. *The Gardens, A Poem.* Translated from the French of the Abbé DeLille. London: Printed by T. Bensley, 1798.

Delille, Jacques. *Les Jardins.* Paris: Michaud Frères, 1813.

Downing, A. J. *A Treatise on the Theory and Practice of Landscape Gardening adapted to North America; with a view to the Improvement of Country Residences.* New York & London: Wiley & Putnam, 1841; Boston: C. C. Little & Co., 1841.

Landscape Gardening. 2d ed., enlarged, revised and newly illustrated. New York & London: Wiley & Putnam, 1844.

Landscape Gardening. 4th ed., enlarged, revised, and newly illustrated. New York: George P. Putnam, 1849; London: Longman, Brown, Green & Longmans, 1849.

Landscape Gardening. 5th ed. New York: G. P. Putnam & Co., 1853.

Landscape Gardening. 6th ed., enlarged, revised, and newly illustrated. With a supplement by Henry Winthrop Sargent. New York: A. O. Moore & Co., 1859.

Landscape Gardening. 10th ed. revised by Frank A. Waugh. New York: John Wiley & Sons, Inc., 1921.

Landscape Gardening. With the 1859 6th ed. supplement by Henry Winthrop Sargent and a special appreciation by John O. Simonds, Jr. New York: Funk & Wagnalls, 1967.

Landscape Gardening. New York: Orange Judd Company, 1875. 9th ed. with supplement [1859] and second supplement [1875] by Henry Winthrop Sargent; reprint, Sakonnet: Theophrastus Publishers, 1977.

Landscape Gardening. With an introduction by Therese O'Malley. New York: George P. Putnam, 1850; reprint, Washington, D.C.: Dumbarton Oaks, 1991.

Landscape Gardening and Rural Architecture. With a new introduction by George B. Tatum. New York: Orange Judd, 1865; reprint, New York: Dover Publications, 1991.

Cottage Residences: or, a Series of Designs for Rural Cottages and Cottage-Villas, and Their Gardens and Grounds, Adapted to North America. New York & London: Wiley & Putnam, 1842.

Cottage Residences. 2d ed. New York: Wiley & Putnam, 1844.

Cottage Residences. 3d ed. New York: Wiley & Putnam, 1847.

Cottage Residences. 4th ed. New York: John Wiley, 1852.

Victorian Cottage Residences. New York: John Wiley & Son, 1873; reprint, with a new preface by Adolf K. Placzek, New York: Dover Publications, 1981.

The Fruits and Fruit-Trees of America. New York & London: Wiley & Putnam, 1845.

The Architecture of Country Houses; including Designs for Cottages, Farm Houses, and Villas, with Remarks on Interiors, Furniture, and the Best Modes of Warming and Ventilating. New York: D. Appleton & Co., 1850; reprint, Dover Publications, 1969.

Rural Essays. Ed., with a memoir of the author, by George William Curtis, and a letter to his friends by Fredrika Bremer. New York: George P. Putnam & Co., 1853.

ed. *The Horticulturist and Journal of Rural Art and Rural Taste. Devoted to Horticulture, Landscape Gardening, Rural Architecture, Botany, Pomology, Entomology, Rural Economy, &c.* July 1846 to July 1852.

Dwight, Theodore. *Summer Tours; or, Notes of a Traveler Through Some of the Middle and Northern States.* 2d. ed. New York: Harper & Bros., 1847.

Dwight, Timothy. *Travels in New England and New York.* 1821. Ed. Barbara Miller Solomon. 4 vols. Cambridge: Belknap Press of Harvard University Press, 1969.

Emerson, G. *Lecture on the Advantages Derived from Cultivating the Arts and Sciences.* Philadelphia: n.p., 1840.

Address delivered before the Delaware Horticultural Society at Wilmington, on the 24th of September, 1851. Philadelphia: n.p., 1851.

Emerson, Ralph Waldo. *Nature* and "The American Scholar." In *The Complete Works of Ralph Waldo Emerson.* With a biographical introduction and notes by Edward Waldo Emerson. Vol. 1. Boston & New York: Houghton Mifflin Co., 1903.

Fessenden, Thomas G. *The New American Gardener.* Boston: J. B. Russell, 1828.

Gardiner, Robert Hallowell, *Early Recollections of Robert Hallowell Gardiner, 1782–1864.* Hallowell, Maine: White & Horne Co., 1936.

Gilpin, William. *A Dialogue Upon the Gardens . . . at Stow.* London: Printed for B. Seeley, 1748; reprint, Los Angeles: William Andrews Clark Memorial Library, University of California, 1976.

Remarks on Forest Scenery. London: Printed for R. Blamire, Strand, 1791; reprint, with a new introduction by Sutherland Lyall, Richmond, Surrey: Richmond Publishing Co., 1973.

Three Essays; on Picturesque Beauty; on Picturesque Travel; and on Sketching Landscape; to which is added a poem on Landscape Painting. 2d ed. London: R. Blamire, 1794; reprint, Westmead, Farnborough, Hants, England: Gregg International Publishers, 1972.

Gilpin, William S. *Practical Hints Upon Landscape Gardening.* 2d ed. London: Printed for T. Cadell, 1835.

Girardin, R. L. *De La Composition des Paysages.* Genève: n.p., 1777.

BIBLIOGRAPHY

Good, John Mason. *The Book of Nature.* From the last London edition. New York: J. & J. Harper, 1831.

Griscom, David. *Descriptive Catalogue of Foreign and Native Evergreen and Deciduous Trees.* Woodbury, N. J.: Evergreen Nursery, 1855–56.

Grund, Francis J. *The Americans in Their Moral, Social, and Political Relations.* 2 vols. London: Longman, Rees, Orme, Brown, Green, & Longman, 1837.

Hirschfeld, C. C. L. *Théorie de l'Art des Jardins.* Traduit de l'Allemand. Leipzig: Chez les Heritiers de M. G. Weidmann et Reich, 1779.

Hofland, Mrs. *A Descriptive Account of the Mansion and Gardens of White-Knights, A Seat of His Grace the Duke of Marlborough.* London: Printed for His Grace the Duke of Marlborough, [1819].

Hogarth, William. *The Analysis of Beauty.* London: Printed by J. Reeves for the author, 1753; reprint, Menston, Yorkshire, England: Scolar Press, 1971.

Home Book of the Picturesque. [1852] A facsimile reproduction with an introduction by Motley F. Deakin. Gainesville, Florida: Scholars' Facsimiles & Reprints, 1967.

Howitt, William. *The Rural Life of England.* From the 2d London ed. Corrected and revised. Philadelphia: Carey and Hart, 1841.

Humboldt, Alexander von. *Cosmos.* Trans. E. C. Otte. 2 vols. New York: Harper & Bros., 1849.

Hume, David. "Of the Standard of Taste." In *Four Dissertations.* London: Printed for A. Millar, 1757; reprint, New York: Garland Publishing, 1970.

Irving, Washington. *The Complete Works of Washington Irving.* Ed. Richard Dilworth Rust. *Letters, Volume II, 1823–1838.* Boston: Twayne Publishers, 1979.

The Complete Works of Washington Irving. Ed. Richard Dilworth Rust. *Letters, Volume IV, 1846–1859.* Boston: Twayne Publishers, 1982.

Knight, R. P. *The Landscape, a Didactic Poem.* London: Printed by W. Bulmer & Co., 1794.

Lauder, Thomas Dick, ed. *Sir Uvedale Price on the Picturesque.* With an Essay on the Origin of Taste and Much Original Matter, by Sir Thomas Dick Lauder. Edinburgh: Caldwell, Lloyd, & Co.; London; Wm. S. Orr & Co., 1842.

Lieber, Francis. *The Stranger in America: Comprising Sketches of the Manners, Society, and National Peculiarities of the United States.* 2 vols. London: Richard Bentley, 1835.

Lindley, John. *The Theory of Horticulture: or, An Attempt to Explain the Principal Operations of Gardening upon Physiological Principles.* First American Edition, with Notes, Etc., by A. J. Downing and A. Gray. New York: Wiley & Putnam, 1841.

Loiseleur-Deslongchamps, M. *L'Herbier général de l'amateur.* Paris: H. Cousin, 1839–44.

Loudon, J[ohn]. [Claudius]. *Observations on the Formation and Management of Useful and Ornamental Plantations; on the Theory and Practice of Landscape Gardening; and on Gaining and Embanking Land from Rivers or the Sea.* Edinburgh: Printed for Archibald Constable & Co., 1804.

An Encyclopedia of Gardening. 2d ed. London: Longman, Hurst, Rees, Orme, Brown, and Green, 1824.

An Encyclopedia of Gardening. New ed. London: Longman, Rees, Orme, Brown, Green, & Longman, 1835; reprint, New York: Garland Publishing, 1982.

Arboretum et Fruticetum Britannicum. 8 vols. London: n.p., 1838.

The Suburban Gardener, and Villa Companion: Comprising the Choice of Suburban or Villa Residence, or of a Situation on which to Form One; the Arrangement and Furnishing of the House; and the Laying Out, Planting, and General Management of the Garden and Grounds. London: Longman, Orme, Brown, Green & Longmans, 1838.

The Landscape Gardening and Landscape Architecture of the Late Humphry Repton, Esq. being his Entire Works on these Subjects. A New Edition: With an Historical and Scientific Introduction, A Systematic Analysis, A Biographical

Notice, Notes, and a Copious Alphabetical Index. London: Longman & Co., 1840.

On the Laying Out, Planting and Managing of Cemeteries, and on the Improvement of Churchyards. London: Longman, Brown, Green & Longmans, 1843.

Lowell, James Russell. *The Complete Poetical Works of James Russell Lowell.* Ed. Horace E. Scudder. Cambridge: Riverside Press of Houghton Mifflin Co., 1897.

Lyell, Charles. *Travels in North America: with Geological Observations on the United States, Canada, and Nova Scotia.* 2 vols. London: John Murray, 1845.

Marryat, Captain. *A Diary in America with Remarks on its Institutions.* 2 vols. Philadelphia: Carey & Hart, 1839.

Martineau, Harriet. *Society in America.* 3 vols. London: Saunders & Otley, 1837.

Mason, George. *An Essay on Design in Gardening.* London: Printed for Benjamin White, 1768; reprint, New York: Garland Publishing, 1982.

Mason, William. *The English Garden: A Poem.* London: Pall-Mall, 1783; reprint, New York: Garland Publishing, 1982.

Meigs, Henry. *An Address, on the Subject of Agriculture and Horticulture, Delivered in the Church of the Messiah, on Thursday, October 9th, 1845.* New York: James Van Norden & Co., 1845.

Agricultural Address, delivered in Castle Garden by Direction of the American Institute, October 9th, 1846. New York: Joseph H. Jennings, 1846.

Milton, John. *Paradise Lost.* New ed., ed. Merrit Y. Hughes. New York: Macmillan Publishing Co., 1985.

M'Mahon, Bernard. *The American Gardener's Calendar; adapted to the Climates and Seasons of the United States.* Philadelphia: Printed by B. Graves, for the Author, 1806.

Morel, J.-M. *Théorie des Jardins, ou l'Art des Jardins de la Nature.* 2d ed. 2 vols. Paris: La Ve Panckoucke, 1802.

Murray, Charles Augustus. *Travels in North America During the Years 1834, 1835, & 1836.* 2 vols. London: Richard Bentley, 1839.

North, Christopher [John Wilson]. *The Recreations of Christopher North.* New York: D. Appleton & Co., 1860.

Parsons, S. B. *An Address Delivered at the Annual Fair of the New Haven County Horticultural Society, September 26, 1849.* New Haven: n.p., 1849.

Pope, Alexander. *The Works of Alexander Pope.* Introduction and notes by Rev. Whitwell Elwin and William John Courthope. 10 vols. London: John Murray, 1886.

Epistles to Several Persons. Ed. F. W. Bateson. New Haven: Yale University Press, 1951.

Price, Sir Uvedale. *An Essay on the Picturesque, as Compared with the Sublime and the Beautiful; and, on the Use of Studying Pictures, for the Purpose of Improving Real Landscape.* 3 vols. London: Printed for J. Mawman, 1810.

Pückler-Muskau, Prince von. *Hints on Landscape Gardening.* Trans. Bernhard Sickert, ed. Samuel Parsons. Boston & New York: Houghton Mifflin Co., 1917.

Quatremère de Quincy, [A. C.] *An Essay on the Nature, the End, and the Means of Imitation in the Fine Arts.* Trans. J. C. Kent. London: Smith, Elder & Co., 1837.

Repton, H. *Sketches and Hints on Landscape Gardening collected from Designs and Observations now in the Possession of the Different Noblemen and Gentlemen, for whose use they were originally made. The whole tending to establish Fixed Principles in the Art of Laying Out Ground.* London: Printed by W. Bulmer & Co., [1794].

Observations on the Theory and Practice of Landscape Gardening. London: Printed by T. Bensley, 1803.

An Enquiry into the Changes of Taste in Landscape Gardening. To which are added, some Observations on its Theory and Practice, including a Defence of the Art. London: Printed for J. Taylor, 1806.

assisted by his son J. Adey Repton. *Fragments on the Theory and Practice of Landscape Gardening.* London: Printed by T. Bensley & Son, 1816.

BIBLIOGRAPHY

The Art of Landscape Gardening. Ed. John Nolen. Boston & New York: Houghton Mifflin Company; Cambridge: Riverside Press, 1907.

Reynolds, Sir Joshua. *Discourses on Art.* Ed. Robert R. Wark. New Haven: Yale University Press, 1975.

Robinson, Solon. *Solon Robinson: Pioneer and Agriculturist.* Selected writings, ed. Herbert Anthony Kellar. Vol. 1, *1825–1845.* Indiana Historical Collections, vol. 21. Indianapolis: Indiana Historical Bureau, 1936.

Ruskin, John. *Modern Painters.* Vol. 1. In *The Works of John Ruskin.* Vol. 3. Ed. E. T. Cook and Alexander Wedderburn. London: George Allen, 1903.

Modern Painters. Vol. 2. In *The Works.* Vol. 4.

Scott, Frank J. *The Art of Beautifying Suburban Home Grounds of Small Extent.* New York: D. Appleton & Co., 1870; reprint, American Life Foundation, n.d.

Sill, Joseph. Diary in 10 vols. Manuscript Collection, Historical Society of Pennsylvania, Philadelphia.

[Smith, John Jay]. *Guide to Laurel Hill Cemetery near Philadelphia.* For Sale at the Cemetery, and by the Treasurer, etc. C. Sherman, Printer, 1844.

Designs for Monuments and Mural Tablets: adapted to Rural Cemeteries, Church Yards, Churches, and Chapels. With a Preliminary Essay on the Laying Out, Planting and Managing of Cemeteries and on the Improvement of Church Yards on the basis of Loudon's Work. New York: Bartlett & Welford, 1846.

Recollections. 3 vols. Manuscript copy, extra illustrated. The Library Company of Philadelphia.

Recollections of John Jay Smith written by himself. Philadelphia: Privately printed, 1892.

Story, William W. *Address Delivered Before the Harvard Musical Association in the Chapel of the University at Cambridge, August 24, 1842.* Boston: n.p., 1842.

Tappan, Henry P. *A Step from the New World to the Old, and Back Again.* 2 vols. New York: D. Appleton & Co., 1852.

Tocqueville, Alexis de. *Democracy in America.* 2 vols. The Henry Reeve Text as revised by Francis Bowen, corrected and edited with introduction, editorial notes, and bibliographies by Phillips Bradley. New York: Alfred A. Knopf, 1945.

Democracy in America. Ed. J. P. Mayer, trans. George Lawrence. New York: Harper & Row Perennial Library, 1988.

Vaux, Calvert. *Villas and Cottages; A Series of Designs Prepared for Execution in the United States.* New York: Harper & Brothers, 1857.

Wainwright, Nicholas B., ed. *A Philadelphia Perspective: The Diary of Sidney George Fisher, Covering the Years 1834–1871.* Philadelphia: Historical Society of Pennsylvania, 1967.

Walpole, Horace. *On Modern Gardening,* 1780; reprint, with preface and bibliographical note by W. S. Lewis. New York: Young Books, 1931.

Waugh, Frank A. *The Landscape Beautiful.* New York: Orange Judd Co., 1912.

Whately, Thomas. *Observations on Modern Gardening.* London: Printed for T. Payne, 1770; reprint, New York: Garland Publishing, 1982.

Wightwick, George. *Hints to Young Architects; together with a model specification, etc. And Hints to Persons About Building in the Country.* by A. J. Downing. New York: Wiley & Putnam, 1847.

Willis, N[athaniel]. P[arker]. *American Scenery.* 2 vols. Illustrated in a series of views by W. H. Bartlett. London: George Virtue, 1840.

Out-Doors at Idlewild-or, the Shaping of a Home on the Banks of the Hudson. New York: Charles Scribner, 1855.

Wordsworth, William. *A Guide through the District of the Lakes.* London: Longman, 1835; reprint, London: Rupert Hart-Davis, 1951.

Secondary Sources

Periodicals Consulted as Primary Sources

American Gardener's Magazine 1 (November 1835) to 2 (December 1836).

Architectural Magazine 1 (1834) to 5 (1838).

Boston Miscellany of Literature & Fashion 1 (January–July 1842) to 2 (1842–43).

Columbian Lady's and Gentleman's Magazine 5 (1846) to 7 (1847).

Cultvator, n.s. 2 (1845) to n.s. 5 (1848).

Farmer's Library 1 (July 1845–June 1846).

Gardeners' Chronicle 1 (1841) to 8 (1848).

Gardener's Magazine 1 (1826) to 19 (1843).

Gardeners' Magazine, n.s. 1 (January–June 1850) to n.s. 3 (January–December 1851).

Godey's Lady's Book, and Ladies' American Magazine 20 (1840) to 27 (1843).

Godey's Magazine and Lady's Book 28 (1844) to 41 (1850).

Godey's Lady's Book 42 (1851) to 45 (1852).

Graham's Lady's and Gentleman's Magazine 19 (1841) to 35 (1849).

Literary World 1 (1847) to 7 (1850).

Magazine of Horticulture 3 (January 1837) to 9 (1843); 25 (1859).

New-York Mirror 10 (1833) to 19 (1841).

North American Review 52 (April 1841) to 59 (October 1844).

United States Magazine and Democratic Review 5 (April 1839) to 21 (November 1847).

Secondary Sources

Adams, William Howard. *Nature Perfected.* New York: Abbeville Press, 1991.

Allen, B. Sprague. *Tides in English Taste (1619–1800).* 2 vols. Cambridge: Harvard University Press, 1937.

Andrews, William, and Deborah Andrews. "A. J. Downing: The Architect as Man of Letters." *Journal of the Society of Architectural Historians* 33 (October 1974): 235.

Appleton, Jay. "Some Thoughts on the Geology of the Picturesque." *Journal of Garden History* 6 (July–September 1986): 270–91.

Aristotle. *Aristotle's "Poetics."* Trans. with an introduction and notes by James Hutton. New York: W. W. Norton & Co., 1982.

"At the Highlands Estate near Philadelphia." *Historic Preservation News,* November 1991, 11.

Auser, Cortland P. *Nathaniel P. Willis.* New York: Twayne Publishers, 1969.

Babbitt, Irving. *The New Laokoon: An Essay on the Confusion of the Arts.* Cambridge: Riverside Press, 1910.

Barbier, Carl Paul. *William Gilpin: His Drawings, Teaching, and Theory of the Picturesque.* Oxford: Clarendon Press, 1963.

Baridon, Michel. "Ruins as a Mental Construct." *Journal of Garden History* 5 (January–March 1985): 84–96.

Barnes, Howard A. "Horace Bushnell: Gentleman Theologian." In *Ideas in America's Cultures: from Republic to Mass Society,* ed. Hamilton Cravens, 27–44. Ames: Iowa State University Press, 1982.

Barth, Gunther. *City People: The Rise of the Modern City Culture in Nineteenth-Century America.* New York: Oxford University Press, 1980.

Bate, Walter Jackson. *From Classic to Romantic: Premises of Taste in Eighteenth-Century England.* Cambridge: Harvard University Press, 1949.

Bender, Thomas. *Toward an Urban Vision: Ideas and Institutions in Nineteenth Century America.* Baltimore: Johns Hopkins University Press, 1982.

Berg, Donald J., ed. *How to Build in the Country.* Berkeley: Ten Speed Press, 1986.

Berger, Max. *The British Traveller in America, 1836–1860.* Studies in History, Economics and Public Law, no. 502. New York: Columbia University Press, 1943.

BIBLIOGRAPHY

Beveridge, Charles E. "Frederick Law Olmsted's Theory of Landscape Design." *Nineteenth Century* 3 (Summer 1977): 38–43.

——— and David Schuyler, eds. *The Papers of Frederick Law Olmsted*. Vol. 3, *Creating Central Park: 1857–1861*. Baltimore: Johns Hopkins University Press, 1983.

Bode, Carl, ed. *American Life in the 1840s*. New York: New York University Press, 1967.

Booth, Edward Townsend. *God Made the Country*. New York: Alfred A. Knopf, 1946.

Boyett, Tanya. "Thomas Handasyd Perkins: An Essay on Material Culture." *Old-Time New England* 70 (1980): 45–62.

Boyle, Robert H. *The Hudson River: A Natural and Unnatural History*. New York: W. W. Norton & Co., 1969.

Brandt, Clare. *An American Aristocracy: The Livingstons*. Garden City, New York: Doubleday & Co., 1986.

Brownell, Morris R. *Alexander Pope and the Arts of Georgian England*. Oxford: Clarendon Press, 1978.

Brownlee, David Bruce. *The Law Courts: The Architecture of George Edmund Street*. New York: Architectural History Foundation; Cambridge: MIT Press, 1984.

———, ed. *Friedrich Weinbrenner: Architect of Karlsruhe*. Philadelphia: University of Pennsylvania Press, 1986.

Bullion, Brenda. "Hawthorns and Hemlocks: The Return of the Sacred Grove." *Landscape Journal* 2 (Fall 1983): 114–24.

———. "Early American Farming and Gardening Literature: 'Adapted to the Climates and Seasons of the United States.'" *Journal of Garden History* 12 (January–March 1992): 29–51.

Bunkse, Edmunds V. "Humboldt and an Aesthetic Tradition in Geography." *Geographical Review* 71 (April 1981): 127–46.

Bushman, Richard L. *The Refinement of America: Persons, Houses, Cities*. New York: Vintage Books, 1993.

Callow, James T. *Kindred Spirits: Knickerbocker Writers and American Artists, 1807–1855*. Chapel Hill: University of North Carolina Press, 1967.

Carmer, Carl. *The Hudson*. Fiftieth Anniversary ed. New York: Fordham University Press, 1989.

Chadwick, George F. *The Park and the Town: Public Landscapes in the 19th and 20th Centuries*. New York: Praeger, 1966.

Chambers, Douglas. *The Planters of the English Landscape Garden: Botany, Trees, and the Georgics*. New Haven: Yale University Press, 1993.

Chambers, Frank P. *The History of Taste*. New York: Columbia University Press, 1932.

Charvat, William. *The Origins of American Critical Thought, 1810–1835*. New York: Russell & Russell, 1968.

Chase, David B. "The Beginnings of the Landscape Tradition in America." *Historic Preservation* 25 (January–March 1973): 34–41.

Chase, Isabel Wakelin Urban. *Horace Walpole: Gardenist*. Princeton: Princeton University Press, 1943.

Chidsey, Donald Barr. *And Tyler Too*. Nashville: Thomas Nelson, 1978.

Chielens, Edward E., ed. *American Literary Magazines: The Eighteenth and Nineteenth Centuries*. New York: Greenwood Press, 1986.

Clark, H. F. "Eighteenth Century Elysiums: The Role of 'Association' in the Landscape Movement." *Journal of the Warburg and Courtauld Institutes* 6 (1943): 165–89.

———. "The Sense of Beauty in the 18th, 19th, and 20th Centuries." *Landscape Architecture* 47 (July 1957): 465–69.

Clement, Walter B. "A Treatise on Building a New-Old Downing Cottage Adapted to the Late-20th Century in South Alabama Including a Downing Doghouse." *Old-House Journal*, May/June 1989, 48–52.

Clifford, Derek. *A History of Garden Design*. Rev. ed. New York: Frederick A. Praeger, 1966.

Secondary Sources

Close, A. J. "Commonplace Theories of Art and Nature in Classical Antiquity and in the Renaissance." *Journal of the History of Ideas* 30 (October–December 1969): 467–86.

Corner, James. "A Discourse on Theory II: Three Tyrannies of Contemporary Theory and the Alternative of Hermeneutics." *Landscape Journal* 10 (Fall 1991): 115–33.

Cranz, Galen. *The Politics of Park Design: A History of Urban Parks in America*. Cambridge: MIT Press, 1982.

Creese, Walter L. *The Crowning of the American Landscape: Eight Great Spaces and Their Buildings*. Princeton: Princeton University Press, 1985.

Crosby, Alfred W. *Ecological Imperialism: The Biological Expansion of Europe, 900–1900*. Cambridge: Cambridge University Press, 1986.

Crotz, Keith. "Andrew Jackson Downing: The Father of American Landscaping." *Fine Gardening*, January/February 1990, 47.

Crowe, Norman. *Nature and the Idea of a Man-Made World*. Cambridge: MIT Press, 1995.

Curl, James Stevens. "John Claudius Loudon and the Garden Cemetery Movement." *Garden History* 11 (Autumn 1983): 133–56.

"The Debt of America to A. J. Downing." *Garden and Forest* 8 (29 May 1895): 211–12.

Downs, Arthur Channing, Jr. "Andrew Jackson Downing & the American Bathroom." *Historic Preservation* 23 (October–December 1971): 31–34.

⸻. "Downing's Newburgh Villa." *APT* 4 (1972): 1–113.

⸻. *Downing & the American House*. Newtown Square, Pa.: Downing & Vaux Society, 1988.

Draper, John W. "Aristotelian 'Mimesis' in Eighteenth Century England." *PMLA* 36 (1921): 372–400.

Earle, Carville, and Ronald Hoffman. "The Foundation of the Modern Economy: Agriculture and the Costs of Labor in the United States and England, 1800–60." *American Historical Review* 85 (December 1980): 1055–94.

Eberlein, Harold Donaldson. *The Manors and Historic Homes of the Hudson Valley*. Philadelphia & London: J. B. Lippincott Co., 1924.

Egbert, Donald Drew. *The Beaux-Arts Tradition in French Architecture*. Princeton: Princeton University Press, 1980.

Ekirch, Arthur Alphonse, Jr. *The Idea of Progress in America, 1815–1860*. Columbia University Studies in the Social Sciences, no. 511. New York: Columbia University Press, 1944; reprint, New York: AMS Press, 1969.

Faris, John T. *Old Gardens in and about Philadelphia and Those Who Made Them*. Indianapolis: Bobbs-Merrill Co., 1932.

Favretti, Rudy J. "The Ornamentation of New England Towns: 1750–1850." *Journal of Garden History* 2 (October–December 1982): 325–42.

Fein, Albert, ed. *Landscape into Cityscape*. New York: Van Nostrand Co., 1981.

Ferber, Linda S. "Themes in American Genre Painting: 1840–80." *Apollo* 115 (April 1982): 250–59.

Fitch, James Marston. *Historic Preservation: Curatorial Management of the Built World*. New York: McGraw Hill, 1982.

Fricker, Laurence. "John Claudius Loudon: The plane truth?" In *Furor Hortensis: Essays on the History of the English Landscape Garden in Memory of H. F. Clark*, ed. Peter Willis, 76–88. Edinburgh: Elysium Press, 1974.

Gates, Paul W. *The Farmer's Age: Agriculture 1815–1860*. Vol. 3, The Economic History of the United States. New York: Holt, Rinehart & Winston, 1960.

Geffen, Elizabeth M. "Joseph Sill and His Diary." *Pennsylvania Magazine of History and Biography* 94 (July 1970): 275–330.

Glacken, Clarence J. *Traces on the Rhodian Shore: Nature and Culture in Western Thought from Ancient Times to the End of the Eighteenth Century*. Berkeley: University of California Press, 1976.

BIBLIOGRAPHY

Gloag, John. *Mr. Loudon's England: The Life and Work of John Claudius Loudon, and His Influence on Architecture and Furniture Design.* Newcastle upon Tyne: Oriel Press, 1970.

Goetzmann, William H. *New Lands, New Men.* New York: Viking, 1986.

Gothein, Marie Luise. *A History of Garden Art.* Ed. Walter P. Wright, trans. Mrs. Archer-Hind. London: J. M. Dent, 1928.

Greiff, Constance M. *John Notman, Architect 1810–1865.* Philadelphia: Athenaeum, 1979.

Griswold, A. Whitney. *Farming and Democracy.* New York: Harcourt, Brace & Co., 1948.

Griswold, Mac, and Eleanor Weller. *The Golden Age of American Gardens: Proud Owners, Private Estates, 1890–1940.* New York: Harry N. Abrams and Garden Club of America, 1991.

Hadfield, Miles. *Pioneers in Gardening.* London: Routledge & Kegan Paul, 1955.

Haley, Jacquetta M., ed. *Pleasure Grounds: Andrew Jackson Downing and Montgomery Place.* Tarrytown, N.Y.: Sleepy Hollow Press, 1988.

Handlin, David P. *The American Home.* Boston: Little, Brown & Co., 1979.

Harris, Neil. *The Artist in American Society: The Formative Years, 1790–1860.* New York: George Braziller, 1966; reprint, Chicago: University of Chicago Press, Phoenix Books, 1982.

Hedrick, Ulysses Prentiss. *A History of Horticulture in America to 1860.* Oxford: Oxford University Press, 1950.

"Here's to You, A. J.!" *Historic Preservation* 43 (November/December 1991): 11.

Hersey, George L. "Associationism and Sensibility in Eighteenth-Century Architecture." *Eighteenth-Century Studies* 4 (Fall 1970): 71–89.

Hess, Jeffrey A. "Sources and Aesthetics of Poe's Landscape Fiction." *American Quarterly* 22 (Summer 1970): 177–89.

Hindle, Brooke. *Emulation and Invention.* New York: New York University Press, 1981.

Hipple, Walter John, Jr. *The Beautiful, the Sublime, and the Picturesque in Eighteenth-Century British Aesthetic Theory.* Carbondale: Southern Illinois University Press, 1957.

Horace. *The Art of Poetry.* Trans. with an introduction by Burton Raffel. Albany: State University of New York Press, 1974.

Howe, Daniel Walker, ed. *Victorian America.* Philadelphia: University of Pennsylvania Press, 1976.

Howett, Catherine M. "Crying 'Taste' in the Wilderness: The Disciples of Andrew Jackson Downing in Georgia." *Landscape Journal* 1 (Spring 1982): 15–22.

——— "Frank Lloyd Wright & American Residential Landscaping." *Landscape* 26 (1982): 33–40.

Hunt, John Dixon. "Gardening, Poetry, and Pope." *Art Quarterly* 37 (Spring 1974): 1–30.

——— *The Figure in the Landscape: Poetry, Painting, and Gardening during the Eighteenth Century.* Baltimore: Johns Hopkins University Press, 1976.

——— *William Kent: Landscape Garden Designer.* New York: A. Zwemmer Limited, 1987.

——— *Gardens and the Picturesque: Studies in the History of Landscape Architecture.* Cambridge: MIT Press, 1992.

——— and Peter Willis, eds. *The Genius of the Place: The English Landscape Garden 1620–1820.* Cambridge: MIT Press, 1988.

Hussey, Christopher. *The Picturesque: Studies in a Point of View.* London: Frank Cass & Co., 1967.

Huth, Hans. *Nature and the American: Three Centuries of Changing Attitudes.* New ed. with an introduction by Douglas H. Strong. Lincoln: University of Nebraska Press, 1990.

Hyams, Edward. *Capability Brown and Humphry Repton.* New York: Charles Scribner's Sons, 1971.

Jackson, J. B. *Landscapes.* Ed. Ervin H. Zube. Amherst: University of Massachusetts Press, 1970.

Secondary Sources

Jackson, Kenneth T. *Crabgrass Frontier: The Suburbanization of the United States.* New York: Oxford University Press, 1985.

Jackson, W. G. "First Interpreter of American Beauty: A. J. Downing and the Planned Landscape." *Landscape* 1 (Winter 1952): 11–18.

Jacques, David. *Georgian Gardens: The Reign of Nature.* London: B. T. Batsford, 1983.

Johnstone, Paul H. "The Rural Socrates." *Journal of the History of Ideas* 5 (April 1944): 151–75.

Jones, Howard Mumford. *O Strange New World: American Culture: The Formative Years.* New York: Viking Press, 1964.

Kelly, Franklin, with Stephen Jay Gould, James Anthony Ryan, and Debora Rindge. *Frederic Edwin Church.* Washington, D.C.: National Gallery of Art, 1989.

Knoepflmacher, U. C., and G. B. Tennyson, eds. *Nature and the Victorian Imagination.* Berkeley: University of California Press, 1977.

Kristeller, Paul Oskar. "The Modern System of the Arts: A Study in the History of Aesthetics." *Journal of the History of Ideas* 12 (October 1951): 496–527; and 13 (January 1952): 17–46.

Kuklick, Bruce. "Myth and Symbol in American Studies." *American Quarterly* 24 (October 1972): 435–50.

Kunstler, James Howard. *The Geography of Nowhere: The Rise and Decline of America's Man-Made Landscape.* New York: Simon & Schuster, 1993.

Laird, Mark. "Approaches to Planting in the Late Eighteenth Century: Some Imperfect Ideas on the Origins of the American Garden." *Journal of Garden History* 11 (July–September 1991): 154–72.

Landow, George P. *The Aesthetic and Critical Theories of John Ruskin.* Princeton: Princeton University Press, 1971.

Lavin, Sylvia. *Quatremère de Quincy and the Invention of a Modern Language of Architecture.* Cambridge: MIT Press, 1992.

Leatherbarrow, David. "Character, Geometry and Perspective: the Third Earl of Shaftesbury's Principles of Garden Design." *Journal of Garden History* 4 (October–December 1984): 332–58.

Lee, Rensselaer W. *Ut Pictura Poesis: The Humanistic Theory of Painting.* New York: W. W. Norton & Co., 1967.

Lees, Carlton B. "The Golden Age of Horticulture." *Historic Preservation* 24 (October–December 1972): 32–37.

Leighton, Ann. *American Gardens of the Nineteenth Century: "For Comfort and Affluence."* Amherst: University of Massachusetts Press, 1987.

Long, Timothy Preston. "The Woodlands: A 'Matchless Place.'" Master's thesis, University of Pennsylvania, 1991.

Longstreth, Richard, ed. *The Mall in Washington, 1791–1991.* Studies in the History of Art, no. 30. National Gallery of Art. Hanover, N.H.: University Press of New England, 1991.

Lovejoy, Arthur O. *Essays in the History of Ideas.* Baltimore: Johns Hopkins University Press, 1948; reprint, New York: Capricorn Books, 1960.

Lowen, Sara. "The Tyranny of the Lawn." *American Heritage,* September 1991, 45–55.

Lynes, Russell. *The Tastemakers.* New York: Harper & Bros., 1949.

Maccubbin, Robert P., and Peter Martin, eds. *British and American Gardens in the Eighteenth Century.* Williamsburg, Va.: Colonial Williamsburg Foundation, 1984.

MacDougall, Elisabeth B., ed. *John Claudius Loudon and the Early Nineteenth Century in Great Britain.* Dumbarton Oaks Colloquium on the History of Landscape Architecture, VI. Washington, D.C.: Dumbarton Oaks, 1980.

Machor, James L. *Pastoral Cities: Urban Ideals and the Symbolic Landscape of America.* Madison: University of Wisconsin Press, 1987.

MacLaren, I. S. "The Limits of the Picturesque in British North America." *Journal of Garden History* 5 (January–March 1985): 97–111.

Major, Judith K. "Fairmount Park's Changing Role in City Life." *Urban Land* 44 (February 1985): 18–21.

———. "The Downing Letters." *Landscape Architecture* 76 (January/February 1986): 50–57.

Malins, Edward. *English Landscaping and Literature 1660–1840.* London: Oxford University Press, 1966.

Manwaring, Elizabeth Wheeler. *Italian Landscape in Eighteenth Century England.* New York: Oxford University Press, 1925.

Marranca, Bonnie, ed. *American Garden Writing: Gleaning from Garden Lives Then and Now.* New York: PAJ Publications, 1988.

Martin, Peter. *Pursuing Innocent Pleasures: The Gardening World of Alexander Pope.* Hamden, Conn.: Archon Books, 1984.

Marx, Leo. *The Pilot and the Passenger: Essays on Literature, Technology, and Culture in the United States.* New York: Oxford University Press, 1988.

Massachusetts Horticultural Society. *Keeping Eden: A History of Gardening in America.* Walter T. Punch, general editor. Boston: A Bulfinch Press Book of Little, Brown and Co., 1992.

Masteller, Richard N., and Jean Carwile Masteller. "Rural Architecture in Andrew Jackson Downing and Henry David Thoreau: Pattern Book Parody in *Walden*." *New England Quarterly* 57 (December 1984): 483–510.

Matthiessen, F. O. *American Renaissance: Art and Expression in the Age of Emerson and Whitman.* New York: Oxford University Press, 1941; reprint, New York: Oxford University Press, 1980.

McLaughlin, Charles Capen, ed. *The Papers of Frederick Law Olmsted.* Vol. 1, *The Formative Years: 1822 to 1852.* Baltimore: Johns Hopkins University Press, 1977.

McMurry, Sally. *Families and Farmhouses in Nineteenth-Century America: Vernacular Design and Social Change.* New York: Oxford University Press, 1988.

Miller, Perry. *Nature's Nation.* Cambridge: Belknap Press of Harvard University Press, 1967.

Miller, Ross L. "The Landscaper's Utopia Versus the City: A Mismatch" *New England Quarterly* 49 (June 1976): 179–93.

Moehring, Eugene P. *Urban America and the Foreign Traveler, 1815–1855.* New York: Arno Press, 1974.

Monk, Samuel H[olt]. *The Sublime, a Study of Critical Theories in XVIII-Century England.* New York, 1935; reprint, Ann Arbor: University of Michigan Press, 1960.

———. "A Grace Beyond the Reach of Art." *Journal of the History of Ideas* 5 (April 1944): 131–50.

Morgan, Keith N. "The Emergence of the American Landscape Professional: John Notman and the Design of Rural Cemeteries." *Journal of Garden History* 4 (July–September 1984): 269–89.

Mosser, Monique, and Georges Teyssot, eds. *The Architecture of Western Gardens: A Design History from the Renaissance to the Present Day.* Cambridge: MIT Press, 1991.

Mott, Frank Luther. *A History of American Magazines: 1741–1850.* 2 vols. New York: D. Appleton & Co., 1930.

Müllenbrock, Heinz-Joachim. "The 'Englishness' of the English Landscape Garden and the Genetic Role of Literature: A Reassessment." *Journal of Garden History* 8 (October–December 1988): 97–103.

Mulvey, Christopher. *Anglo-American Landscapes: A Study of Nineteenth-Century Anglo-American Travel Literature.* Cambridge: Cambridge University Press, 1983.

Myres, Sandra L. *Westering Women and the Frontier Experience, 1800–1915.* Albuquerque: University of New Mexico Press, 1982.

Nash, Roderick. *Wilderness and the American Mind.* 3d ed. New Haven: Yale University Press, 1982.

Secondary Sources

Naude, Virginia Norton. "Lemon Hill." *Antiques,* November 1962, 531–33.

Nevius, Blake. *Cooper's Landscapes: An Essay on the Picturesque Vision.* Berkeley: University of California Press, 1976.

Newton, Norman T. *Design on the Land: The Development of Landscape Architecture.* Cambridge: Belknap Press of Harvard University Press, 1971.

Norris, Mary Win Walter. "A Present From the Past: 138-Year-Old Garden Lives On." *Fine Gardening,* January/February 1990, 46–50.

Novak, Barbara. *Nature and Culture: American Landscape and Painting 1825–1875.* New York: Oxford University Press, 1980.

Nye, Russel Blaine. *Society and Culture in America: 1830–1860.* New York: Harper & Row, 1974.

Nygren, Edward J. *Views and Visions: American Landscape before 1830.* Washington, D.C.: Corcoran Gallery of Art, 1986.

O'Malley, Therese. "'A Public Museum of Trees': Mid-Nineteenth Century Plans for the Mall." *Studies in the History of Art* 30 (1991): 60–76.

———. "Art and Science in the Design of Botanic Gardens, 1730–1830." In *Garden History: Issues, Approaches, Methods,* ed. John Dixon Hunt, 279–302. Dumbarton Oaks Colloquium on the History of Landscape Architecture, XIII. Washington, D.C.: Dumbarton Oaks, 1992.

Panofsky, Erwin. *Idea: A Concept in Art Theory.* Trans. Joseph J. S. Peake. Columbia: University of South Carolina Press, 1968.

Pattee, Sarah Lewis. "Andrew Jackson Downing and His Influence on Landscape Architecture in America." *Landscape Architecture* 19 (January 1929): 79–83.

Paulson, Ronald. *Emblem & Expression: Meaning in English Art of the 18th Century.* London: Thames & Hudson, 1975.

Pessen, Edward, ed. *The Many-Faceted Jacksonian Era: New Interpretations.* Contributions in American History, no. 67. Westport, Conn.: Greenwood Press, 1977.

Pevsner, Nikolaus. *The Englishness of English Art.* Middlesex: Penguin Books, 1963.

———. *Some Architectural Writers of the Nineteenth Century.* Oxford: Clarendon Press, 1972.

———, ed. *The Picturesque Garden and Its Influence Outside the British Isles.* Washington, D.C.: Dumbarton Oaks, 1974.

Pilcher, Donald. *The Regency Style: 1800 to 1830.* London: B. T. Batsford, 1948.

Placzek, Adolf K., ed. *Macmillan Encyclopedia of Architects.* Vol. 3. New York: Free Press of Macmillan Publishing Co., 1982.

Price, Martin. "The Picturesque Moment." In *From Sensibility to Romanticism: Essays Presented to Frederick A. Pottle,* ed. Frederick W. Hilles and Harold Bloom, 259–92. New York: Oxford University Press, 1965.

Quaintance, Richard E. "Walpole's Whig Interpretation of Landscaping History." *Studies in Eighteenth-Century Culture* 9 (1979): 285–300.

Reps, John W. "Downing and the Washington Mall." *Landscape* 16 (Spring 1967): 6–11.

Roquet, Claude-Henry. "Vocabulary: Four Entries for a Dictionary." *Lotus International* 32 (1981): 80–81.

Saisselin, R. G. "The French Garden in the Eighteenth Century: From Belle Nature to the Landscape of Time." *Journal of Garden History* 5 (July–September 1985): 284–97.

Schlesinger, Arthur M., Jr. *The Age of Jackson.* Boston: Little, Brown & Co., 1945.

Schmitt, Peter J. *Back to Nature: The Arcadian Myth in Urban America.* New York: Oxford University Press, 1969.

Schneider, René. *Quatremère de Quincy et son Intervention dans les Arts (1788–1830).* Paris: Librairie Hachette, 1910.

Schuyler, David. "The Evolution of the Anglo-American Rural Cemetery: Landscape Architecture as Social and Cultural History." *Journal of Garden History* 4 (July–September 1984): 291–304.

―――. *The New Urban Landscape: The Redefinition of City Form in Nineteenth-Century America*. Balitmore: Johns Hopkins University Press, 1988.

―――. *Apostle of Taste: Andrew Jackson Downing 1815–1852*. Baltimore: Johns Hopkins University Press, 1996.

―――, and Jane Turner Censer, eds. *The Papers of Frederick Law Olmsted*. Vol. 6. *The Years of Olmsted, Vaux & Company: 1865–1874*. Baltimore: Johns Hopkins University Press, 1992.

Scourse, Nicolette. *The Victorians and Their Flowers*. Portland, Oreg.: Timber Press, 1983.

Seaburg, Carl, and Stanley Paterson. *Merchant Prince of Boston: Colonel T. H. Perkins, 1764–1854*. Cambridge: Harvard University Press, 1971.

Sears, John F. *Sacred Places: American Tourist Attractions in the Nineteenth Century*. New York: Oxford University Press, 1989.

Shi, David E. *The Simple Life: Plain Living and High Thinking in American Culture*. New York: Oxford University Press, 1986.

Simo, Melanie Louise. *Loudon and the Landscape: From Country Seat to Metropolis: 1783–1843*. New Haven: Yale University Press, 1988.

Smith, David L., ed. *Horace Bushnell: Selected Writings*. Chico, Calif.: Scholars Press, 1984.

Smith, Henry Nash. *Virgin Land: The American West as Symbol and Myth*. Cambridge: Harvard University Press, 1950.

Spann, Edward K. *The New Metropolis: New York City 1840–1857*. New York: Columbia University Press, 1981.

Spencer, Benjamin T. *The Quest for Nationality: An American Literary Campaign*. Syracuse, N.Y.: Syracuse University Press, 1957.

Spingarn, J. E. "Henry Winthrop Sargent and the Landscape Tradition at Wodenethe: An English Inheritance Becomes an American Influence." *Landscape Architecture Quarterly* 29 (October 1938): 24–39.

Steil, Lucien. "On Imitation." In *Imitation & Innovation. Architectural Design*. Profile 75. New York: St. Martin's Press, 1988.

Stein, Roger B. *John Ruskin and Aesthetic Thought in America, 1840–1900*. Cambridge: Harvard University Press, 1967.

Stilgoe, John R. *Borderland: Origins of the American Suburb, 1820–1939*. New Haven: Yale University Press, 1988.

Streatfield, David C., and Alistair M. Duckworth. *Landscape in the Gardens and the Literature of Eighteenth-Century England*. Los Angeles: University of California, 1981.

Stroud, Dorothy. *Capability Brown*. London: Country Life, 1950.

―――. *Humphry Repton*. London: Country Life, 1962.

Tatarkiewicz, Wladyslaw. *A History of Six Ideas: An Essay in Aesthetics*. Warsaw: Polish Scientific Publishers, 1980.

Tatum, George Bishop. "A. J. Downing: Arbiter of American Taste, 1815–1852." Ph.D. diss., Princeton University, 1950.

―――. "The Beautiful and the Picturesque." *American Quarterly* (1953): 36–51.

―――. "The Emergence of an American School of Landscape Design." *Historic Preservation* 25 (April–June 1973): 34–41.

―――. "New Introduction." In Andrew Jackson Downing, *Rural Essays*. 1853. Ed. George William Curtis, with a memoir of the author by George William Curtis and a letter to his friends by Fredrika Bremer. New York: Da Capo Press, 1974.

―――, and Elisabeth Blair MacDougall, eds. *Prophet with Honor: The Career of Andrew Jackson Downing 1815–1852*. Dumbarton Oaks Colloquium on the History of Landscape Architecture, XI. Washington, D.C.: Dumbarton Oaks, 1989.

Thomas, Keith. *Man and the Natural World: A History of the Modern Sensibility.* New York: Pantheon Books, 1983.

Thornton, Tamara Plakins. *Cultivating Gentlemen: The Meaning of Country Life among the Boston Elite 1785–1860.* New Haven: Yale University Press, 1989.

Tishler, William H., ed. *American Landscape Architecture: Designers and Places.* Washington, D.C.: Preservation Press, 1989.

Toole, Robert. M. "Springside: A. J. Downing's Only Extant Garden." *Journal of Garden History* 9 (January–March 1989): 20–39.

———. "An American Cottage Ornée: Washington Irving's Sunnyside, 1835–1859." *Journal of Garden History* 12 (January–March 1992): 52–72.

Truettner, William, and Alan Wallach, eds. *Thomas Cole: Landscape into History.* New Haven: Yale University Press, 1994.

Turner, Roger. *Capability Brown and the Eighteenth-Century English Landscape.* New York: Rizzoli, 1985.

Turner, T. H. D. "Loudon's Stylistic Development." *Journal of Garden History* 2 (April–June 1982): 175–88.

Tuveson, Ernest Lee. *The Imagination as a Means of Grace: Locke and the Aesthetics of Romanticism.* Berkeley: University of California Press, 1960.

Upton, Dell. "Pattern Books and Professionalism." *Winterthur Portfolio* 19 (Summer/Autumn 1984): 107–50.

Vidler, Anthony. "The Idea of Type: The Transformation of the Academic Ideal, 1750–1830." *Oppositions* 8 (Spring 1977): 95–115.

———. "The Hut and the Body: The 'Nature' of Architecture from Laugier to Quatremère de Quincy." *Lotus International* 33 (1981): 102–11.

———. "The 'Art' of History: Monumental Aesthetics from Winckelmann to Quatremère de Quincy." *Oppositions* 25 (Fall 1982): 52–67.

Walker, Peter, and Melanie Simo. *Invisible Gardens: The Search for Modernism in the American Landscape.* Cambridge: MIT Press, 1994.

Ward, John William. "The Politics of Design." In *Who Designs America?,* ed. Laurence B. Holland, 51–85. Princeton Studies in American Civilization, no. 6. Garden City, N.Y.: Anchor Books, 1966.

Washburn, Wilcomb E. "Vision of Life for the Mall." *AIA Journal* 47 (March 1967): 52–59.

Watkin, David. *The English Vision: The Picturesque in Architecture, Landscape and Garden Design.* New York: Harper & Row, 1982.

Welter, Rush. "The Idea of Progress in America." *Journal of the History of Ideas* 16 (June 1955): 401–15.

———. *The Mind of America: 1820–1860.* New York: Columbia University Press, 1975.

White, Morton, and Lucia White. *The Intellectual Versus the City: From Thomas Jefferson to Frank Lloyd Wright.* Cambridge: Harvard University Press & MIT Press, 1962.

Wiebe, Robert H. *The Opening of American Society: From the Adoption of the Constitution to the Eve of Disunion.* New York: Alfred A. Knopf, 1984.

Wiebenson, Dora. *The Picturesque Garden in France.* Princeton: Princeton University Press, 1978.

Wilkinson, Jeff. "A. J. Downing." *Old-House Journal,* May/June 1989, 53.

Willey, Basil. *The Eighteenth Century Background: Studies on the Idea of Nature in the Thought of the Period.* New York: Columbia University Press, 1962.

Williams, Raymond. *Keywords.* New York: Oxford University Press, 1976.

Williams, Robert. "Making Places: Garden Mastery and English Brown." *Journal of Garden History* 3 (October–December 1983): 382–85.

Wittkower, R. "Imitation, Eclecticism, and Genius." In *Aspects of the Eighteenth Century,* ed. Earl R. Wasserman, 143–61. Baltimore: Johns Hopkins University Press, 1965.

Architectural Principles in the Age of Humanism. 4th ed. New York: St. Martin's Press, 1988.

Woloch, Nancy. *Women and the American Experience.* New York: Alfred A. Knopf, 1984.

Woodbridge, Kenneth. "William Kent's Gardening: The Rousham Letters." *Apollo* 100 (October 1974): 282–91.

Woodburn, Elisabeth. "Horticultural Heritage: The Influence of U.S. Nurserymen." In *Agricultural Literature: Proud Heritage-Future Promise,* ed. Alan Fusonie and Leila Moran. Washington, D.C.: Associates of the National Agricultural Library & Graduate School Press, U.S. Department of Agriculture, 1977.

Worster, Donald. *Nature's Economy: A History of Ecological Ideas.* New York: Cambridge University Press, 1977.

Young, Terence. "Trees, the Park and Moral Order: The Significance of Golden Gate Park's First Plantings." *Journal of Garden History* 14 (July–September 1994): 158–70.

Zaitzevsky, Cynthia. *Frederick Law Olmsted and the Boston Park System.* Cambridge: Belknap Press of Harvard University Press, 1982.

Zukowsky, John, and Robbe Pierce Stimson. *Hudson River Villas.* New York: Rizzoli, 1985.

INDEX

Académie Royale des Beaux-Arts, 55

Adams, Charles Francis, 8

Adams, John, 119

Adams, John Quincy, 2–3, 17–18

Addison, Joseph, 63, 71, 140–141
  Spectator, 41, 140–141

Albany (New York), 99
  country residences near, 16–17, 67, 74

Alison, Archibald, 37, 56, 64, 69–70
  Essays on Taste, 62, 79
  influence on Downing, 62, 79–80

Allegheny Mountains (Pennsylvania), 143

Allen, Lewis F., 20

American Gardener's Magazine, 8. See also *Magazine of Horticulture*

Angling, 133

Apollo (Vatican), 96

Architectural Association (London), 100

Architectural Magazine, 55, 59. See also Loudon, John Claudius

Architecture, and landscape gardening, 11, 44, 67, 83, 110–111, 128, 133

Architecture of Country Houses (Downing), 4, 28, 30, 86–87, 100, 111, 128

Aristotle
  Poetics, 54

Ashridge (H. Repton), 42, 52

Association, in aesthetic theory, 62, 80

Astor, John Jacob, 111

Babylon, hanging gardens of, 70

Bacon, Francis, 11
  "Of Gardens," 41

INDEX

Barnard, Henry
    Practical Illustrations of School Architecture, 115

Barton, Cora Livingston, 87

Bartram's Botanic Gardens (Philadelphia), 43

Batteux, Charles
    Les Beaux Arts réduits à un même principe, 54

Beau ideal, 54, 57, 59, 63–64, 79, 84, 87, 95, 96, 109, 137, 154, 157

Beaumont, Francis, and John Fletcher, 132

Beautiful, the, 29–30, 47–53, 61, 62, 80, 87, 91, 94, 95, 96, 136–137, 145, 156

Beaverwyck (estate of William P. Van Rensselaer), 74

Beecher, Henry Ward, 6

Belle nature, 54, 63, 83

Bellori, Giovanni Pietro
    Le vite de' Pittori, Scultori et Architetti, 54

Belmont (estate of J. P. Cushing, near Boston), 76–78

Belmont (residence of Judge Peters, Schuylkill River), 75

Blackstone, Sir William, 128

Blenheim, 42

Blithewood (estate of Robert Donaldson, Hudson River), 18, 45, 46

Bonaparte, Joseph, Count de Survilliers, estate of, 46

Book of Nature, 26

Bordentown (New Jersey), estate at, 46

Boston, 66, 110, 132
    country seats near, 46, 76–78
    lack of green space, 22–23
    suburban residences near, 73, 107

Bremer, Fredrika, 17, 113, 124, 126, 132

Brentwood (England), school near, 115

Brookline (Massachusetts), country seats at, 46, 76, 78

Brookwood (estate of C. H. Fisher, Philadelphia), 33

Brown, Lancelot (Capability), 47, 49, 52, 53, 71, 72, 83
    Downing criticizes, 52, 71

Bryant, William Cullen, 33, 91, 132

Buist, Robert, nursery of, 59

Burke, Edmund, 83
    A Philosophical Inquiry into the Origin of Our Ideas of the Sublime and Beautiful, 32, 47–48

Burton, Warren
    District School as It Was, 26

Bushnell, Horace, 115

Butler, Mrs. C. H., 25

Camac, Mrs. William M. (Elizabeth Markoe), residence of, 74–75

Canada (steamer), 101

Catskill Mountains, 107

Cedar Grove (seat of DeWint family), 3

Central Park. *See* New York City

Chambers, William
    Designs of Chinese Buildings, 41

Channing, William Ellery, 129–130

Chatsworth (seat of the Duke of Devonshire), 43, 101–102, 105, 106–107, 109, 162

Chaucer, Geoffrey, 132

Chevalier, Michael, 29

Choules, Reverend, 123–124

Class structure, 17, 26–30, 43, 106–113
    emulation, spirit of, 27–28, 105, 119–124, 162
    first class, defined, 28

Claude. *See* Lorrain, Claude

Clay, Henry, 21

Climatic causality, 138–140

Cole, Thomas, 91

Index

Colman, Henry
    European Agriculture, 24, 129
    as the "Traveller," 110, 115–117, 121, 159, 163

Columbian Magazine, 25

Concord (Massachusetts), 17

Cooper, Susan Fenimore, 110, 126
    Rural Hours, 12

Cottage Residences (Downing), 4, 29, 45, 67, 99

Country and city life, compared, 22–26, 111

Cousin, Victor, 145

Cowley, Abraham, 109

Cowper, William
    The Task, 22

Cultivator, 13, 27, 33–34, 86, 99. *See also* Tucker, Luther

Curtis, George William, 203n1

Cushing, John Perkins, 46, 76–78

Darwin, Charles
    Journal of Researches . . . From 1832 to 1836, 155

Davis, Alexander Jackson, 8

Delille, Jacques
    Les Jardins, 38, 39, 42

Democratic Review, 9, 15, 19, 24–25, 26, 27, 33, 124

Devonshire, William Cavendish, 6th Duke of, 101, 162, 207n6

DeWint, John Peter, 203n1

Dexter, Franklin B., 156–157

Dolci, Carlo, 95

Domesticity, 10, 17–21, 124–126

Donaldson, Robert, 18, 45

Douw, Gerard, 95

Downing, Andrew Jackson. *See also* Architecture of Country Houses; Cottage Residences; Fruits and Fruit-Trees of America; Horticulturist; Rural Essays; Treatise on the Theory and Practice of Landscape Gardening
    Anglophilia, 37, 132, 137–141
    birth, 2
    correspondence, 8, 11, 32, 59, 61, 66–69, 73–74, 86–87, 89, 100, 132, 143, 203n1, 206n5, 206–207n6
    death, 100, 158, 159
    early writings, 7–8
    early years, 3
    education, 3
    landscape gardening commissions, 32, 33, 45, 66, 67, 78, 159–163
    nursery business, 3–4, 7, 59, 86, 149, 158
    as "An Old Digger," 100
    as pomologist, 99–100, 130–131
    practice, 113, 129, 141, 143, 144–145
    residence, 4
    reviews Beecher, 6
    reviews Colman, 24, 129
    reviews Cooper, 12, 126
    reviews Gray, 6
    signature, 2
    trip to England, 17, 43, 100–105, 148, 149
    and the Whig party, 3

Downing, Caroline DeWint, 2, 3, 17

Downing, Charles, 7, 126, 158

Downing, Samuel, 3

Dropmore, 101

Durand, Asher B., 89, 91
    Kindred Spirits, 91
    "Letters on Landscape Painting," 157

Dwight, Theodore, 113–115

Dwight, Timothy
    Travels, 114, 123

East Hartford (Connecticut), 130

Eaton Hall, 105

Egalitarianism, 28–29

INDEX

Emerson, Ralph Waldo, 9, 17, 132
    Nature, 23

Epicurus, garden of, 70

Exotic plants, 37–38, 59, 61, 69, 79, 82, 128–129, 148–157, 158, 165

Expression, in aesthetic theory, 37, 46–47, 61–64, 69–70, 78, 84, 94, 95, 96, 136

Far west, 13, 14, 155

Faulkner, Johnaphene, 13

Fayetteville (Kentucky), correspondent from, 159

Fessenden, Thomas G.
    New American Gardener, 7

Fillmore, Millard, 159, 162

Fisher, Charles Henry, 33

Fisher, Sidney George, 16–17, 33, 74

Flora, 126

Florence, villas, 138

France and the French, 64, 121, 130–131, 138, 139, 141, 151

Frankfurt, parks, 115

Fruits and Fruit-Trees of America (Downing), 4, 86, 99

Gardeners' Chronicle. 87, 91, 144. *See also* Lindley, John

Gardener's Magazine. See Loudon, John Claudius

Gardenesque, 37, 58, 61, 62, 80, 84

Gardening, 29. *See also* Landscape gardening
    difference between British and American, 2, 133

Gardiner, Robert Hallowell, estate of, 78

Gardiner (Maine), 78

General nature, 54, 63, 79, 95, 137, 152

Geneseo (estate of Wadsworth family, Genesee River), 30, 89–90

Geneva (New York), villas, 16

Germany and the Germans, 121–122, 146, 151

Gilpin, Reverend William, 57, 94
    Essay on Picturesque Beauty, 48–49

Girardin, R. L.
    De la Composition des Paysages, 42

Godey's Magazine, 19, 21, 22, 23, 25, 139

Godwin, Parke, 12

Goethe, Johann Wolfgang von, 29

Graceful, the, 69, 80–84

Graham's Magazine, 18, 46

Gray, Asa, 6

Greenough, Horatio
    "Remarks on American Art," 11, 14–15

Greenwood Cottage (residence of Sarah and J. I. Taylor, Illinois), 28

Guardian. See Pope, Alexander

Guyot, Arnold, 139

Hague, The, parks, 115

Hamilton, William, estate of, 75

Hardwicke, Earl and Countess of, 103, 207n6

Harrison, William Henry, 11

Hartford (Connecticut), 78

Henry Clay (steamboat), 159

Hillhouse, James, 123

Hofland, Barbara
    White-Knights, 38–39

Hogarth, William, 83, 95
    Analysis of Beauty, 48

Home Journal, 163. *See also* Willis, Nathaniel Parker

Hooker, Sir William Jackson, 206n5, 206–207n6. *See also* Royal Botanic Gardens, Kew

Index

Horace (Quintus Horatius Flaccus)
    Ars poetica, 54
    Sabine Farm, 21

Horticulture, professional, 7–8, 99–100, 113, 120, 130, 132

Horticulturist (ed. Downing), 2, 4, 5, 6, 21, 44, 46, 75, 76, 86, 87, 89, 91, 97, 99–165
    audience, 106, 124–126
    English poets quoted in, 132
    landscape gardening, defined in, 136, 154–155, 157
    language, 106, 129–134, 158
    "Mr. Downing's Letters from England," 101–105
    reviews of, 99

Hosack, David, estate of, 44

Hovey, C. M., 8. *See also Magazine of Horticulture*

Hovey, P. B., Jr., 8

Hudson (New York), estate near, 73

Hudson Highlands, 4, 81

Hudson River, 78, 158
    estates on, 16–17, 21–22, 30, 44–46, 66, 73, 87–89, 107, 131, 147–148
    as setting for Downing's life, 3

Hudson River School, 91, 137

Humboldt, Alexander von, 139
    Cosmos, 139–140, 162

Hunt, Leigh, 132

Hyde Park (estate of David Hosack, Hudson River), 44, 46

Idealist aesthetics, 37, 53–54, 58, 63–64, 95, 154, 157

Idlewild (estate of N. P. Willis, Hudson River), 30–31, 33

Imitation, in aesthetic theory, 37, 53–64, 69, 78–79, 95

Independence (Missouri), 13

Indigenous plants, 38, 61, 87, 91, 95, 105, 128–129, 136, 137, 148–157, 158–159, 161–163

Irish immigrants, 146

Irving, Washington, 16, 28
    correspondence, 22
    Sunnyside, residence of, 21–22

Isle of Wight, houses and gardens, 103, 105

Isola Bella, 70

Italian garden, 138, 141

Jackson, Andrew, 2–3

Jefferson, Thomas, 28

Jupiter Olympus, Temple of, 96

Karlsruhe (Germany), 59

Kennebec River, 78

Kent, J. C., 57

Kent, William, 39, 41, 71

Kenwood (residence of Joel Rathbone), 30

Kew. *See* Royal Botanic Gardens, Kew

Knight, Richard Payne, 47, 52, 57, 64
    influence on Downing, 52, 71
    The Landscape, 49, 57, 71

Labor costs, 29, 105, 141–142, 145–146, 147

Land ownership, 10, 17–19, 29, 43

Landscape gardening
    and academic doctrine, 37, 54–59, 63–64, 79, 83, 137
    adapted to North America, 4–6, 36–38, 66–70, 87, 91, 97, 105, 133, 136–165
    amateurs, as practiced by, 11, 30–33, 46, 94, 126–129, 134
    American national style, 136–141, 159–165
    ancient/formal/geometric style, 37, 38–43, 46, 64, 70, 71–72, 137–140
    Anglo-Chinese fashion, 41–42, 71
    difference between American and British, 2, 43, 132, 142, 144, 147, 148

INDEX

difference from gardening, 29
Dutch school, 70
and economy, 81, 87, 105, 108–113, 136, 137, 141–148
as a fine art, 29–30, 32, 37–38, 57, 64, 154
as a harmony between the real and the ideal, 136–137, 154, 157
and ladies, 103, 124–126
and landscape painting, 32, 94, 137, 156
modern/natural/irregular style, 37, 38–43, 61, 64, 70–71, 87, 136–141
moral effects of, 105, 106, 113–119, 134
novices, as practiced by, 126–129, 143, 145
as a profession, 11, 30–33, 66, 94, 126–129

Laocoön, 96

Lauder, Sir Thomas Dick
Price on the Picturesque, 69–70, 79–81

Lawn, 73, 75, 81, 82, 137, 142–143, 144–145, 146, 147–148

Leasowes, the (estate of William Shenstone), 70–71

Lee, Thomas, cottage of, 78

Lemon Hill (estate of Henry Pratt, Schuylkill River), 46

Le Nôtre, André, 39, 83

Leveling of ground, 141

Lindley, John, 72–73, 87, 91, 94, 144

Linnaeus, Carolus (Carl von Linné), 63

Literary World, 36

Liverpool (England), 100, 151

Livingston, Mrs. Edward (Louise Davezac), 87, 107

Livingston, Mrs. Mary, 73

Livingston family, residences of, 45

Livingston Manor (estate of Mrs. Mary Livingston), 73, 143

Log cabins, 11, 13, 33

London, George, 70

London, 101
parks, 102, 115–116, 121

Lorrain, Claude, 52, 53, 59, 91, 94, 156

Loudon, John Claudius, 4, 9, 32, 37, 40, 53–61, 62, 63–64, 67–68, 72–73, 79, 80, 83, 84, 124, 143, 148
Arboretum et Fruticetum Britannicum, 55, 58
Architectural Magazine, 55, 59
Encyclopedia of Gardening, 9, 41, 44, 46, 70, 72, 87
Gardener's Magazine, 37, 43, 55, 56, 72, 151
influence on Downing, 4, 37, 38, 40, 41, 53, 54, 59, 61, 72–73, 148–149
Landscape Gardening of Humphry Repton, 72, 82–83
Suburban Gardener, 8, 57–58, 61

Louis XIV, 39

Louisville (Kentucky), correspondent from, 159

Lowell, James Russell, 132
"The Rural Cot of Mr. Knott," 132
"The Vision of Sir Launfal," 132

Lowell, John, estate of, 46

Lyell, Charles, 143–144

Macon (Georgia), correspondent from, 159

Magazine of Horticulture, 8. See also *American Gardener's Magazine*

Malthus, Daniel, 42

Manifest destiny, 19–21

Marryat, Frederick, 19, 29

Marsh-Caldwell, Mrs. Anne ("the authoress"), 207n6

Martineau, Harriet, 8–9, 17, 43

Mason, George
Design in Gardening, 42

Mason, William, 41, 71
The English Garden, 42

Massachusetts, as exemplar, 117–118

Meigs, Henry, 20

238

Index

Messina (estate in the Livingston family, Hudson River), 46

Milton, John
    Paradise Lost, 41

Mississippi, correspondents from, 24, 117

Missouri, correspondent from, 147

M'Mahon, Bernard, 39
    American Gardener's Calendar, 7

Moderation, 87, 106–113, 134, 136

Monte Video (estate of Daniel Wadsworth, Connecticut), 46

Montgomery, Janet Livingston, estate of, 107

Montgomery Place (estate of Louise Davezac Livingston, Hudson River), 46, 87–89, 107, 127

Mount Vernon, 44

Munich, parks, 115

Murillo, Bartolomé Esteban, 96

Murray, Charles Augustus, 19–20

Nahant (Massachusetts), residence in, 127

National Academy of Design (New York), 91

Nationalism, 2, 9, 33, 130–133, 136, 153, 154

Newburgh (New York), 3

New Haven (Connecticut), 123

New Jersey, 155

New Orleans, 99
    Battle of, 2

Newport (Rhode Island), 153

New York Agricultural Society, 133

New York City, 24, 66, 120
    Battery, 22
    Broadway, 24
    Central Park "Greensward" plan, 162–163
    City Hall open space, 22
    Trinity Church, 78
    Wall Street, 24

New-York Mirror, 11–12, 22, 23–24, 110

Niagara Falls, 101–102

North American Review, 7–8, 9, 32, 119–120, 143, 156

Northampton (Massachusetts), Ornamental Tree Society, 122

Northfield (Illinois), correspondent from, 159

Oaklands (estate of R. H. Gardiner, Maine), 78

Old and New Worlds, compared, 101–103, 110, 120–121, 146, 159

Olmsted, Frederick Law, 162–163

Oregon country, 13

Pacific (steamer), 100

Paris
    parks, 115
    revolution of 1848, 110

Parks, public, 113, 115–117, 119, 121, 159–163

Parmentier, André, 44
    "Landscapes and Picturesque Gardens," 7

Patrick, Major Marsena Rudolph, 133–134

Paulding, James K., 18

Perkins, Thomas Handasyd, estate of, 46, 76

Peters, Judge Richard, residence of, 75

Philadelphia, 24, 44, 46, 149, 151
    houses and gardens, 16, 17, 43, 46, 66, 67, 74–75
    lack of green space, 22–23
    nursery in, 59

Picturesque, 37, 47–53, 61, 62, 69, 80–84, 87, 91, 94, 95, 96

INDEX

Plato, garden of, 70

Pomona, 109–110

Pope, Alexander, 132
   "Epistle to Lord Burlington," 41, 70
   Guardian essays, 41, 70

Poughkeepsie (New York), 33

Poussin, Nicolas, 59, 156

Pratt, Henry, 46

Price, Sir Uvedale, 47, 56, 57, 64, 69, 79–80, 94, 124, 162
   Essay on the Picturesque, 9, 42, 47–52, 71, 81
   influence on Downing, 47, 52, 69–70, 71, 79–81

Primogeniture, 43, 103, 108–109

Princeton (Illinois), cottage in, 28

Prior, Matthew, 132

Progress, idea of, 10, 11–17, 28

Propriety, 30, 110–111

Provincial Law Association (Britain), 128

Pückler Muskau, Hermann, Fürst von, 30

Pugin, A. W. N., 128

Quatremère de Quincy, Antoine Chrysosthôme, 58, 59, 79
   Essai sur la nature, le but et les moyens de l'imitation dans les beaux-arts, 55–56, 57, 64
   influence on Downing, 56, 57
   "On the Principles of Taste," 55
   quoted by Downing, 56

Racism, 153

Raphael (Raffaello Sanzio), 59, 96

Rathbone, Joel, estate of, 30

"Recognition of art" (Loudon), 37–38, 58, 63, 69, 79, 83–84

Repton, Humphry, 47, 52–53, 64, 69, 72, 80, 83, 94, 124
   Downing criticizes, 53
   influence on Downing, 52–53, 72, 80–83
   Landscape Gardening of Humphry Repton, 72, 80, 82–83 (*see also* Loudon, John Claudius)
   Observations on the Theory and Practice of Landscape Gardening, 42, 52
   Sketches and Hints on Landscape Gardening, 42

Republicanism, 30, 103, 106, 107–113, 121, 131, 145, 159

Restlessness, of Americans, 18–21

Reynolds, Sir Joshua, 59, 113, 128
   Discourses on Art, 33, 55

Robinson, Solon, 13–14

Rome, villas, 138

Rosa, Salvator, 52, 53, 94, 156

Roxbury (Massachusetts), country seat in, 46

Royal Botanic Gardens, Kew, 58, 102, 159, 162, 206n5, 206–207n6

Rural Essays (Downing), 167–168

Rural life, 10, 21–26

Ruskin, John, 136, 137, 148, 152, 155, 156, 163–164
   influence on Downing, 87, 95–96, 136, 137, 138, 148, 152, 154–155
   Modern Painters I, 94, 156–157
   Modern Painters II, 87, 95–96, 138
   Modern Painters IV, 96

Sacramento (California), 13

Sandwich Islands, 139

San Francisco, 159

Saratoga (New York), 123–124

Sargent, Henry Winthrop, 131

Schoolhouses and grounds, 26, 113, 115, 119

Schuylkill River, country residences on, 46, 75

Scott, Frank J., 97

Index

Sedgwick, Catharine Maria, 26

Shakespeare, William, 39

Sheaff, George, country seat of, 67, 74

Shenstone, William, 57, 71

Sigourney, Lydia, 19, 115

Sill, Joseph, 16, 17

Simplicity, ideal of, 30, 87, 105, 106, 109–113, 134, 136

Smith, John Jay, 32, 59, 66, 73–74, 86, 89

Spectator. See Addison, Joseph

Spenser, Edmund, 39, 132

Springside (estate of Matthew Vassar), 33

Stereotyping, racial and ethnic, 41–42, 139, 141, 146, 153, 155

St. Leon Loud, Mrs., 19

Sublime, the, 47–48, 80

Sunnyside (residence of Washington Irving, Hudson River), 21–22

Survilliers, Count de. *See* Bonaparte, Joseph

Switzerland, 138

Tappan, Henry P., 19

Taste, 30, 32, 126–129, 140–141, 145

Taylor, Sarah and J. I., cottage of, 28

Temple, William
    Upon the Gardens of Epicurus, 41

Terre Haute (Indiana), 145

Tierra del Fuego, 155

Tocqueville, Alexis de, 8, 20, 21, 24, 43
    Democracy in America, 19

Toledo (Ohio), 145

Treatise on the Theory and Practice of Landscape Gardening (Downing), 2, 4, 6, 7–97, 99, 105, 109, 113, 134, 137, 159, 162
    American poetry quoted in, 33
    audience, 10–11, 26–30, 87, 106
    British poetry quoted in, 33
    contents, 37
    dedication to John Quincy Adams, 3
    edition of 1841, 8, 36–64, 72, 73, 81, 84, 134, 148, 158–159
    edition of 1844, 5, 66–84, 87, 91, 97, 109, 110, 148
    edition of 1849, 5, 84, 86–97, 100, 107, 108, 136, 148, 154
    on estate size, 26–30, 73, 109
    and European gardening literature, 36–42, 47–53, 56–61, 72–73, 79–84, 91, 94
    first conception of, 8
    foreign phrases used in, 33–34
    language, 11, 33–34, 99
    price, 33
    reviews of, 7–8, 9, 10, 11, 12, 18–19, 24–25, 32, 33–34, 71–73, 87, 91, 94, 163–164

Trees, 61, 140–141, 144, 147, 149
    Ailanthus, 149, 152, 153–154, 158
    and American destructiveness, 143–144, 145
    American Elm, 87, 95, 149, 157
    Cedar of Lebanon, 149
    Chili Pine, 149
    Douglas Fir, 101
    English Elm, 101
    European Linden, 149
    Horse-chestnut, 152
    Japanese Ginkgo, 75
    Magnolia grandiflora, 149
    Noble Fir, 101
    Norway Spruce, 149
    Pepperidge, 152
    and pruning, 140–141, 156
    Sassafras, 152
    Silver Fir, 149
    Silver Poplar (Abele), 153–154, 158
    Sugar Maple, 149
    transplanting, 146–147
    Tulip Tree, 149, 151, 152, 155, 158, 159, 161

INDEX

and type-form, 155–157, 161
White Pine, 149

Trinity Church (R. Upjohn), 78

Tucker, Luther, 6, 99, 100, 134, 137

Tuckerman, Henry T., 137

Tudor, Frederic, residence of, 127

Turner, Joseph M. W., 94, 156

Tyler, John, 11

"Typical Beauty" (Ruskin), 87, 95–96, 138, 148, 155

Upjohn, Richard, 78

Van Buren, Martin, 29

Van Rensselaer, William P., estate of, 67, 74

Van Rensselaer family, residence of, 67

Variety, 63, 79

Vassar, Matthew, estate of, 33

Vaux, Calvert, 3, 100–101, 113, 129, 159, 161–163

Versailles, 39, 63, 64, 70

Villages, 113, 117–119

Vitruvius (Marcus Vitruvius Pollio), 30, 128

Wadsworth, Daniel, estate of, 46

Wadsworth, James S., 89. *See also* Geneseo

Walpole, Horace
On Modern Gardening, 42

Ward, Samuel G., 100

Warwick Castle, 42, 43, 101

Washington, George, 75

Washington, D.C.
Mall, after Downing, 162
Public Grounds (Downing), 33, 159–163

Watertown (Massachusetts), country seat in, 46

Webster, Daniel, 21

Weinbrenner, Friedrich, 59
Architektonisches Lehrbuch, 59

West Point (New York), 24

Whately, Thomas, 56, 64, 71
Observations on Modern Gardening, 9, 42–43

William and Mary, 87

William the Conqueror, 87

Willis, Nathaniel Parker, 21, 33
Home Journal, 21
Out-Doors at Idlewild, 30–31

Wimpole (seat of the Earl and Countess of Hardwicke), 103

Wise, Henry, 70

Woburn Abbey, 42–43, 101

Wodenethe (estate of H. W. Sargent, Hudson River), 131

Woodlands, the (estate of William Hamilton, Schuylkill River), 75

Zenobia, 159

Zeuxis, 54

www.ingramcontent.com/pod-product-compliance
Lightning Source LLC
Chambersburg PA
CBHW080732300426
44114CB00019B/2558